WHAT WOULD
JESUS *REALLY* DO?

WHAT WOULD JESUS *REALLY* DO?

The Power and Limits of Jesus' Moral Teachings

ANDREW FIALA

ROWMAN & LITTLEFIELD PUBLISHERS, INC.
Lanham • Boulder • New York • Toronto • Plymouth, UK

ROWMAN & LITTLEFIELD PUBLISHERS, INC.

Published in the United States of America
by Rowman & Littlefield Publishers, Inc.
A wholly owned subsidiary of The Rowman & Littlefield Publishing Group, Inc.
4501 Forbes Boulevard, Suite 200, Lanham, Maryland 20706
www.rowmanlittlefield.com

Estover Road
Plymouth PL6 7PY
United Kingdom

Distributed by National Book Network

British Library Cataloguing in Publication Information Available

Library of Congress Cataloging-in-Publication Data
Fiala, Andrew G. (Andrew Gordon), 1966–
  What would Jesus really do? : the power and limits of Jesus' moral teachings /
Andrew Fiala.
    p. cm.
  Includes bibliographical references and index.
  ISBN-13: 978-0-7425-5260-9 (hardback : alk. paper)
  ISBN-10: 0-7425-5260-8 (hardback : alk. paper)
  1. Jesus Christ—Teachings 2. Jesus Christ—Example. 3. Christian ethics. I.
Title.
  BS2415.F45 2007
  241—dc22   2006036667

Printed in the United States of America

♾™ The paper used in this publication meets the minimum requirements of
American National Standard for Information Sciences—Permanence of Paper for
Printed Library Materials, ANSI/NISO Z39.48-1992.

For my Sunday school teachers

CONTENTS

PREFACE

You will know the truth, and the truth will make you free.

—John 8:32

This book is about what Jesus does and does *not* teach us about ethics. Jesus is the paradigm for morality in the Christian West. His idea that we should love our neighbors is the very heart of ethics, and his life of love and self-sacrifice provides a model to which we all should aspire. But the Golden Rule and Jesus' model do not provide sufficient guidance for answering the tough questions about morality in the contemporary world. The complex ethical issues of our time require further guidance than Jesus can provide. The purpose of this book is to discuss Jesus as a moral teacher, while also showing why we need to go beyond Jesus in thinking about morality.

Religion and ethics have always been intimately connected. Americans have been reminded of this recently: religious and ethical controversies have been front-page news. Conservative American Christians have made a sustained effort to bring Christian ethics into the public sphere. President George W. Bush once claimed that his favorite philosopher was Jesus. Bush has justified a "war on terrorism" by claiming that God wants democracy to spread throughout the nations. And his veto of legislation that would have provided federal support for embryonic stem cell research is seen as an example—for better or worse—of Bush's religious convictions. There have been recent legal battles about whether the Ten Commandments could be displayed in public places and about whether the United States really is "one nation under God." Politicians routinely reach out to religious believers by making arguments about ethical issues that are grounded in religious belief. Such arguments were heard, for example, in the case of Terri Schiavo, a young woman diagnosed as being in a persistent vegetative state. Christian opponents of euthanasia appealed to scripture to argue that her feeding tube should not be removed. Christian arguments, grounded in scripture, continue to be heard in discussions of abortion, same-sex marriage, and the death penalty. One has only to skim the letters to the editor of the local paper in order to see that ethical discourse is thoroughly infused with religious language and that the Christian scriptures are seen by many as the source—for many, the *only* source—of ethical wisdom.

Christians are not united in their thinking about ethics. The late Pope John Paul II advocated what he called "the gospel of life," which was opposed to abortion and euthanasia. But unlike some religious conservatives, the pope was also opposed to the death penalty and to war, including President Bush's expansive war on terrorism. Evangelical Protestants have become better organized in recent years, and their voices are heard more clearly in our culture as they argue vociferously against homosexuality, abortion, and euthanasia. But other Christians—such as former President Jimmy Carter—offer a more progressive agenda for Christian ethics that includes openness to individual choice on these issues and a firm commitment to the separation of church and state. American Christian voices range across the political spectrum. It is important to remember that the big tent of Christianity includes African American civil rights leaders such as Martin Luther King Jr. and Jesse Jackson. It also includes progressives such as Jim Wallis and Episcopalian Bishop John Shelby Spong. And it includes conservatives such as James Dobson and Pat Robertson, as well as those politicians—such as George W. Bush and former Senator Bill Frist—who align themselves with this brand of conservative Christianity. The diversity we find within Christianity results from the vagueness of Jesus' ethical teaching: it is possible to interpret the ethics of Jesus in a variety of ways.

One difficulty of looking to Jesus for answers about the questions of ethics is that our sources of information about Jesus are limited. Moreover, the texts and traditions that tell us about Jesus were created in a world that was quite different from our own. Our ideas about society and politics have progressed substantially since biblical times. Slavery has been abolished. Women have been liberated. Literacy has spread. We no longer have kings. And we no longer believe in social hierarchies based on family or caste. The world of Jesus was patriarchal, hierarchical, and undemocratic. One wonders whether Jesus can provide us with guidance for the quite different social world in which we live.

Moreover, scientists are making great strides in exploring the genetic bases of life on earth and in understanding the complexity of the universe. The rapid development of science has created complicated ethical issues. Stem cell research, genetic engineering, and cloning create ethical problems that didn't exist in Jesus' time. Just as Jesus did not know about the dinosaurs or the age of our planet or the structure of the solar system, Jesus could not have anticipated the ethical issues that arise from prenatal testing or from our ability to sustain dying bodies with life-support technology. Again, one wonders how Jesus can help us to think about topics that would not even have been imagined in his time.

This is not to say that Jesus is wrong or that we should ignore Christian sources in thinking about ethics. Rather, my thesis is that there are limits to what Jesus can teach us about contemporary issues. Jesus' idea of loving your neighbor is a great moral principle. But to apply this idea to complex issues of contemporary concern, we need knowledge, imagination, and reason. The philosophical tradition of Western humanism helps us develop these capacities of critical thought.

THE AUTHOR'S CONFESSION

I teach ethics for a living. This book is written for my students and for people like them. Two different sorts of students frequently show up in my classes: Christians and relativists. I hope in this book to address both of these sorts of people.

On the one hand, my Christian students usually have the idea that all of the answers to life's questions can be found in the Bible. I admire these students' piety, and I appreciate their commitment to the idea that there must be an absolute foundation for ethics. But these students often refuse to go beyond Jesus, and they also tend to credulously submit to religious authority. This book is intended to help Christians think more clearly about the limits of the Christian approach to ethics. I do not mean to imply that Christian ethics is wrongheaded. But I do want to argue that Christians need to look beyond Jesus for ethical insight. This idea of going beyond Jesus is, by the way, an important part of the sort of Christian ethics that follows in the natural law tradition of Christian philosophers such as Thomas Aquinas. Christians long ago realized that the ethical model of Jesus needed to be supplemented by the use of reason. One of my goals here is to remind Christians of this fact.

On the other hand, the relativists in my classes usually think that there are no final answers to the questions of ethics. I admire the tolerant and open spirit that leads many students to relativism. But relativism provides no ultimate answers to the questions of ethics. Indeed, a sincere relativist has no reason to be tolerant or open-minded—if all values are relative, then there is no good reason to be tolerant of others. Many people who espouse relativism do so because they are fed up with the closed-minded and self-righteous moralizing that they often hear from some outspoken Christians. This book sympathizes with this critique of Christian moral superiority. But it begins with the belief that some moral ideas do in fact have a near-absolute value. Of course, one of these important moral ideas is the idea that one should not be self-righteous and censorious. This message about modesty and tolerance is, in fact, found in Jesus' model.

I personally identify with both sorts of students. I was raised as a Christian—Presbyterian to be exact—and I flirted with relativism during college. I wrote this book to help both sorts of audiences figure out what to think about the relation between Christianity and ethics.

My Sunday school teachers taught me to respect the Bible—even hold it in awe. But Sunday school involved very little critical or philosophical analysis. Luckily my parents—who also taught my Sunday school class one year at our church—encouraged me to continue to ask questions about the tradition I was inheriting. I learned at some point that not everything written in the Bible is literally true. But this realization can lead to a quick slide down the slippery slope toward relativism. Fortunately, philosophy stopped me on this slide and I came to realize, along with Socrates, that reason shows us what is true and that scriptures and religious beliefs must be criticized from the standpoint of reasonable truth. When I read that Jesus says "you will know the truth, and the truth will make you free" (John 8:32), I interpreted this as the command to pursue philosophy. Philosophy is the love of wisdom, and wisdom will set us free: it frees us to know the truth, and it frees us from the bondage of authority and tradition. I believe that the spirit of criticism can be found in the Christian tradition itself. Jesus enjoins us, after all, to think critically about false prophets and about wars and rumors of wars. And he himself models a critical encounter with his own tradition: he questions and reinterprets the texts and conventional wisdom of the Hebrew tradition, and he stands up to those authorities who claim to have a monopoly on religious and ethical truth.

The primary Bible that I consulted in writing this book was one that was given to me at the First Presbyterian Church. This Bible was inscribed on its first page with a quote from Paul's letter to Timothy (1 Timothy 4:12): "Let no one despise your youth, but set the believers an example in speech and conduct, in love, in faith, in purity." I suppose that the church elders intended this quote to inspire a life of Christian discipleship. But my passion for the truth led me to read more in pursuit of the true meaning of love, faith, and purity. The whole of this chapter from Paul's letter to Timothy includes an exhortation to "train yourself in godliness." But how does one do this, and what exactly is godliness? Earlier in this chapter, Paul writes, "Have nothing to do with godless and silly myths." But he also maintains in the same chapter, "Everything that is created by God is good, and nothing is to be rejected if it is received with thanksgiving." All of this raises more questions than it answers. Exactly which myths are godless and silly? What is the difference between good and evil?

When one begins to reflect on such questions, relativism looms. There were other religions in the ancient world, just as there are other religions today. Which one is true? Jesus claims: "If you continue in my word, you are truly my disciples, and you will know the truth, and the truth will make you free" (John 8:31–32). But what, then, are we to make of the other religions that claim to have access to a truth that is quite different from the truth of Jesus: the Muslims, the Hindus, the Buddhists, the Native Americans, and so on? Of course, one need not look far to see the problem: there are major differences among those who claim to be "Christian." In college I became aware of this problem as I studied history, anthropology, and other social sciences. And as I studied the Bible and its history, I learned that the Bible was written over the course of centuries in response to a variety of historical and political events, including ultimately the subjugation of the Hebrews under Rome. Jesus was a product of this political context: he was identified as the messiah who was expected to liberate the Jews from the Romans. But others claimed to be liberators, and others were more zealous in their pursuit of Jewish emancipation—even taking up arms against the Romans.

Further inquiry shows that the Gospels were written decades after Jesus was killed, after the Romans asserted their power over the Jews by destroying Jerusalem and its temple. Stories about Jesus had to reflect this reality: the reality of a liberator who promised a different sort of emancipation and who could make sense of the disrupted world of first-century Judaism. Early Christian ethics developed within this context. Choices were made by the authors, who wrote these texts in order to tell this particular story. Moreover, the Gospels were directed toward audiences that had certain expectations and ideas about ethics as well as about the nature of religious emancipation. Further choices were made in deciding what to include in the canon once Christianity began to spread and develop. These human choices have continued throughout the 2,000 year history of Christianity.

Such historical awareness can lead to full-blown relativism. It seems that the ethics of Jesus is one possible approach to morality among others, constructed by a group of men at a given time in history. When one begins to understand the vast range of cultural and historical diversity that we find in the human world, it appears that there is no final answer to the question of which ethical ideas are the right ones. Such a realization led me to study philosophy. Philosophy aims beyond historical and cultural relativism toward a truth that transcends history and context. What one discovers as one works one's way beyond relativism is that if ethical ideas are supposed to be good, they are good not because Jesus (or some other authority) said them. Rather, an authority like Jesus is to be admired because he articulated ethical ideas that are true independent of the fact that he said them. This was the basic idea taught by Socrates centuries before Jesus, and it was also articulated by Kant and others in the centuries that followed him. If the truth will set you free, it is the truth itself that has this power and not the person who says it.

When I began teaching ethics on a regular basis, I discovered that students were still struggling with the Christian texts, just as I had. I have published two books on ethical topics that took me back to Christian sources: one on pacifism and another on tolerance. The Christian tradition is a key source for thinking about peacefulness and tolerance. My reflection on these virtues led me toward the present critical interaction with Jesus. As I reread the Bible with adult eyes, I noted that Jesus advocates these virtues without providing a full defense of them. I found that I agreed with much of what Jesus said in key places like the Sermon on the Mount. But I wished that he had said more. And I was troubled by some of the other things he said—such as his prophetic vision of God's vengeance.

As I returned to the Bible in order to discover what Jesus actually said about ethics, I also returned to the philosophical sources that have inspired my own thinking to see what relation these texts have to Christianity. I rediscovered that most of the philosophers in the Western tradition up through the nineteenth century took it for granted that Jesus was the primary ethical paradigm. Moral philosophers such as Kant and Mill both claimed that what they were doing was in line with the basic message that Jesus had postulated. Respecting others, loving our neighbors, and the virtues of generosity, mercy, tolerance, and peace form a common thread that links Christianity and modern ethical philosophy. Of course, there are thinkers who eventually turned away from Jesus and Christianity. But one of the reasons for this is that philosophers began to see that there were limits to how far the original Christian texts can lead us. Jesus was, quite simply, silent about many important ethical questions.

Philosophy takes us further than Jesus can. Modern philosophy responds to uniquely modern problems. And philosophy is a more refined instrument with which to think about ethics. Where Jesus offers exhortations and admonitions, philosophy offers principles, arguments, and an analysis of evidence. There is a time and place for parables and sermons. But we also need careful definitions, systematic theories, rigorous arguments, and in general a more sustained defense of the values that are central to our lives. We also need a healthy dose of humility to realize that no human being has all of the answers to the tough questions of ethics. Even Jesus does not have all the answers. This is why we need to continue to reflect on these questions for ourselves.

I intend this book to address both Christians and non-Christians. My goal is to stimulate dialogue and thought. And, hopefully, my approach will elevate the level of discourse in our culture about ethics and about religion.

If you are a Christian, I hope that this book will inspire you to read the Bible with more care. I also hope that it will lead you to recognize the complexity of the ethical issues that we must confront today. And I hope that it will teach you the need for tolerance for those with diverse answers to the questions of ethics. Tolerance is a key virtue for Jesus, along with virtues such as mercy, forgiveness, and love. Christians can benefit from recalling the importance of these virtues.

If you are not a Christian, I hope that this book will educate you about the foundational ideas of Western culture. I also hope that it will cause strident atheists and anti-Christians to look again at the model provided by Jesus—not with the goal of converting you to Christianity, but simply to encourage you to recognize that Jesus did articulate some very important ethical ideas. I also hope that it will inspire you to be more tolerant and to better understand the Christians with whom you disagree. At the same time, I hope you will also appreciate that although the issues we must confront have no easy answers, we must strive to find answers and avoid the temptations of relativism.

We can all benefit from more and better dialogue. I hope that this book stimulates a more enlightened conversation about Jesus and that it helps you think more clearly about contemporary moral problems.

NOTE ON THE TEXT

The chapters in this book fall into five groups. Chapters 1 and 2 introduce my humanistic approach to ethics and the Bible. Chapters 3, 4, and 5 clarify general ethical concepts with a special focus on virtue ethics. Chapters 6 through 11 delve into several applied issues. Chapters 12 through 14 consider what modern philosophers have thought about Jesus and Christian ethics. And chapter 15 concludes with a discussion of liberal politics and where we can go from here. Each of the groups is independent, and each chapter should, I hope, make sense independently of the other chapters. Thus you might choose to skip around in the book in search of the ethical issues or questions you are interested in.

The version of the Bible that I have used is the Revised Standard Version. I have occasionally consulted the original Greek and other translations by using a useful Internet tool, "The Blue Letter Bible," where it seemed appropriate to do so. But this book is not an attempt to provide detailed scholarship of the Bible. There is an entire industry of Bible scholars out there and I don't presume to compete with them. I realize that there is a complex debate about the status of biblical texts and about the question of the historical Jesus. But my approach here is to read the Bible as a non-scholar would, in search of Jesus' ethical teaching. I do not claim to offer new insights into the history of the Bible or the pursuit of the historical Jesus. Rather, I want to enter into a conversation about ethics with those who take the Bible seriously.

My assumption is that most people focus primarily on the Gospels, so I will focus on the Gospels as well. While we know that Paul's letters were written prior to the Gospels, Paul does not attempt to portray Jesus as a character in a story. The Gospels show us Jesus as a preacher, a teacher, a miracle worker, and a martyr. And the Gospels show us a rich and coherent ethical ideal lived in the life of Jesus himself. Most Christians believe that the Gospels present, for the most part, a historically accurate portrait of Jesus. I will go along with this assumption in what follows and will focus on the ethical teaching and model that Jesus provides.

Although I am trained as a philosopher, I have attempted to avoid extensive reference to the philosophical literature on general ethics, on the applied issues discussed here, and on the history of philosophy. As with biblical scholarship, there is a whole industry of philosophers who spend their energies pondering the questions of ethics. I don't claim that this book offers any new insight into these deep questions. Rather, my goal is to summarize the results of philosophical reflection on ethics in order to help foster a more intelligent conversation about ethics among non-philosophers.

ACKNOWLEDGMENTS

This project developed through conversations with many people in classrooms, at conferences, and over coffee. One never works alone when one has the support and inspiration of good friends and family. Special thanks are due to: Worth Hawes, Derek Jeffreys, Hye-Kyung Kim, David Galaty, Trudy Conway, Lani Roberts, John Lachs, Robert Maldonado, Terry Winant, Jason Smick, Charlie Recksieck, Peter Lenz, David Snow, and Steve Meyer; and Valerie, Julaine, Gordon, Peggy, Don, Tahoe, and Bodhi.

1

JESUS AND ETHICS

> You shall love the Lord your God with all your heart and with all your soul, and with all your mind. This is the great and first commandment. And a second is like it. You shall love your neighbor as yourself. On these two commandments depend all the laws and the prophets.
>
> —Matthew 22:37–40 (see Mark 12:29–31; Luke 25:27)

Jesus claims that there are two commandments: love God and love your neighbor. Jesus derives these basic commandments from the Jewish tradition, echoing claims that were made in both Deuteronomy (19:18) and Leviticus (6:5). In thinking about the ethics of Jesus, it is natural to ask whether it is possible to disentangle these two commandments and think about ethics without also thinking about God. But Christians believe that the two commandments are so closely connected that they might actually be one commandment. As the current pope, Benedict XVI, said in his encyclical *God Is Love* (*Deus Caritas Est*): "Love of God and love of neighbor are thus inseparable, they form a single commandment." The idea is that we develop the strength and the will to love our neighbors by learning to love God, and we learn what love is by receiving the love of God and by contemplating the love that we see in the life and works of Jesus.

Most Christians believe that the ethical content of the Gospels is secondary to the claims that are made about Jesus' divinity. It is difficult to focus only on the ethics of Jesus because the Gospels also aim to establish that Jesus is the Christ, the messiah, the son of God, the light of the world, or simply, the Lord. It appears that ethics is made possible by proper devotion to God: love of God seems to be a prerequisite for love of one's neighbor. And if Jesus is the Lord, then ethics is made possible by properly understanding and loving Jesus, the son of God. Nonetheless, we can avoid these theological questions and focus directly on Jesus' ethical vision. The question that guides this endeavor is not how Jesus was related to God, but what Jesus had to say about ethics. If Jesus was the Christ, then perhaps his moral teachings become that much more important. But these teachings are of value even if we remain undecided on the theological question.

Jesus offers us three basic moral lessons. First, he states the Golden Rule: we should love our neighbors as ourselves. Second, he celebrates a set of virtues that include charity, forgiveness, mercy, tolerance, pacifism, and love. And third, he shows us in his life and works the importance of service and sacrifice.

DIVINE COMMAND ETHICS

Although almost everyone knows these basic truths about the ethics of Jesus, these lessons are sometimes hard to find in the Gospels. The Bible is a big book and it cannot easily be read from cover to cover. The Gospels themselves can be hard to decipher: they are repetitious and occasionally dull. And they are full of scriptural allusions and strange language. Moreover, if you are looking for ethics, you have to dig through other stories about Jesus' life, his career as a healer and miracle worker, his preaching and teaching practice, and his death and resurrection. My aim here is to focus on the ethical teachings that can be found in certain key passages like the Sermon on the Mount, without getting sidetracked or bogged down by the rest of the information in the Gospels.

I teach ethics to college students. Every semester I encounter students who claim that Jesus is the basis of their ethical system. One of the mottoes for this idea is the question "What would Jesus do?" This book is an effort to answer this question. However, my conclusion is that the question is often not easy to answer. In my introductory ethics classes, we briefly consider the "divine command" theory of ethics, which is the idea that ethics is based on God's commandments. In most contemporary ethics textbooks, the divine command theory is mentioned only in passing. Indeed, most contemporary philosophers simply dismiss it with a shrug and move on. I should admit that I am no fan of the divine command theory. Indeed, this book attempts to argue for the limitations of such an approach. One of the biggest limitations is that it is often not clear what God wants us to do. Divine command theory is not much good if it cannot provide an answer to the question "What would Jesus do?"

But philosophers should take the divine command theory seriously, because most of us begin our moral education with some version of the divine command theory. And many people seem to think that without a firm foundation in God, there can be no ethics at all. As Dostoevsky famously put it, "If there is no God, then everything is permitted."

One of the chief problems of the divine command theory is that there are ethical disagreements *within* religious traditions as well as between rival traditions. So even if there is a God, it is often not clear what is permitted or not permitted. Some Christians deplore homosexuality; others accept it. Some Christians forbid abortion; others permit it. Some Christians condemn euthanasia; others allow it. The problem of the divine command theory is thus that there is no univocal sense of what God commands. And the problem is exacerbated if we open our vistas beyond Christianity and take into account global religious diversity. For this reason, we need to find ethical ideas that can be shared by all without an exclusive appeal to any given set of divine commandments.

Although Jesus stated a few basic principles, he did not say a lot about the tough cases of ethical decision-making, like abortion, the death penalty, or euthanasia. Reasonable people can reach divergent conclusions about what Jesus would have thought about the hard cases. The religious diversity of the contemporary world reminds us that it is best to remain tolerant. Indeed, this is one of the virtues that Jesus advocates.

Ethics is about the question of how to lead a good life in community with others. Theories of ethics are grounded in larger metaphysical ideas about the meaning and purpose of life. Thus ethics is linked to religion. But as a method of dealing with the big questions, religion usually relies on appeals to authority. Usually there is an ancient teacher, prophet, or text that tells the authoritative story of humanity's place and purpose within the God-created cosmos. The approach I advocate—what I call philosophical humanism—is skeptical of such appeals to authority. I think it is possible for human beings to discover the truth about the good life without appeals to divine revelation or ancient tradition. Indeed, this is the way most of us proceed—even those who are devout. Our work lives, our family lives, and our social lives require constant ethical judgment. And we make these judgments within the context of the natural and social worlds in which we dwell, based on the evidence of our senses and the basic structure of reason. While some consult ancient texts for advice in making these judgments, even this approach requires us to make reasonable interpretations of these texts.

Ancient prophets and texts do not by themselves provide a useful guide for daily living. Jesus did not provide a set of rules that tell us what to think in every possible situation. Rather, like other moral teachers, Jesus articulated general rules. But it is up to individuals to apply these rules in the context of daily life. Revelation does not help you decide what job to take, whether to call in sick, or how much time to devote to family and friends. These decisions require the good habits of living that are developed by thinking and reflecting on self, world, and others. While religion can provide guidelines and models, it is up to you to apply these guidelines and make decisions for yourself. Many of my religious students seem to believe that the answers to all of life's questions can be found in the Bible. While I admire the piety and calm assurance of such students, the belief that any one text or tradition can answer all of our questions is a bit naïve.

There are several limitations to an approach to ethics that relies entirely on Jesus and the Bible. First, our record of the historical Jesus is fragmentary and confused. One can admit this without thinking that the Christian faith is irrational. Indeed, Christians have long recognized that interpretation and argument are necessary precisely because of the fragmentary nature of the Christian record. In fact, one of the long-standing disputes is what exactly belongs within the Bible. The Old Testament of the Revised Standard Version of the Bible, which is the version I will quote here, does not include the books of the Apocrypha, even though these books are part of the traditional Old Testament. And choices are made about the New Testament: for example, whether to include the passage in John (7:52–8.11) where Jesus defends the woman who is about to be stoned for adultery.

Second, Jesus and the entire biblical tradition were completed in another time and another place. As we shall see, the biblical tradition presents us with ideas that we no longer accept. The most obvious of these are biblical ideas about human rights, democracy, and the state. The world of the Bible was one in which slavery was an accepted practice. Jesus does not explicitly condemn it. Moreover, Jesus does not defend the democratic ideals that are shared by most Americans. Indeed, he seems to advocate submission and obedience to tyrants—as seen in his submission to Pilate and the authorities who execute him.

Third, we have much better systems of thinking about ethics in the developed traditions of Western philosophy. The Catholic Church has long emphasized that natural law is a source of ethics that must be consulted in addition to the word of God as revealed in the Bible. This tradition of thinking about ethics using reason developed in modern times into systematic philosophical ethics. These systems are much better than divine command theory at answering questions about basic values. This is true despite the fact that disputes remain, even within philosophical ethics.

Fourth, at least some of our ethical problems are unique to the modern world. Jesus and his contemporaries were simply not confronted with the range of issues that concern us: same-sex marriage, cloning and genetic research, women's rights, medical abortion, environmental degradation, nuclear war, terrorism. These new problems need new thinking. While the Bible can provide us with guidelines and ideas, it cannot provide us with final answers about these complex issues.

FUNDAMENTALISM AND PHILOSOPHY

The predominant tradition in Christian ethical thinking maintains that Jesus' ethical message cannot be divorced from the theological context. The basic idea of this tradition—as found in Augustine, for example—is that ethics must begin with an account of the highest good, which is God. To be good is to be with God, while evil is conceived as a distance from God. This idea is linked to Jesus' claim that the first commandment is to love God: virtue follows from proper piety.

The primacy of the first commandment is connected to claims that are made about Jesus as a moral authority. After Matthew recounts the Sermon on the Mount—Jesus' most important statement on ethics—he ends with the following claim: "He taught them as someone who had authority" (Matthew 7:29). The reason to take Jesus' moral vision seriously is that he speaks with divine power. To love God—as the first commandment requires—is to love Jesus and to follow his ethical commandments.

Christians have to explain what it means "to love God" and what it means to "love your neighbor." Such explanations require considerable philosophical effort. The goal of finding a more detailed account of these two commandments points us toward a rationally developed ethical system that explains both the nature of goodness in general (as one of the attributes of God—or as that which God loves) and the idea of love itself. Such a fully developed system is lacking in the original Christian texts, even though these texts provide us with a few interesting hints. My aim in this book is to examine these hints in order to uncover the ethical heart of Jesus' teachings while also showing the limits of an approach that relies exclusively on Jesus.

Christian ethicists have long argued that one could employ reason to discover ethical and metaphysical truth. Augustine, Aquinas, and others in the Christian tradition freely employed reason to interpret sacred scriptures. One influential recent example of such a Christian approach to ethics is found in the writings of Pope John Paul II. In his encyclical *Evangelium Vitae: On the Value and Inviolability of Human Life* (1995), the pope explains and defends the view that human persons are of infinite worth. The metaphysical and theological context for the pope's remarks is one that emphasizes the immortality of the soul and God's love for persons. This forms the basis of what he calls the "Gospel of Life," which leads to the Catholic Church's stance against abortion, euthanasia, and the death penalty.

The difficulty of this approach is that, even if one accepts the idea that the soul is immortal or that God loves persons, this still tells us very little about the morality of euthanasia or abortion, for example. The crucial question with regard to abortion is not whether the soul is immortal but whether the fetus is a person in the moral sense. And the crucial question with regard to euthanasia is not whether God loves the old and dying but whether actively killing another person or passively letting them die expresses respect for their dignity. Unfortunately, Jesus did not tell us whether the fetus has a soul, nor did he tell us whether it is permissible to respect an individual's request to be allowed to "die with dignity." To answer such questions, we need to go beyond Jesus and beyond the general ideas of Christian ethics and develop a more concrete understanding of the world via the natural and social sciences.

There are many things that Jesus did not tell us, although some Christians are fond of claiming otherwise. Jesus did not tell us whether homosexuality should be accepted. He did not tell us whether cloning should be allowed. But he did explicitly state some ideas that run counter to the ethical ideas of most modern Americans. In addition to condemning "murder, adultery, fornication, theft, false witness, and slander" (Matthew 15:19), Jesus also condemned divorce except in cases of adultery. And he said, "Whoever marries a divorced woman commits adultery" (Matthew 5:31; Matthew 19:9). Moreover, Jesus emphasized our obligations to the poor; he condemned the idolatry of money, and he generally assailed the rich, the powerful, the hypocritical, and the self-righteous. I should note that I agree with most of these values and that I also concur with the pope and other Christians about the importance of respecting persons. However, I think we must distinguish the basic ethical teachings that are broadly shared by Christian and non-Christian ethics from the more complex and contentious claims that are found in specific Christian dogmas. And we must use reason as we critically interpret the Christian scriptures.

I realize that this runs counter to some currents of Christian thought. Some fundamentalists appear to maintain that we can make no progress beyond the biblical texts, for these texts are the word of God, and God's word does not change over time. This idea is a postulate of faith for many Christians. One particular version of this general idea is known as "inerrancy." The basic idea is that the scriptures are the absolute truth and contain no error. A related idea says that the scriptures are "infallible." Some versions of this idea go so far as to claim that the Bible is the very word of God, which the divine author prompted in the minds of those who actually wrote the texts. This idea is often linked to the idea that there is no further progress to be made beyond the revelation given in the New Testament. Article V of the "Chicago Statement on Biblical Inerrancy" states, "We deny that any normative revelation has been given since the completion of the New Testament." The gist of this is that there is no progress to be made beyond the scriptures: they contain all that God intended us to know about him and his plan for human life. Subsequent ideas about theology or ethics must thus be firmly grounded in the biblical texts. Moreover, there can be no progress toward truth without this basis in the Bible. This is often further linked to the idea that the words of the Bible are literally true. Thus creationism holds that the words of Genesis record the literally true story of the origin of life on earth, including the true story of the great flood as well as the true story of God's unique covenant with Abraham and his descendants. Anything that falls outside of this history—the traditions of India, China, Africa, and the Americas—is irrelevant to the true history of God and his chosen people.

A more complex approach might supplement biblical literalism with prayer and direct communication with God. When asking "What would Jesus do?" such an approach would look both to the biblical texts and toward a direct and continued revelation from God that is available through meditation and prayer. Indeed, one might argue that it is God's presence and inspiration that allows one to correctly interpret the biblical texts. The difficulty of this appeal to revelation still remains: such a direct revelation has no authority whatsoever for those who have not experienced it.

Fundamentalism can be understood as a reaction against modern ideas such as the scientific method. But it is absurd to reject modern science. Science has made massive progress in terms of knowledge, and scientists have discovered truths unimaginable in Jesus' time. And modern philosophical reflection has led to profound ethical and political developments, including the abolition of slavery, the spread of representative democracy, and the liberation of women. But fundamentalists cannot appreciate these developments from within the confines of their reading of scriptures. Moreover, the fundamentalist approach also neglects the vast richness of global human culture, when it argues that Jesus alone is the true and final revelation of God.

For these reasons we should reject fundamentalism. The Bible should be open to rational critical interpretation. And we should open our minds to the philosophical and religious wisdom of global culture. But if the scriptures are not literally true, do they have any value whatever? Christians claim that the Bible is of value because it represents God's revelation to humankind and the Gospels are the final revelation of God. The stories of Jesus' miraculous and healing powers, including his resurrection, are intended to lead the reader to the conclusion that Jesus is the son of God and that what he says is the direct revelation of God's will. But one can believe that Jesus' basic ethical teachings are valid without deciding the question of whether Jesus had divine power. Indeed, the philosophical approach is interested in the truths of ethics while downplaying the significance of the person who states these truths. It seems fairly obvious that Jesus—like Socrates and other teachers such as the Buddha, Lao-Tsu, Confucius, and Muhammad—had wisdom and personal charisma. But if the wisdom he possessed is of value, it is valuable independent of his personal attributes.

It is difficult to know how to assess the claims that are made about Jesus' miraculous powers. The world in which Jesus lived was one permeated by magic and by a limited understanding of the natural world. The ancients did not know the causes of the weather or understand the structure of the solar system. But we now know more about how to rationally critique a miracle such as the calming of the storm (Matthew 8:23–27; Mark 4:35–41; Luke 8:22–25): the weather is an interconnected system that is fueled by both global and local circulations of moisture and energy. Jesus' followers also knew little of biology and medicine. It is not surprising, then, that Jesus' healing powers are described as a process of casting out demons (Matthew 8:28–34; Mark 5:1–20; Luke 8:26–39). But we know more now: diseases are caused by germs and other biochemical processes. Jesus and the authors who told stories about him did not know this.

Moreover, these miraculous stories are intended by the Gospel authors to prove that Jesus was the messiah. This attempt to establish Jesus' power of salvation occurs in the context of turmoil in Israel as a result of Roman rule, ongoing Jewish rebellion against the Romans, and the eventual destruction of the temple in Jerusalem. The messianic movement and apocalyptic vision of the first century must be understood in this context. The Gospel texts were written decades after Jesus' death and are based on an oral tradition that was passed down and modified according to the needs of the incipient Christian community as it struggled to define itself both in the context of reforming Judaism and against the larger forces of Greco-Roman culture.

My approach seeks to downplay the miraculous element in the original Christian texts in an effort to unpack Jesus' ethical vision. I assume that it is possible to think about Jesus' ethical wisdom without deciding the question of theology. This admittedly humanistic approach will offend some Christians, as it seems to ignore the first commandment, which is to "love God." However, in order to love God, we must know him, and it is reason that allows this to happen. Jesus' ethical vision is compelling because it is, for the most part and within limits, reasonable. Those who interpret and apply Christian texts must use reason in the project of constructing a Christian ethic from amid the fragments and hints found in Jesus' teachings.

CONCLUSION

There have been numerous attempts in the last 2,000 years to discover the truth about Jesus and to systematize Christian ethics. The present effort is thus a drop in a large ocean of thought. However, my approach differs from many explicitly "Christian" attempts to discover a Christian ethic because my aim is neither to formulate an apology for Christianity nor to construct a catechism or code of Christian principles. In fact, my goal is to show the limits of such a dogmatically Christian approach. At the same time, however, my aim is to provide a sympathetic reading of the Christian texts. I think there is room for Christian ethics within the larger philosophical discourse on ethics, even though I think that ethics cannot be grounded solely in the Christian scriptures. The Christian approach is valuable for reminding us of the importance of the Golden Rule and for showing us the value of certain key virtues.

While considering these basic ideas from Jesus' teaching, I will also consider the relation between these ethical teachings and other philosophical theories of ethics. But I will also criticize those who claim that the Bible provides definitive conclusions about contemporary ethical issues. Jesus states basic principles of good behavior, but there is no definitive way to apply these general principles to contemporary issues. This is not a failing that is unique to Christian ethics. Indeed, it is a problem for philosophical ethics as well. There is a space between principles and their application that allows for different interpretations of the way such principles should be applied. This is especially true of principles that were articulated thousands of years ago in the midst of a foreign culture.

The biblical texts were written in a different time and addressed to audiences who had different interests and ideas than our own. They do not, then, provide us with easy answers to complicated questions of contemporary concern. The idea that we could obtain a definitive answer to the question "What would Jesus do?" is too simple. Indeed, Jesus himself implied that life was complicated and that basic principles can be bent according to the demands of specific situations. In the famous scene where Jesus is anointed by a woman at Bethany, Jesus tells his disciples that there is a time to care for the poor and a time to attend to other things.

While I agree with much of Jesus' teachings, I also argue that these teachings are limited. Jesus did not provide us with specific answers to our questions about the death penalty, homosexuality, pornography, abortion, cloning, stem cell research, euthanasia, or a variety of other complicated issues. And he did not tell us what to think about complicated political questions about the separation of church and state or about political toleration in the context of radical pluralism. Part of the problem is that these issues could not have come up for Jesus, given his historical setting. He did not foresee the developments of science and technology that would create many of our questions, nor did he foresee the historical and political developments of the last two millennia.

Jesus was addressing his contemporaries with regard to issues that were important for them. His discussions of dietary customs, his reconsideration of the importance of the Sabbath, and his attack on the "money-changers" in the temple provide us with concrete examples: these issues were important for Jews living 2,000 years ago. They do not directly apply to us.

Jesus tells us to be generous and kind, to turn the other cheek, to forgive, to be humble and tolerant, and to be courageous in pursuit of the good. All of this is part of what might be called the "perennial" moral philosophy. This perennial moral vision is not unique to Jesus. It can be found in Buddhism, Stoicism, and in other great moral traditions. And it is part of the ethical vision that has been developed by the Western philosophical tradition. My goal here is to return us to the perennial moral vision that Jesus articulates, while arguing that there is often no clear conclusion about how this general view of ethics is supposed to be applied in the contemporary world.

2

HUMANISM AND CHRISTIAN FAITH

> As to Jesus of Nazareth . . . I think the system of morals and his
> religion, as he left them to us, the best the world ever saw or is
> likely to see; but I apprehend it has received various corrupt-
> ing changes, and I have some doubts as to his divinity.
>
> —Benjamin Franklin[1]

The basic idea of what is known as "divine command" ethics is that God is the source of the moral law and that he gives this law to human beings through a direct revelation to some mediator: a prophet, priest, or messiah who has divine authority. In the Hebrew tradition, God revealed the law to Moses on the mountaintop. Christians claim that Jesus represents a new and final revelation and that Jesus' Sermon on the Mount is the new location at which God brings ethical wisdom to human beings.

The approach that I take to ethics rejects the idea that a particular person has special access to the truth and that the rest of humanity gains access to the truth only through the mediator. One might say that the emphasis on revelation and authority is typical of what is called "religion." The approach that I take is not religious in this sense. Rather, it is humanistic. I assume that human beings have access to the truth without appealing to revelation. I also assume that each human being can find the truth for himself or herself without divine intervention.

This is the approach of most of Western philosophy, which holds that human reason shows us the truth and that each one of us possesses the ability to use reason in this way. But this is not the idea of most forms of Christian faith. Christian faith usually maintains that human beings are fallen, sinful, and in error. We need grace to help us overcome these limitations so that we might find the truth. One aspect of grace is the Bible itself—it is given by God as a tool to help us overcome our limitations. The idea that we can attain righteousness by our own efforts is in fact identified as a specific heresy: the Pelagian heresy. One of the reasons that most Christian faiths reject this view is that if it is true that human beings can attain righteousness through their own efforts, then there is no need for Jesus or forgiveness. It is original sin that creates the necessity of God's intervention and forgiveness.

ANCIENT PHILOSOPHY

The ancient Greek philosophical tradition that gives rise to humanism begins with the basic premise that the key to a good life is to "know thyself." Self-knowledge is the beginning of genuine wisdom. And wisdom develops as we use reason to interrogate ourselves and the world around us. Human beings are able to discover the objective truth by themselves, without divine intervention. But this idea runs counter to the tradition that we find in much of the Christian scriptures. In Proverbs (9:10) we read that "the fear of the Lord is the beginning of wisdom." And in Job we see this explained (28:12–13): "But where shall wisdom be found? And where is the place of understanding? Man does not know the way to it, and it is not found in the land of the living." Job learns in the end that he knows nothing. Job concludes with a phrase that is typical of the anti-humanist idea of much of Christianity: "Therefore, I despise myself, and repent in dust and ashes." The basic idea that human beings should despise themselves and that they can do nothing for themselves without the intervention of God runs counter to the humanistic faith in the power of human reason.

This conclusion may seem extreme to modern Christians who are sympathetic to the Greek philosophical tradition. Indeed, the history of Christianity has shown us many ways in which faith and reason work together, especially within the natural law tradition developed by Thomas Aquinas. However, the original sources contain much that is directly antagonistic to the humanistic spirit of the Greek philosophical tradition. Paul writes, for example: "See to it that no one makes a prey of you by philosophy and empty deceit, according to human tradition, according to the elemental spirits of the universe, and not according to Christ" (Colossians 2:8–9). He also writes: "For Jews demand signs and Greeks seek wisdom, but we preach Christ crucified, a stumbling block to Jews and folly to Gentiles, but to those who are called, both Jews and Greeks, Christ the power of God and the wisdom of God. For the foolishness of God is wiser than men, and the weakness of God is stronger than men (1 Corinthians 1:22–25).

Paul's use here of the term "wisdom"—or *sophia*—demands to be compared with the Greek idea of *sophia* that is found in the very idea of *philosophia*, or "love of wisdom." Paul's point is that human beings are not wise enough by themselves to achieve wisdom. Nor are we good enough to achieve virtue by ourselves. Rather, wisdom must be revealed to us by God, and God must intervene to allow us to overcome our sinfulness. As Paul puts it, "He is the source of your life in Christ Jesus, whom God made our wisdom, our righteousness and sanctification and redemption" (1 Corinthians 1:30). In this important passage, Paul indicates that Jesus is the Christ or messiah who provides wisdom (*sophia*) and justice or righteousness (*dikaiosyne*) as well as redemption. What is especially interesting here is that these two words—wisdom and justice—are words that are crucial for Plato and the Greeks. Indeed, for Plato, wisdom and justice were two of the four cardinal virtues (along with courage and moderation). But unlike Paul, Plato thought that at least some human beings—those who were in love with wisdom—could redeem themselves by following this love through the upward path of education that leads us out of darkness and into the light of truth.

The Christian religion is—by definition—a religion that is about the Christ or messiah. The idea that we need a messiah to provide us with wisdom and righteousness is opposed to one degree or another to a humanistic philosophy that believes that human beings can achieve wisdom without divine intervention. We should thus contrast the idea of the Christ or messiah with the idea of a moral teacher. If we conceive of Jesus as the messiah, then *he is the truth*. In the Gospel of John, Jesus says, "I am the way, and the truth, and the life: no one comes to the Father but by me" (John 14:6). In other places in John—chapter 8, for example—Jesus claims that his message is true because it comes directly from "the Father." He also claims, "I and the Father are one" (John 10:30). On the standard interpretation of these ideas, Jesus is more than a teacher; he is also the very object—the source and the content—of what is to be taught. Socrates, on the other hand, is a mere teacher; he does not present himself as the object of contemplation and worship. Rather, Socrates conceives of himself as a midwife whose teaching method is devoted to helping individuals give birth to the truth by helping individuals discover and develop the truth that is found through reason. The idea of the messiah is that the faithful are born again, in and through the messiah; the idea of a teacher is that the teacher helps us to give birth to the truths of reason.

Although many Christians believe that Jesus' ethical teachings are intrinsically related to claims about his divinity or his status as a prophet or messiah, his ethical ideas can be divorced from these other theological claims. In other words, we can consider Jesus as a *moral teacher*, while avoiding more speculative claims about whether Jesus was the son of God, whether he was resurrected, or even whether Jesus actually existed.

Now this may seem like the wrong way to go about an inquiry into "the ethics of Jesus." It might seem that we should first establish whether Jesus actually existed, and that we should also establish the veracity and authenticity of the biblical texts. From this perspective, the truth of ethics depends on the truth of the source: we may want to know exactly what Jesus actually said. A group of scholars known collectively as "the Jesus Seminar" have endeavored to do just this. They have examined the Gospels in an effort to verify and authenticate the words and acts of Jesus. Such a project is instructive. However, it is still limited to a theological principle: that it is Jesus' genuine voice that is the source of ethics.

It might seem, then, that we should get our theology straight first. We should first decide whether Jesus was in fact the son of God who was given by a loving God so that "whoever believes in him should not perish but have eternal life" (John 3:16). It might seem that to ignore the theological question is blasphemous, or at least woefully misguided. Many Christians seem to think that once we get the theology right and once we authenticate the texts, then ethics will follow.

However, disputes remain—even among Christians—about the authenticity of the texts and about the truth of the Christian revelation. One might then simply focus on what Jesus says about ethics in the texts that form the core of the tradition, while ignoring the more contentious claims about theology. Indeed, the scholars of the Jesus Seminar argue that the ethical pronouncements of the New Testament are the most authentic words attributed to Jesus. But often these pronouncements are not unique to Jesus. Rather, they are part of the developed Hebrew tradition that was shared by Jesus and the authors of the Gospels. For example, the two essential commandments given by Jesus in Matthew 22:37–39—to love God and love your neighbor—have also been attributed to Hillel, a Judean rabbi who was a near contemporary of Jesus. Moreover, it is possible that claims about Jesus' divinity and stories of his miracles are creations of the early Christian community and of the imaginations of the authors of the Gospels.

These authors wanted to establish Jesus' religious authority as they wrote the Gospels in the generations after Jesus' death.

PHILOSOPHICAL HUMANISM

The philosophical tradition has long maintained that ethical wisdom is prior to religious speculation. In the dialogue *Euthyphro*, Socrates argues that the will of God does not make something good. Rather, ethics is, in a sense, prior to God: God wills the good because it is good (and because God is good). Thus to understand God we need first to understand the good. More concretely, Plato argues in the *Republic* that we should use reason to criticize even stories about the gods. Some religious stories have the gods doing horrible things. Zeus and the other Greek gods were jealous, partial, and vengeful. It should be noted, of course, that these characteristics also apply to the God of the Old Testament. Plato argues that since the gods are moral beings, stories that make them appear to be immoral are false. Human reason provides us with a standard according to which we should evaluate stories and revelations about God. A god who is worthy of worship must be good. Thus, in order to discover the proper object of worship, we must first ask the basic questions of ethics. In short, humanistic ethics is important and cannot be overlooked by Christians who want to return to biblical texts, because a humanistic account of ethics helps us to decide how we are to interpret and criticize the biblical texts.

Humanism is a method that uses human reason to evaluate ideas. But there is a long and contentious history of humanism. The ancient Greek philosophers Socrates, Plato, and Aristotle were humanists, as were the Stoics, Skeptics, and Epicureans. In the Renaissance, Pico della Mirandola, Leonardo da Vinci, and others represented a brand of humanism that sought to bring back the traditions of ancient philosophy. Almost every modern philosopher could be called "humanist": from Descartes to Kant and beyond. The eighteenth-century thinkers typical of the era known as the "Enlightenment"—including the founders of the United States—were thoroughly humanistic. In short, the basis of modern Western culture is humanistic.

Humanism does not necessarily lead to atheism, nor is it explicitly anti-Christian. The ancient Greek philosophers did not deny the existence of the gods. Pico argued that philosophy could lift us toward God. Descartes sought to prove the existence of God using reason. Even skeptics such as Voltaire were aware of the importance of the Christian teaching. Of course, there are some contemporary authors who use "humanism" in a way that equates it with atheism (Paul Kurtz, for example). However, humanism simply means a commitment to the human capacity to know the truth by the employment of reason. This truth may include truths about divinity.

But humanism is at least partially antagonistic to religion. Indeed, a humanistic approach will ask critical questions of "revealed religion." Revealed religion is the set of views about divinity that are "revealed" to a few select witnesses or prophets. These ideas are then disseminated by way of oral or written communication. The difficulty of revealed religion is that its truth is based on the authority of the witness or author. Since Socrates, philosophers have criticized such authorities. The basic question a humanist asks of authority is "Why should I believe you?" This question asks for justification by way of arguments that appeal to general reasons and readily available evidence. Humanists want a good reason to believe something, and they think that appeal to authority is not an adequate reason.

There are reasonable sources for claims about moral value. We can look at our own experience or at the experience of others to discover what is good. And we can employ reason to evaluate the coherence of claims that are made about what is good. It turns out that much of what we would arrive at using this approach is similar to Jesus' ethical vision. Indeed, there is a vast consensus among ethical philosophers about moral values. And Jesus' ideas about ethics are part of the mainstream of this consensus.

Yes, disagreements remain. But these disagreements are part of the very process of doing ethics from a humanistic perspective. We must argue our way through disagreements in order to find truth. And here is a crucial difference between humanistic ethics and an approach that appeals to "divine command." The divine commandments may not be subjected to critical analysis. When Moses returned from the mountain, he spoke with the authority of God, and this authority was not to be questioned. However, the humanistic approach would question those who claim to speak with God's authority. "How do you know that this is God's will?" the humanist would ask. And indeed, a humanist would be willing to compare rival claims about the will of God in order to arrive at the truth.

It is important to note that we see a version of humanism even in the Christian Gospels. This shows up in two ways. First, Jesus uses parables to teach: this shows us that his goal is for human beings to understand. It is not enough that human beings follow the ethical commandments; they must also understand these commandments to the best of their ability. Of course, Jesus does claim that there are some who can see and hear better than others (Matthew 13), but his goal is for everyone to understand as best they can. Second, Jesus engages in dialogues with the Pharisees and others who either want to be taught or want to prove him wrong. Although these dialogues fall short of the sort of dialogues that Socrates engaged in, the presence of these dialogues in the stories of Jesus' teaching show us that Jesus was willing to engage in a rational process of dialogue and debate. Indeed, these dialogues occasionally had to do with the proper interpretation of the Hebrew scriptures. Jesus thus hints that it is proper to use reason to interrogate sacred texts.

WHAT WAS JESUS: SON OF GOD OR SON OF MAN?

Christians think that Jesus is the "son of God," which is usually thought to mean that Jesus shares in God's substance. Christians also think that Jesus is a "son of man," which is usually thought to indicate Jesus was not only God but also human. The supposed conjunction of God and man in Jesus is one of the most complex and subtle problems in Christian theology.

If Jesus is God, then his ethical pronouncements carry the full force of divine command; to disobey the commandments would be to turn away from God. One of the appeals of the divine command approach to ethics is that it provides a source of enforcement for ethics. The fear of God's displeasure at unethical actions and the hope for an eternal reward for good behavior can serve to inspire people to conform to basic ethical principles. However, the method of the present account attempts to sidestep such religious claims and the theological structure of reward and punishment. Even if it were true that Jesus spoke with divine authority, the humanist assumption is that we can use reason to evaluate and understand Jesus' words. There is a long and complicated philosophical and psychological dispute about motivation for ethics. But the basic assumption of the humanist approach is that the human search for truth is enough to foster an ethical life: our greatest goal is to know the good and to develop habits that allow us to become good.

There may be some basis for humanism in the Gospel texts. Jesus refers to himself as the "son of man" in numerous places in the Gospels.

Usually this is interpreted as merely another title by which we can identify the messiah, along with the "son of God," "the light of the world,"
the "word of God," or the "wisdom of God." Biblical scholars such as
Marcus Borg and those who make up the Jesus Seminar argue that the
claims about Jesus' identity that are found, for example, in the Gospel
of John are attempts by the early Christian community to explain what
they experienced in and through Jesus. Indeed, some of these scholars
claim that Jesus never said such things about himself—they are later
interpretations of Jesus' identity made by his followers. There is thus a
long-standing dispute among scholars about the relationship between
the eschatological and apocalyptic claims that we find in the Bible and
the claims that we find about the human concerns of ethics. One of
the difficulties of the "son of man" language is that it can be traced in
multiple directions. In the Old Testament, Daniel recounts an apocalyptic dream in which the son of man comes out of a cloud and is given
everlasting dominion over all peoples (Daniel 7). And this language is
echoed in the apocalyptic vision of the book of Revelation.

Appellations and epithets like "son of God" and "son of man" thus
indicate a connection between the rhetoric of the New Testament and
the language of the Jewish tradition of the prophets. Ezekiel uses the
phrase "son of man" repeatedly: it is the phrase that God uses in addressing his words to Ezekiel and through Ezekiel to the people of Israel. But
for Ezekiel it is connected to a sense of human frailty and distance from
God. We see this also in Job, where one of Job's companions reminds Job
of how worthless human beings are: "How then can man be righteous
before God? How can he who is born of woman be clean? Behold
even the moon is not bright and the stars are not clean in his sight; how
much less man, who is a maggot, and the son of man who is a worm!"
(Job 26:4–6). The idea of the "son of man" is thus used to establish the
distance between humans and God. With this in mind, it is possible that
when Jesus calls himself (or is called by the authors of the Gospels) the
"son of man," he is modestly expressing his connection to humanity.

But when Jesus is also called the son of God, we have the possibility
of a remarkable revaluation: that which is worthless—the human alienated from God—is redeemed. The idea that Jesus is the "son of God"
might be interpreted as a metaphorical claim that Jesus possessed a spark
of the divine that is found in wisdom. While Jesus appeared to his followers to have possessed wisdom, it is possible that all human beings
possess a spark of the divine: we are all, in this sense, sons and daughters
of God. But it is important to note that the Christian tradition holds that

this redemption cannot be accomplished without divine intervention.

The phrase "son of man" helps situate Jesus within the Jewish prophetic tradition. But much of this tradition is full of metaphor. Ezekiel claims, for example, that God gave him a scroll, which he ate and which then filled his mouth with words. And Isaiah speaks in oracles and parables that use vivid poetic imagery. The Gospel of John is full of such poetic imagery, especially in describing Jesus. Jesus is described as the word that was with God, as the light of the world, as the lamb of God, as the living water, as the good shepherd, as the door of the sheep, as the true vine, and as the son of God.

What are we to make of these names and metaphors? What does it mean to claim to be a "son of God" in this metaphorical sense? The humanist interpretation is that this points to the spark of the divine within the human. This spark is reason. When John calls Jesus the "word" of God, he uses the word *logos*, which is the Greek word for "reason." As the Renaissance humanist Pico della Mirandola puts it, it is reason that allows us to transcend our animal condition and commune with God. The idea here is that God is reasonable and we can commune with God (or even become like God) when we employ reason. Since God is conceived as an ethical being, we commune with God (and even become like God) when we understand and do the good. This idea can be derived from the "wisdom" tradition of the Old Testament. In the apocryphal book Wisdom of Solomon, the idea is expressed in a prayer: "May God grant to me to speak properly, and to have thoughts worthy of what he has given me, for it is he that guides wisdom, and directs the wise."[2] This tradition does not reject the pursuit of human wisdom, although it does suggest that human wisdom must be open to and guided by God.

There are a variety of ways to understand who or what Jesus was. The Bible scholar John Dominic Crossan summarizes biblical scholarship in his book *The Historical Jesus* and indicates a variety of interpretations of Jesus that include the following: Jesus as political revolutionary, as magician, as charismatic leader, as rabbi, as Hillelite or proto-Pharisee, as Essene, and as eschatological prophet. We might also include Jesus as healer and miracle worker. Crossan indicates that Jesus could also be considered a peasant Jewish Cynic. There is no easy way to resolve the question of who or what Jesus was. My choice here is to focus on Jesus as an ethical teacher.

If we make this interpretive choice, then we can look to Jesus as a model for *human* behavior and wisdom. Jesus' example may be more meaningful if we conceive of him as a man and not as a god. A god who has to sacrifice, suffer, and die at least knows in advance the outcome of this tribulation. If we emphasize the divinized Jesus, then Jesus knows in advance that he will be betrayed, that he will die, and that he will be resurrected. The later chapters of John show us a Jesus who knows the drama that is about to be enacted. But if the outcome is known in advance, one wonders whether the tribulation would in fact cause much suffering. Suffering is exacerbated when the outcome is in doubt; but when we know that there will be a reward at the end of an ordeal, pain becomes more bearable. If Jesus were a god, and if he knew himself to be one, then his passion would seem to lack the human element of doubt, despair, and loss that creates genuine suffering and is part of a genuine sacrifice. The model that Jesus provides for a human life of service and sacrifice is more inspirational and effective if we conceive of Jesus as a man and not as a god.

THE ANALOGY WITH SOCRATES

So far I have spoken of Jesus as if he were a real man. I have no reason to doubt that he actually existed. However, it is important to note that the mere fact of his existence tells us nothing about his divinity. Indeed, what we know about Jesus is mediated through the authors of the Gospel accounts of his life and teachings. But these accounts are merely the written words of human beings. It is nevertheless appropriate to treat Jesus as a person in the same way that philosophers and historians treat Socrates as a person. The basic method here is to approach Jesus as a literary hero in the same way that one would approach Socrates as a literary hero. By saying that Jesus is a literary hero, my aim is to focus on the moral vision that is exemplified in his story. Literary heroes can utter profound truths and they can provide models for the ethical life. The truths uttered by such heroes remain true despite questions we might have about the existence of the person who is the model for the literary character.

It is useful to consider the analogy between Jesus and Socrates because this analogy reminds us of the value of critical reading and of the way in which literary heroes can be guides for the ethical life.

We have only a tenuous grasp of "the real" Jesus or Socrates. It is as difficult to establish what Jesus actually said and did as it is to establish facts about Socrates' life and teaching. There are important limits here that must be acknowledged, such as the fact that the Gospels only give us a basic outline of the last years of Jesus' life. Nonetheless, we can still take the stories of Jesus' teaching and life seriously. If philosophers take Socrates seriously, despite our limited evidence about his actual life and thought, then we should also take Jesus seriously.

Our knowledge of Socrates and his teachings is indirect because he wrote nothing himself. The most influential source of information about Socrates is Plato, and there are a few other sources such as Aristophanes and Xenophon. Nonetheless, philosophers continue to use Socrates as *the* model for ancient Greek philosophy. The historic Socrates is probably best represented in Plato's early dialogues (such as the *Apology* or the *Charmides*). However, we must admit that Socrates has been presented to us by an author who has his own interests. Indeed, Plato's later dialogues (such as the *Republic*, *Phaedrus*, or *Statesman*) feature a character named Socrates who is different in significant ways from the Socrates of the early dialogues. In these differences we witness the development of Plato's ideas, but this has little to do with the historic Socrates. Despite this, the consensus among scholars is that Socrates did in fact profess a kind of skepticism conjoined with an irritating habit of questioning authority. And Socrates used this method in service of Athens and in hope of a better life.

Like Socrates, Jesus wrote nothing himself. And the Gospels present Jesus in different ways. There are lapses and differences even among the Gospel books. For example, it is not exactly clear whether Jesus was born in Bethlehem, as the Christmas tradition claims. The Gospel of Mark is thought to be the earliest account of the historic Jesus. But this Gospel does not contain an account of Jesus' birth; there is no Christmas story in this text. Nor is there one in the Gospel of John.

The different accounts of Jesus' life and teaching vary according to the interests of the authors. The books of Matthew, Mark, and Luke are considered to be "synoptic" Gospels—they provide similar accounts that focus on the concrete events of Jesus' life. The differences between Matthew and Luke, on the one hand, and Mark, on the other, are attributed by scholars to an oral tradition (and possibly lost written source) that scholars call Q. While Mark emphasizes Jesus' powers of healing and his ability to exorcize demons, Matthew emphasizes Jesus' ethical teachings, and Luke includes stories about Jesus' mother, Mary, that are not repeated elsewhere. But the Gospel according to John contains abstract metaphysical speculation about the nature of Jesus and his relation to God. Despite these differences, there are some obvious common themes. The story of Jesus' betrayal, death, and resurrection is the climax of all of the Gospels. And Jesus' miraculous powers to heal, to walk on water, to turn water into wine, and to bring about other phenomena are attested to throughout. Moreover, Jesus' ethical vision is presented in all four of the Gospels.

The analogy between Socrates and Jesus can be pushed further by considering the content of their ideas and the trajectory of their lives, as established in the literary record. Both of these characters claim to have a sort of wisdom that runs counter to the orthodox authorities of their communities. Both are eventually killed for this anti-authoritarian stance. More importantly, Jesus and Socrates both challenge the established authorities because of a profound concern for justice and the ethical life. And both link this concern to a kind of transcendence that culminates in a vision of immortality. Socrates tells us that the just are most likely rewarded in the next life. Jesus also tells us that the key to immortal happiness is the ethical life. And both are interested in the importance of piety and commitment to virtue.

One important difference is that Socrates never claims to be a god, nor did Plato make any claims about Socrates' resurrection. Mythical stories about the afterlife and transmigration of souls can be found in Plato's works, including the "myth of Er" in the concluding book of the *Republic*. However, the Gospel writers systematically emphasize the resurrection and divinity of Jesus. This crucial difference cannot be overlooked. Indeed, Christians will claim that this difference makes all the difference: as the incarnation of God and the pathway to eternal life, Jesus has ultimate authority.

CONCLUSION

My goal here is to consider Jesus' ethical pronouncements in the same way that one would consider the ideas of some other literary figure: we must look at the content of the claims and analyze them reasonably. A Christian may claim that reason has no place in an analysis of Jesus, since faith in Jesus is sufficient for living well. But even Jesus claims that we must "beware of false prophets" (Matthew 7:15). This implies that we must use reason to criticize and evaluate the claims made by those who claim to be prophets or philosophers—the claims of Jesus included. One way we do this is by looking for consistency within the claims that Jesus makes and by coordinating them with the broader set of principles that we derive from reason. Jesus tells us quite clearly what his first principles are. But these principles are acceptable not because Jesus says them. Rather, if they are acceptable it is because they form part of a coherent ethical system. In approaching Jesus in this way, I ally myself with Socrates and the long tradition of humanistic philosophy in thinking that human reason is the key to interpreting even the pronouncements of God.

NOTES

1. Benjamin Franklin, Letter to Ezra Stiles (1790), in *The Portable Enlightenment Reader*, ed. Isaac Kramnick (New York: Penguin, 1995).

2. *The Wisdom of Solomon*, chap. 7 in *The Apocrypha: An American Translation* (New York: Vintage, 1959), 190.

3

JESUS' GOLDEN RULE:
ALTRUISM AND UNIVERSALITY

> Love your enemies, do good to those who hate you, bless
> those who curse you, pray for those who abuse you. To him
> who strikes you on the cheek, offer the other also; and from
> him who takes away your coat do not withhold even your
> shirt. Give to every one who begs from you; and of him who
> takes away your goods do not ask them again. And as you wish
> that men would do to you, do so to them.
>
> —Luke 6:27–31

Jesus' primary moral teaching is the Golden Rule: "love your neighbor as yourself," or "as you wish that men would do to you, do so to them." This moral rule is stated as a commandment, second only to the commandment to love God. One might argue that the first commandment is in fact logically prior to the second: in order to love our neighbor, we must first love God. It is important not to overlook the crucial place of piety in the ethics of Jesus: the Christian ethic is intimately connected with Christian worship and theology. To love our neighbor in the sense that Jesus intends may imply a radical redistribution of wealth that is only possible if we transcend our attachment to the material goods of this world. We may be enjoined to give everything away. At least it is probable that Jesus thought affluence was a sin, especially when others were poor and suffering. Pious love of God—which directs our attention away from material goods—may make it easier to give others what they need.

We see the primacy of piety if we return to the Old Testament, especially to the Ten Commandments. The first four commandments focus on the relation between humans and God. The struggle of the Old Testament is to convince the Israelites to remain committed to Yahweh and not to be tempted by rival gods. Old Testament texts address a community of believers with the goal of reminding them of their duties to God and to each other.

This ethical focus permeates the prophetic tradition. The first chapter of Isaiah emphasizes justice. "Wash yourselves; make yourselves clean; remove the evil of your doings from before my eyes; cease to do evil, learn to do good; seek justice, correct oppression; defend the fatherless, plead for the widow." Similar passages could be cited from the other prophets. The basic idea here is that we are commanded to do good and seek justice. This is also the heart of Jesus' ethical teaching. We are to focus on becoming virtuous and we are to care for the weak and the oppressed. This is what *altruism* is: caring for others (as opposed to caring only for oneself).

It should be remembered, however, that the Hebrew idea of justice was often confined to justice *within* the community. The prophets addressed a closed community united under the same God. The same could be said of Jesus: he talked to Jews about Jewish concerns. Nonetheless, the germ of a more universal ethical message can be found in Jesus' teaching. This extension of moral concern beyond the community of believers represents a substantial development in the direction of the universalism that is characteristic of contemporary humanist ethics.

The Golden Rule is an elegant expression of altruism: we are to care for others as we would care for ourselves. However, there are two difficult questions that must be answered in order to properly apply this time-honored principle. Who is my neighbor? And what should I do to love him or her?

WHO IS MY NEIGHBOR?

This question is traditionally answered by focusing on a community of believers united under God. In the Old Testament, there was an exclusive focus on the members of the religious community. Nonbelievers were not considered neighbors to whom love was owed. But should we love those with whom we share little in common? A "neighbor" seems to be someone we are close to, for example, a member of our family, village, or religious/ethnic group. Foreigners or those who worship other gods are not necessarily considered neighbors in this sense. At least there is no explicit demand in the standard formulation of the moral law—"love your neighbor as yourself"—that we consider foreigners or strangers.

The Greek word for neighbor is *plesion,* which is translated in Latin as *proximus,* which literally means "one who is near." It is important to remember that Jesus does articulate a parable—the parable of the Good Samaritan—that calls for the extension of the idea of the neighbor to include those who are not members of the religious or ethnic community. However, this parable is only recorded in Luke. And Jesus does not emphasize—even in this parable—a truly *universal* extension of altruism. In other words, although the Good Samaritan story shows us that foreigners should be considered as neighbors, Jesus nowhere states that all human beings have an inherent right to be cared for, regardless of race, ethnicity, or religious affiliation.

Jesus did not invent the Golden Rule. Nor did he invent the first commandment regarding piety. He inherited them from Old Testament texts. And Hillel and other contemporaries of Jesus had the same idea. The Gospel texts quote the Old Testament directly, even as they reinterpret these ancient Hebrew ideas. The first commandment as stated by Moses in Deuteronomy (6:5) is "love the Lord your God with all your heart and with all your soul and with all your might." The context of this passage is one that focuses on the sin of worshiping other gods. Later in this same chapter, Moses tells the people that God is a "jealous God," and he claims that if the people were to worship other gods, God will "destroy you from the face of the earth" (Deut. 6:15). He further states that the love of God will culminate in political power, as God will provide the Israelites with the power to take possession of the land of Canaan. Moses then says the following of the enemies whom the Israelites will fight for the land:"When the Lord your God gives them over to you and you defeat them; then you must utterly destroy them; you shall make no covenant with them, and show no mercy to them" (Deut. 7:2). The brutal stories of destruction that are found in the book of Joshua represent the fulfillment of this mission to slaughter the enemies of Israel and occupy the land of Canaan. Here the first commandment to love God is linked to the commandment to kill your enemies; it is not linked to the idea of loving your neighbor. Nor can it be linked to Jesus' even more radical idea of loving your enemy.

Despite the brutal implications of the commandment of piety in the Old Testament, the Golden Rule is found there as well, and it is extended in a direction that points beyond the ethnocentric violence of Deuteronomy and Joshua. The formulation that Jesus uses is found in Leviticus (19:18), and it is even extended in this chapter to the idea of loving the "stranger who sojourns with you in your land" (19:33). In the difference between Deuteronomy and Leviticus we see the problem of turning to scripture for ethical advice. The contradictions between these passages are stark. And these contradictions are not easily resolved by turning to Jesus as the reconciling principle, for we still wonder whom we should love and how we should love them. The point here is that the Bible is a compilation of sources, written for specific purposes at specific times. These sources occasionally conflict with one another, as the interests and contexts of the authors of these texts lead to different conclusions. The Bible is not a *systematic* treatise on ethics—or on religion for that matter. Rather, it represents an evolving attempt to understand ethics and God's will.

Jesus' understanding of the Golden Rule is not that different from what we find in Leviticus. It is useful to consider the original formulation of this rule in Leviticus in full. The key passage occurs in a longer list of ethical commandments. The Golden Rule is then stated as follows (Lev. 18:17–18): "You shall not hate your brother in the heart, but you shall reason with your neighbor, lest you bear sin because of him. You shall not take vengeance or bear any grudge against the sons of your own people, but you shall love your neighbor as yourself; I am the Lord." The point here is that the Golden Rule is applied *within* the community of the people of Israel—a community whose members could be called "brothers." But in the formulation of this in Luke, Jesus expands on the idea of the "neighbor." In the passage in Luke, after having recited the two commandments, Jesus is challenged by an expert in religious law who asks him, "And who is my neighbor?" Jesus replies with the parable of the Good Samaritan, where the Samaritan goes out of his way to help someone who was not a member of his community. The gist of this story is that the neighbor is the one who is in need of assistance—regardless of our relationship with him or her. The germ of this idea is already contained in the idea in Leviticus that we should love the "stranger who sojourns with you in your land."

This understanding of the Golden Rule as applying beyond the community of believers points to a unique emphasis for later Christian ethics and toward the development of a truly universal notion of human rights. But it should be noted that the Gospels are not entirely clear about the universal application of the Golden Rule. The story of the Good Samaritan is, after all, a parable: Jesus does not directly state that ethical concern should be applied universally. In the Matthew version (23:34–40) of the story of Jesus' discussion with the expert on religious law (who is now explicitly identified as a Pharisee), the conversation ends simply with Jesus' statement of the two commandments. There is no parable of the Good Samaritan in Matthew. However, in Matthew's Sermon on the Mount, Jesus gives an indication of a further extension of the Golden Rule. He says, "You have heard that it was said 'you shall love your neighbor and hate your enemy.' But I say to you, Love your enemies and pray for those who persecute you" (5:43–44). Moreover, Jesus makes the commandment to "love your enemies" in at least two places in Luke (6:27, 6:35). Thus there are several indications that Luke and Matthew aim to extend the application of the Golden Rule beyond its application within the community. The Golden Rule is to apply to everyone: friend and enemy, community member or stranger. At least this seems to be the gist of the idea that can be derived from these texts.

For the tradition—as found in Deuteronomy and Joshua—that aimed to slaughter enemies in the name of God, the idea of loving enemies is radically subversive. In the nineteenth century, Tolstoy claimed that the essence of the Gospel message was to "resist not evil." This idea involves much more than merely loving your neighbor. It also involves pacifism and a sort of love that runs counter to the tradition of retributive justice, where the idea of justice was "an eye for an eye." Indeed, Jesus tells us that the old idea of *lex talionis* no longer applies. We will consider this in more detail in subsequent chapters.

Three philosophical concepts might help to explain this expansion of the Golden Rule: the ideas of universality, impartiality, and equality. Universality means that moral principles should apply to each and every person. Impartiality means that they should be applied in an unbiased way. And equality means that these ideas apply equally to everyone. These concepts are cornerstones of philosophical ethics as it has developed in the modern West, and they are essential to the idea of human rights. This idea was expressed, for example, by Jefferson in the Declaration of Independence: "All men are created equal and they are endowed by their Creator with certain inalienable rights." Here equality and universality are linked: all have equal rights under God. Immanuel Kant, the most important modern proponent of "deontology" (moral obligation) in ethics, maintains that universality is the key to understanding the moral law. The moral law, for Kant, is the demand that we do nothing that cannot be considered as a universal law for humankind. The "utilitarian" approach of John Stuart Mill claims that we should consider the greatest good for the greatest number, and that this calculation of utility should focus on the largest possible social unit while ignoring partial interests. Likewise, the ideas of universality, impartiality, and equality can be found in Thomas Nagel's recent attempt to return to the idea of the Golden Rule by asking: "How would you like it if someone did that to you?" Nagel claims that this is the basic question of ethics, a question that forces us to imagine the perspective of the other. These values have also been advocated recently by John Rawls, who claims that in order to decide about the principles of justice, we should ignore our particular interests and affiliations under what he calls a "veil of ignorance." This idea is supposed to help us obtain an impartial and universal perspective in which everyone has equal consideration.

Contemporary ethicists have pondered the problem of extending basic altruism in a universal direction. The philosopher Peter Singer claims that we have an obligation to all suffering others. In an influential article on global poverty, "Famine, Affluence, and Morality," Singer claims that we have an obligation to give away everything up to the point of what he calls "marginal utility." The idea here is that those of us in affluent nations should give away our wealth up to the point at which we create more suffering for ourselves than we alleviate in others. Singer's point is, however, that we would not be obligated to give away quite this much. Rather, if every affluent person gave a bit, global poverty could easily be eliminated, and the amount that would be needed to eliminate poverty would not be so much that it would substantially disrupt the way of life of the affluent. This argument makes use of concepts such as universality, equality, and impartiality. The idea is that everyone's interests matter equally, and that we should impartially judge how distributions of goods are to be made.

Jesus would appear to concur with Singer when he claims that we should give to those who are in need. But Jesus did not use concepts such as universality or impartiality in his ethical teaching. The ideas of the philosophers mentioned here do share much in common with Jesus. However, they go beyond Jesus in attempting to systematically explain the idea of "loving your neighbor." Concepts such as universality, equality, and impartiality require detailed exposition. Jesus simply says, "Love your neighbor"; philosophical ethics asks what this means.

Let us return to the idea of the neighbor as "one who is near." The claim that altruism only applies within a community is easy enough to understand. We do have positive duties toward those with whom we are intimately connected—our family, friends, and co-workers. But we usually do not feel compelled to help suffering others in distant places. One could argue that the idea of loving your neighbor as yourself only works when you and the neighbor live in a close community. We need to have enough in common that it makes sense to say that we love one another. For me to love a neighbor as myself, the neighbor must be a self who is similar to me in important ways. One of these important similarities may in fact be our similar religious experience: we are the same because we both worship the same God. It is possible to imagine two moral rules: "love family members and co-religionists" but "treat strangers differently." Indeed, much of the history of the world has been based on these two rules. Something like these two rules were stated, for example, in Plato's *Republic* by Polemarchus, who argued that justice was "doing good to friends and harm to enemies" (332 ff.). Traditional accounts of ethics make an implicit distinction between *us* and *them*. Thus the Golden Rule does not necessarily have universal scope—unless we radically reinterpret the idea of "the neighbor" to include those with whom we have very little in common. It is often suggested that this is what Jesus had in mind in the parable of the Good Samaritan. While Jesus' reinterpretation of the idea of the neighbor in this parable is provocative, it needs further development. This is why the Golden Rule has been supplemented in contemporary ethics with the idea of universal human rights, which ought to be respected despite our differences.

HOW SHOULD I LOVE MY NEIGHBOR?

The second problem for interpreting the Golden Rule is related to the first: it is not clear exactly what it means to love another. The commandment to "love your neighbor" is vague and does not tell us how to behave in concrete cases. My neighbor may have stored his weapons in my house—to paraphrase an example used by Socrates—but should I return these weapons to him when he arrives at my house raging drunk? As Socrates shows, we need a more concrete idea of harm and benefit if we are to know how properly to apply the idea of love. It might, for example, be perfectly fine to ignore suffering strangers because they would want to be left alone to be cared for by their families, or because helping them may offend their sense of pride. In the same way, love might be expressed by allowing a stranger to worship his own god in his own way. But it might also require me to force the other to come to God in order to save his eternal soul. A proper understanding and application of the Golden Rule requires a substantial amount of further reflection about the nature of harm, the importance of autonomy, and the proper relation between self and other.

Jesus explains love in a commonsense way by linking it to the idea of alleviating suffering by helping the poor and the weak. In Luke (6:30–31), Jesus says, "Give to every one who begs from you; and of him who takes away your goods do not ask them again. And as you wish that men would do to you, do so to them." This formulation of the Golden Rule is in the form of "do unto others as you would have them do unto you." Here the context is one of poverty: if you were poor, you would want to be assisted, so if you find someone who is poor, help them out.

The idea that we ought to care for others as much as we care for ourselves runs counter to an egoistic perspective that maintains that we each should mind our own business and pursue our own self-interest. The altruistic perspective is most easily derived from the idea of a shared community: when the members of the community help each other, we all do better. Such a view, which emphasizes the mutual benefit of the Golden Rule, might be called "reciprocal altruism." Reciprocal altruism means "I'll help you if you help me." This is the basic idea of a capitalist economy: trade is a sort of reciprocal altruism. However, as we shall see, Jesus' idea points beyond reciprocity. Genuine Christian altruism asks nothing in return. As Jesus says in the passage from Luke cited above: "Of him who takes away your goods, do not ask them again."

Pure Christian altruism thus appears to run counter to the competitive and individualistic ethic of modern capitalism, where the presupposition is that we all do better when we develop the economy by competing with one another. Jesus, however, does not praise those who are successful in business. Instead, in the Sermon on the Mount, Jesus blesses the poor and the meek. These are not the winners in the struggle for survival; rather, Jesus turns his attention to the losers. The connection between altruism and helping the poor is made explicit in Matthew 19. Jesus is asked what one must do to gain eternal life. Jesus says that one must keep the commandments, especially the commandment "love your neighbor as yourself." In order to do this properly, Jesus says that we should sell what we possess and give to the poor. And immediately following this passage is Jesus' famous claim that it is easier for a camel to go through the eye of a needle than for a rich man to enter heaven.

Jesus' concern with alleviating poverty thus expresses the specific content of a general sort of altruism. While Jesus does not directly answer the question of how far we are to extend our altruistic concern for the poor, it is quite clear that within the immediate neighborhood, Jesus intends us to do as much as we can to help the poor. We might presume that Singer's idea of giving to the point of "marginal utility" applies.

However, we may be required even to go beyond this: Jesus himself gave more than he received, and his example of self-sacrificial love might be the primary model.

The difficulty of this view is that Jesus does not look deeper into the social and political questions of how best to alleviate poverty, nor does he have a clearly developed understanding of economics. Will direct handouts to the poor work in the long run to reduce poverty? Is it really a good idea to let those who steal our goods keep them? Jesus claims that if someone takes your coat, you should also give him your shirt. But will this work in the long run to alleviate suffering?

The idea of tolerating the thievery of those in need that is found in the Sermon on the Mount in Matthew and in the Sermon on the Plain in Luke is connected with the larger context of these passages: the idea of "loving your enemies" and "turning the other cheek" (Matthew 5:38–46; Luke 6:27–29). I'll return to this pacifist ideal and its connection with a larger utopian view in the next chapter. The question there will be: "But will it work?"

Jesus' altruism may actually lead us to condemn the modern ideal of private property on which the egoistic pursuits of capitalism are grounded. It is private property that creates the possibility of thievery: a needy person who takes a coat only commits a crime if the coat is thought to belong to someone else, and in our capitalist system we assume that all material goods belong to someone until they are traded to someone else. In a society based on altruism and motivated by Jesus' concern for the poor, private property may have to be abolished and we might want to organize ourselves according to the Marxist idea: "From each according to their ability, to each according to their need." This is not as far-fetched as it sounds. In Acts, the apostles are described as living together in a communal arrangement. In this community of believers, the members cared for each other as genuine altruists. Each member sold his belongings and gave everything to the community. From this fund, "distribution was made to each as any had need" (Acts 4:35). It might come as a surprise to Americans that the basic principles of Marxism were employed by the members of the early church. But it should be no surprise that our emphasis on private property may in fact be one of the things that leads us away from the good life and indeed away from God.

From Jesus' perspective, what we own in this life is trivial in comparison with our relation to God and the treasures we will inherit in heaven. Here again, the theological context cannot be divorced from Jesus' ethical vision. When Jesus tells us to "render to Caesar the things that are Caesar's and to God the things that are God's" (Matthew 23:21), his point is that what God values transcends the world of money and property. Money and taxes belongs to Caesar—the ruler of the temporal world—but your soul belongs to God. Jesus is more explicit in his rejection of the money system and its exaltation of private property in his claim that "you cannot serve God and mammon" (Luke 16:13). The danger of "serving mammon" is that we make an idol out of money and forget God. This claim also has an interesting connection to Marxist critiques of capitalism: Marx conceives of money as a merely apparent value, which serves to conceal the real basis of value. Money, then, becomes a fetish item, which we invest with a kind of magical power. Jesus seems to understand this problem, and his discussions of wealth aim to get us to look beyond the magical power of money toward the infinitely higher value of God. We can see, then, an important reason why Jesus' first commandment—love God—needs to be considered prior to the Golden Rule. If we love God properly, we will see through the vanity of temporal goods and we will not make an idol out of money. This should make it easier to redistribute basic goods to those who need them, and so make it easier to truly love your neighbor.

Nonetheless, this sort of transformational piety is still a poor guide for telling us how best to express love of a neighbor in terms of the structure of our economy. If we refuse to idolize money and if we direct our love to God and to our neighbor, will this produce good for everyone—or will it simply reduce us all to poverty? History appears to show us that communism of the sort hinted at by Jesus may not be the best way to produce long-term benefit for everyone. Contemporary capitalists believe that the prosperity produced by the free market is the key to alleviating poverty. Indeed, Christian philosophers such as John Locke claim that the right to property is a basic right given by God. Locke claimed, in fact, that the introduction of money would allow the creation of surpluses, which would in turn produce more for everyone.

Jesus did not debate the virtues of capitalism per se, and he did not articulate a theory of economics and politics that would explain how best to put his altruistic vision into practice. Indeed, Jesus and his immediate interpreters—Paul and the authors of the Gospels—were apocalyptic thinkers who had little concern for questions about long-term economic development. If the eschatological expectation of these authors—and perhaps the expectation of Jesus himself—was that God was going to institute his reign on earth directly in the near future, questions about long-term economic development would be idle and irrelevant.

Paul claimed: "The form of this world is passing away" (1 Corinthians 7:31). And from this he counseled that we should not be anxious about the structure of worldly affairs. But the kingdom of God has not yet replaced the city of man. Thus we need to attend to "the dismal science" of economics. In this sense, Jesus' noble idea of loving your neighbor by giving everything to one who begs must be supplemented by the critical reflections of humanists who use reason to help us develop a more rational view of how to create social welfare.

CONCLUSION

Jesus elegantly articulates the idea of the Golden Rule. He locates this idea within a theological context and addresses it to a community of co-religionists. Nonetheless, he attempts to expand it beyond a simplistic understanding of what it means to "love your neighbor" by showing us, in the parable of the Good Samaritan, how the idea of the neighbor should be expanded to include whoever is in need. However important the parable of the Good Samaritan is, we must admit that the question of who is a neighbor is not fully resolved by Jesus. Moreover, Jesus did not envision the development of a truly global society in which the affluent on one side of the globe would be able to affect the suffering of the poor on the other side. One suspects that Jesus would have been in favor of a sort of global altruism of the sort imagined by Singer; he might even have been sympathetic to the Marxist vision of global communism. However, we must admit that to claim this is to move beyond the texts to a further interpretation. This further interpretation is best bolstered by considering the concepts developed in philosophical ethics: concepts such as universality, equality, and impartiality. These concepts themselves are important components of ethical theories such as utilitarianism, and they are essential to developing a theory of universal human rights.

Jesus did not develop a sophisticated ethical (or economic) theory. His claims were aimed at a local audience with the intent of inspiring this audience to take up the altruistic perspective already found in the Hebrew scriptures, while opening the possibility of a more universal understanding of this altruistic ideal. While Jesus' altruism is inspiring, it needs to be supplemented by a more fully developed ethical theory, as well as by more complex theories of politics and economics.

4

JESUS VERSUS JOSHUA: CHRISTIAN VIRTUES IN CONTEXT

Father, forgive them; for they know not what they do.

—Luke 23:34

Forgiveness is a primary value for Jesus. We see this value in the passage from Luke where Jesus is crucified. Instead of calling down hellfire and damnation, Jesus prays for forgiveness. It should be noted that this passage is unique to Luke. It does not show up in the other Gospels. Indeed, some scholars argue that the ancient original text of Luke did not contain this particular passage at all. But it fits with the overall narrative of Luke, which emphasizes charity, compassion, and forgiveness. Luke also includes the only accounts of the Good Samaritan and the parable of the prodigal son.

It is remarkable that there are divergent accounts of what Jesus said during his crucifixion. One would think that his final words would be so important that they would be remembered unanimously by his followers. But the Gospels diverge. This shows us a problem of interpretation. Should we take Luke's Gospel message as primary? Or should we focus more on Mark, which is the older of the Gospels but in which Jesus appears more as a miracle worker and prophet than as an ethical teacher? In Mark, Jesus' death occurs without the prayer for forgiveness and with the famous cry of despair: "My God, my God, why hast thou forsaken me?" One must make interpretive choices in thinking about this. The choice that I make here is to focus on the overall character of Jesus. This approach is thus interested in Jesus' virtues: his tendencies, habits, and dispositions, as well as what he said about the sort of character traits and habits that are important for living well.

Jesus did emphasize the importance of forgiveness and of peaceful acceptance of others. He even extended this to include love of and resignation to enemies. We see this in the overall story of his life and death as well as in his words (despite differences in the Gospel accounts). This spirit of forgiveness and acceptance runs counter to our most basic instincts: when one is attacked, beaten, condemned, rejected, and crucified, the most basic instinct is to fight back, to lash out, and to struggle for honor. Ancient warriors such as Achilles or Joshua would not have allowed themselves to be crucified without putting up a fight or at least lashing out with spiteful words. But Jesus represents a different ideal of moral excellence. He does not fight back or call for vengeance. Instead he submits and he forgives.

In Christian theology, forgiveness is more than an ethical ideal. It is also essential for the Christian doctrine of atonement: through his death, Jesus atones for the sins of humankind. Paul explains (for example, in Colossians 2:13–14) that the crucifixion of Christ allowed for "our trespasses" to be forgiven. The passion narrative and the doctrine of atonement are based on the story told about the Hebrews, their sins, and the distance from God that is found throughout the Old Testament. But in one of the final passages from Luke (24:45–47), the resurrected Christ explains that the idea of forgiveness of sins is now opened to all the nations. Thus Jesus' death is supposed to allow for forgiveness to all of humankind.

The theological story of how Jesus' crucifixion allows for sin to be forgiven is fascinating. However, as I noted at the outset, I will attempt to avoid theology here. It is possible to see Jesus' prayer of forgiveness as another example of the simple moral message that permeates Luke and the other Gospels as well: we should forgive those who harm us even unto death. It is, of course, difficult to distinguish the ethics of forgiveness from theology. The importance of the moral act of forgiving others is given a theological basis, for example, in the Lord's Prayer and Jesus' explanation of it. All Christians routinely recite the formula of the Lord's Prayer: "Forgive us our debts as we also have forgiven our debtors" (Matthew 6:12; Luke 11:4). In Matthew, Jesus explains this idea as follows: "For if you forgive men their trespasses, your heavenly Father also will forgive you; but if you do not forgive men their trespasses, neither will your Father forgive your trespasses" (Matthew 6:14–15). The moral idea of forgiveness is thus tied to a kind of cosmic reciprocity: in order to be forgiven, you must forgive others.

Some may claim that the idea of forgiveness only makes sense if we have faith in this sort of cosmic order. But one can argue that forgiveness is good directly, without appeal to theology: forgiveness and related Christian virtues—such as love, mercy, tolerance, and peacefulness—are virtues that are important for living well in community with others. It is possible to see in Jesus an example of the moral life that can be defended on its own, without recourse to theology.

Jesus' example is revolutionary and counterintuitive. The idea of forgiving one's enemies is related to the strange idea of *loving* your enemies. Jesus says in the Sermon on the Mount: "Love your enemies and pray for those who persecute you" (Matthew 5:44; Luke 6:27–28). Jesus' ideas appear odd to those who are raised in a tradition that celebrates the virtues of warriors and conquerors. According to the warrior tradition, enemies are to be killed and reviled. A virtuous warrior exacts revenge against his enemies. He does not forgive and love those who have harmed him.

Virtues are taught by way of example. Philosophers such as Alasdair MacIntyre and Stanley Cavell have reminded us of the importance of stories, exemplars, and traditions: virtues are excellences that are defined within a tradition of stories, rituals, and practices. The Christian stories look to Jesus as the moral exemplar who teaches forgiveness, love, and peace. We are reminded of these virtues when we think of stories such as the one Luke tells about Jesus' death. Virtue is most starkly exhibited when a moral hero is put into conditions of extreme duress. When Jesus is hanging on the cross in agony, we expect screams of pain, anger, and hatred. In Mark and Matthew, Jesus cries out to God because he feels forsaken. These stories seem to undermine the claim that Jesus is a moral exemplar: he succumbs to despair at the end. But in Luke we have the prayer of forgiveness, and Jesus' final words are "Father, into thy hands I commit my spirit" (Luke 23:46). It is interesting that there are discrepancies among the stories of the most important event in Christianity—Jesus' death—and such discrepancies may fuel skepticism about the accuracy of these accounts and their ultimate significance. It is impossible to say whether the Luke story is true or definitive. But the Luke story does remind us of the virtues that Jesus advocated throughout his life.

ANCIENT WARRIOR VIRTUES

The story of Jesus' life presents an idea of the good life that runs counter to a more ancient warrior tradition. The warrior virtues include honor, vengeance, courage, mercilessness, and righteous anger. Jesus' virtues are quite different. Thus an argument must be made about which life is the best life: the life of the warrior or the life of Jesus. Stories of Jesus' resurrection and special relationship to God serve to show that his model is superior to that of the ancient warrior tradition. But it is also possible to see that these virtues are essential to human flourishing, without appealing to resurrection or theology. We must begin this project by explaining the warrior tradition that Jesus was, in effect, arguing against.

The warrior virtues are seen most vividly in the stories of Greek epic poetry and in the stories of the Old Testament. Achilles and Odysseus are the moral heroes of the Greek warrior tradition. Moses and Joshua are the exemplars of the Hebrew warrior tradition. It is easy to romanticize the warrior virtues and make the warrior into a paragon of chivalry and decency. But the warrior virtues are about power and triumph. The virtuous warrior's goal is to seize power, and this requires ferocity and cruelty.

Achilles is the greatest of the Greek warriors. Achilles had a choice between a long life spent at home or a short life spent in pursuit of military power. The first option would have brought pleasure but not lasting fame. The second choice brings misery and death but also glory. Achilles chooses glory. The virtues that he exemplified include courage and physical strength. Indeed, these virtues create in him what might be called his fatal flaw—his tendency toward unbridled rage. The *Iliad* begins with Achilles' rage at being slighted by Agamemnon. And we see Achilles in full fury as he rampages in response to the death of Patroclus, his beloved companion. Achilles slaughters Trojans without mercy in revenge for the death of Patroclus. This slaughter includes the cold-blooded sacrifice of twelve Trojan prisoners on Patroclus' funeral pyre, as well as a horrific massacre in which Achilles kills so many Trojans that the river Scamander is choked with bodies and rebels against Achilles. Throughout this story, various victims—including the Trojan hero Hector—beg Achilles for mercy. Hector pleads with Achilles to be decent enough to allow his body to be properly buried. But Achilles shows no mercy. Indeed, he desecrates Hector's body by dragging it behind his chariot for days. While we may view such stories with disgust, we should recall that these stories *celebrate* Achilles' power. Achilles is the warrior par excellence. His rage, courage, and strength are the key to the glory he earns.

The same sorts of virtues are also found in the stories of Odysseus, with the exception that Odysseus' virtues also include a sort of guile and sneakiness. Like Achilles, Odysseus possesses physical prowess. This power is seen in his performance both in battle and in warlike games.

And his physical power is the key to his return to Ithaca: Odysseus alone is able to bend the bow that he left at home. But Odysseus also is a master of deception. He is the mastermind behind the Trojan horse, and he returns home in disguise. Both of these deceits culminate in slaughter. The Greeks hidden in the Trojan horse use deception to utterly destroy the Trojans, and Odysseus uses deception to set up the slaughter of the suitors who have invaded his house. Like Achilles, Odysseus shows no mercy. He kills all of his enemies whenever he can. Indeed, in one memorable scene, after he has butchered all of the suitors in his home, he orders the twelve maids who were disloyal to clean up the massacre. These maids were then taken outside and hanged. After this, Melanthius, the goatherd who had betrayed Odysseus, was taken outside: his nose and ears were sliced off, his private parts were ripped away as meat for dogs, and finally his feet and hands were lopped off.

Cruelty is not only a virtue of the Greek warriors. We also see it in Moses and Joshua. Moses is remarkably cruel. The indiscriminate slaughter of the firstborn in Egypt is perhaps the most memorable act of cruelty attributed to Moses and his God. Moses is a military leader as well as a religious leader. The parting of the Red Sea was a brilliant bit of military strategy that resulted in the total destruction of the pharaoh's chariots and horsemen. One difference between the Hebrews and the Greeks, however, is that for the Hebrews, victory belongs completely to God, while the Greeks allowed that individuals were, at least in part, responsible for their own virtue. An often overlooked passage in Exodus celebrates the cruel power of God. After the pharaoh's armies have been destroyed, the Israelites sing a song of praise to the God of war that includes the following lines: "Terror and dread fall upon them; because of the greatness of thy arm, they are as still as a stone, till thy people, O Lord, pass by whom thou hast purchased" (Exodus 15:16). Moses' virtue is his piety and his ability to hear the voice of God. But we see a certain mercilessness in Moses and his vision of God. Moses' magical powers help Joshua—his main general—to defeat the people of Amalek. And then God tells Moses: "I will utterly blot the remembrance of Amalek from under heaven" (Exodus 17:14). Toward the end of Moses' career, he preached a final sermon in which he explains the vengeful power of God as he speaks the following in the name of God: "I will take vengeance on my adversaries, and will requite those who hate me. I will make my arrows drunk with blood, and my sword shall devour flesh—with the blood of the slain and the captives, from the long-haired heads of the enemy" (Deuteronomy 32:41–42).

Moses was not destined to enter the Promised Land. He was succeeded by Joshua, who led the Hebrews into Canaan with the power of the sword. Joshua was a conquering warrior king who was empowered by God to slaughter and destroy everyone who dwelled in the land that God had promised to Moses and his people. Like Odysseus, Joshua is not above using guile: he sends spies into Jericho in advance of the attack. But what is most characteristic of Joshua is his mercilessness. At Jericho, the Hebrews "utterly destroyed all in the city, both men and women, young and old, oxen, sheep, and asses, with the edge of the sword" (Joshua 6:21). This sort of slaughter is repeated numerous times. In one battle, Joshua commands the sun to stand still, thus prolonging the day so that the massacre could be completed. In addition to killing men, women, children, and animals, Joshua hung the dead bodies of the defeated local kings on display. Joshua's merciless conquest displayed the warrior virtues of cruelty and ferocity. And these virtues paid off in real terms for Joshua and his people. At the end of his life, Joshua explained the story by attributing the following words to God: "I sent the hornet before you, which drove them out. . . . I gave you a land on which you had not labored, and cities which you had not built, and you dwell therein" (Joshua 24:13). Joshua's ruthlessness paved the way to victory. This victory and the virtues that made it possible were pleasing to God. Indeed, God had ordained that the Hebrews should steal the land from its previous inhabitants at the point of a sword. What was required for the Hebrew victory was absolute devotion to God and a willingness to kill without mercy whoever was in the way of God's plan.

In war, the only thing that matters is victory. The virtues of warriors are evaluated by looking at the triumphs that warriors achieve. Great warriors like Achilles, Odysseus, Moses, and Joshua are alike in their use of violence, in their celebration of vengeance, and their lack of mercy. The virtues of ruthlessness and ferocity, guile and deception do create victory. But these virtues are, for the most part, antithetical to the virtues that are displayed in Jesus' story.

JESUS' VIRTUES

Jesus' transformation of the warrior values is quite startling. We can begin by recognizing that Jesus was, in a certain sense, a descendant of Joshua. Indeed, the name "Jesus" is a derivative form of the name "Joshua." But Jesus is not a ruthless warrior-king. Joshua killed indiscriminately in the name of God; but Jesus told Peter to put away his sword. Joshua, like Moses, was intolerant of religious diversity and was willing to kill in order to establish orthodoxy. Although Jesus speaks of hatred and war in the family, he never explicitly tells his followers to kill family members in the name of religious purity. In fact, Jesus tells us that we should pray modestly and practice piety privately. He also condemns the hypocrisy of those who sanctimoniously condemn others. Moreover, the relation between God and the hero that we see in Joshua is radically different in the story of Jesus. Joshua is given miraculous powers to make the sun stand still so that war may be waged. But Jesus' miraculous powers are only used for healing purposes. He does not wage any battles. Nor does he use his power to harm anyone. Indeed, when Jesus is fasting in the desert in the early part of his story, Luke and Matthew both claim that he was tempted by Satan with worldly power. The price for worldly power is that Jesus must worship Satan. But Jesus refuses this offer, claiming that only God is worthy of worship.

This point is crucial. Both the Old Testament stories and the Greek epics show God intervening in order to give the hero martial power. But this is not true in the New Testament texts. Indeed, when Jesus enters Jerusalem, he hints that the outcome will not be pleasant. He weeps over Jerusalem and addresses the town directly: "Would that even today you knew the things that make for peace! But now they are hid from your eyes. For the days will come when your enemies will ... dash you to the ground, you and your children within you" (Luke 19:41–44). Although Jesus appears to have some popular support that could be used to create an uprising, he does not. And he knows that the outcome will not be victory but death—his own death and indeed death for the children of Jerusalem. It is important to recall at this point that the Gospels were written after the destruction of the temple in Jerusalem. So for their immediate audience, it appears that Jesus' prophecy of violent destruction came true. And significantly, God did not intervene. There was no new Joshua or David to win military victory. Rather, for Christians, the new Joshua was himself crucified, and the vestiges of Jewish political power were eventually destroyed as well.

The miraculous power of God does not prevent this destruction. But Christians believe that it does allow for the possibility of overcoming death itself. Unlike Joshua, then, who uses God's power to create an earthly kingdom, Jesus uses God's power to enter into the kingdom of the next world. Moreover, the brutal imagery of the apocalypse is deferred to the future. Jesus never tells his followers to take up weapons here and now. Although there will be violence, it will come in the future and be led directly by the returning "son of man." Until then, the Christian is to, in Paul's words, "strive for peace with all men, and for the holiness without which no one will see the Lord" (Hebrews 12:14).

In the story of the crucifixion, then, we see the climactic point at which Jesus' character is fully on display together with his virtues. Jesus displays courage, modesty, patience, tolerance, and a commitment to peace throughout his ordeal. His virtues are the virtues of a nonresistant martyr who allows himself to be humiliated and killed without fighting back. Jesus' virtues are radically different from the virtues of Achilles or Joshua. It is difficult to imagine any of the warrior heroes dying without a fight or at least a cruel word, but Jesus quietly submits and, in Luke, prays for God to forgive his enemies.

This difference, of course, makes all the difference. When Tolstoy claims that Jesus' primary teaching is "do not return evil," it is ultimately the scene of Jesus' death that must be kept in mind. Jesus' virtues culminate in a lonely and miserable death. There is no martial pomp and ceremony. Achilles and the Greeks celebrated the deaths of their heroic friends by throwing a celebration that included games, feasts, prizes, and often the ritual sacrifice of their enemies. Jesus is buried in an inauspicious grave. Nor is there immediate retribution or retaliation in the Gospel stories. In the Old Testament, when Samson is enslaved, he pulls the walls of his captors down upon them and on himself in a brutal suicidal slaughter. When Achilles' friend Patroclus is killed, Achilles goes on a murderous rampage. But when Jesus dies, his disciples quietly go forward to tell his story. Indeed, Jesus returns from the dead to give his disciples a message about how to carry on. He does not advocate revenge. Instead, he tells his followers to spread the message of forgiveness of sins.

Even if we discount the Luke story because it occurs only in Luke, the same message of peaceful love is established in the other Gospels. In Matthew, the resurrected Jesus commands his disciples to go on a baptizing and teaching mission. In John, the resurrected Jesus leaves his disciples with the messages "feed my lambs" and "follow me" (John 21:15; John 21:19). It should be obvious that Jesus does not advocate retaliation for his humiliation, although he and his followers fully expected that the apocalypse would come. It is only in Mark that the resurrected Jesus claims: "He who does not believe will be condemned" (Mark 16:16). The message we are left after Jesus' resurrection is that his disciples should take part in his ministry of social justice, should develop his virtues of love and forgiveness, and should follow him in the path of self-sacrifice.

NARRATIVE AND VIRTUE

Virtues are habits of thought and action that work together to produce a good life. Virtue ethics does not give us specific rules for action. Rather, virtues are general dispositions toward right action within the complexity of real life. Different actions are required at different moments, depending on the context. Virtues are adaptable to situations. They point in a general direction, and they indicate a general tendency. But each situation is unique. A virtuous person will respond appropriately to the demands of the situation.

An approach to ethics that emphasizes virtue is thus different from an approach that emphasizes rules, principles, and laws. Aristotle recognized this. He claimed that virtue was the "golden mean," by which he meant that virtue was found in the middle between extremes. Virtue is like the middle point of a target—the bull's eye. There are many ways to miss the bull's eye but only one way to hit it right. To hit the target correctly, one needs to practice and continually correct oneself. If you tend to shoot to the left, you need to correct toward the right, and so on. The virtue of courage, for example, is found in the middle between cowardice and recklessness. Courage is the proper amount of fear and fearlessness. Some fear is good, because fear teaches us respect for the gravity of the situation. But too much fear produces the vice of cowardice, which results in the inability to do what is required by the situation. Similarly, too little fear produces recklessness, which results in risk-taking behaviors that are also inappropriate.

One of the ways we learn how to attain the golden mean is through studying others who know how to hit it. To become courageous, we ponder stories of those who were courageous. We learn virtue by observing the lives and stories of virtuous others. Jesus seems to have known this. He teaches in parables, in part to encourage his audience to think about the nature of the story. And he provides us with memorable exemplars of virtue, such as the Good Samaritan. In Luke (6:39–40), Jesus indicates the way this works. Jesus asks, "Can a blind man lead a blind man? Will they not both fall into a pit?" And Jesus answers, "A disciple is not above his teacher, but everyone when he is fully taught will be like his teacher." The point of this is that we need a good guide—one who is not blind—to lead us. If we follow the right teacher, if we model our own behavior on the behavior of one who is not blind, we will do well.

The first part of this parable—about the blind leading the blind—occurs in Matthew (15:14) in the context of thinking about ancient

Jewish dietary regulations. Jesus hints in this passage that we need to be as careful about what we say and hear as we do about what we eat. The key to this is developing good habits of the heart, for the heart is the source of virtuous thoughts and actions, as well as vicious habits and evil deeds. When Jesus articulates the beatitudes at the beginning of the Sermon on the Mount, he defends a series of virtues, such as peacefulness and mercy. And he says, "Blessed are the pure in heart" (Matthew 5:8).

We develop purity of heart by following good examples. Plato noted this in the *Republic*, where he indicated that a good city should censor the stories that are heard. Bad stories corrupt us by showing us bad models. In Jesus' terms, we should focus on stories of those who are righteous and enlightened, and we should avoid being led by the blind. After all, Jesus says, we become like our teachers. This is why we must choose our teachers and role models well. If our model is Joshua or Achilles, we will learn to be ruthless and cruel. But if our model is Jesus, we will learn to care for the sick and the poor. And we will learn peace, tolerance, forgiveness, and love.

One way that we learn from moral exemplars is through the ritual reenactment of their lives. In the Christian religion, ritual reenactment occurs through the repetition of aspects of Jesus' life. Jesus taught his disciples how to pray, for example, and Christians continually repeat the Lord's Prayer. This is a constant reminder of the basic ideas of Christianity, including the ideal of forgiveness. Other repetitions include the repetition of the story of Jesus' life and death in the Christmas pageant and in the Easter celebration. Moreover, the celebration of communion is a ritual specifically designed as a remembrance. The wine and bread of the Last Supper remind Christians of the self-sacrificial model of Jesus. It is not enough simply to hear a story once or to memorize a set of general principles. Rather, one must cultivate the spirit and dwell within the model of the moral teacher. This is a lifelong endeavor. One does not become virtuous all at once. Rather, we continually work at living up to the model.

Virtue is the knack for doing the right thing at the right time in the right way in the right amount. To do this takes practice and what Aristotle called "practical wisdom." Practical wisdom is the tendency to know what to do and how to do it. It is not enough, however, to know general principles. You must have experience in action. Thus one learns virtue by practicing at being virtuous.

This is why stories are useful. When we read the story of Jesus on the cross, we are carried along with the narrative. And we can begin to imagine how we might react in this situation. This act of imagination is a crucial part of learning virtue. In reading or hearing, we put ourselves in place of the example and begin to develop those habits that will serve when we are confronted with similar situations. The Christian question "What would Jesus do?" asks us to do just this. It is obvious that there are no exact examples of how Jesus would react to the situations of contemporary life. But one can consider the situations that Jesus encountered and imagine how he would respond to other situations.

CONCLUSION

Jesus' virtues include forgiveness, tolerance, patience, generosity, peacefulness, and love. In the next chapters, we will examine these virtues more extensively. Before turning to this task, let us note that there is some ambiguity in the story of Jesus and the model he provides. This is not merely a factor of discrepancies among the Gospel accounts; it is a tension that is internal to the stories themselves. This tension is located in the way in which Jesus' new set of Christian virtues conflicts with the older set of warrior virtues.

While Jesus speaks of forgiveness and love, he also occasionally speaks of condemnation, hatred, and final judgment. One possible interpretation of this problem is that the stories of Jesus' life are in the middle of the process of transformation. In other words, there are rival strains in these stories. Although the loving and peaceful virtues come to predominate, the ancient warrior tradition persists. Indeed, this is one of the difficulties for answering the question of what Jesus would do: sometimes it does appear that Jesus condemns without forgiving. This opens the question of which set of virtues we should emphasize. And this helps to explain the tension within the developed Christian tradition—a tradition that gives rise to witch burnings and the Inquisition, while also giving birth to Tolstoy and Martin Luther King Jr.

My interpretation of the total set of stories of Jesus' life is that the overall tone is one that emphasizes forgiveness, love, peace, and related virtues. We see this most obviously in the passion narratives and especially in Jesus' peaceful acquiescence to the tyrants who kill him on the cross. And his message of peace, love, and forgiveness is the final image that we are left with in the accounts of his post-resurrection appearances.

The narratives of Jesus' life show us virtues that go beyond the Golden Rule. Jesus deliberately submits to evil and refuses the temptation of political power. Jesus advocates an ethic of self-sacrifice that gives further meaning to virtues such as charity, forgiveness, mercy, tolerance, pacifism, and love. These virtues mean more than simply loving your neighbor—they are also applied to enemies in a way that exceeds the standards of common sense usually associated with the Golden Rule. We hear about this idea of excessive love in the Sermon on the Mount. But we see it lived in the flesh, as it were, in the story of Jesus' life and death.

5

JESUS' VIRTUES: PEACE AND LOVE

> Put your sword back into its place; for all who take the sword
> will perish by the sword. Do you think that I cannot appeal
> to my Father, and he will at once send me more than twelve
> legions of angels?
>
> —Matthew 26:52–53

Jesus exemplifies virtues that include love, charity, tolerance, forgiveness, mercy, and peacefulness. And he advocates nonresistance to evil. We see these ideas enacted in the scenes of his capture, trial, and death, where Jesus passively submits to the authorities who threaten him. There is some ambiguity in Jesus' character: Jesus advocates peace and love, but he also flirts with violence and gives hints about divine retribution. One of the most difficult problems for drawing ethical conclusions from Jesus' peaceful and loving virtues is Jesus' supposed divinity: it may be that his model does not pertain to the rest of us. Moreover, even if we accept that his life provides a model for us, Jesus is a private individual who does not hold political power. Indeed, Jesus is an outsider to both the political and religious power structures. Jesus' example tells us very little about how political power should be employed or whether one can enact the principle of nonresistance to evil in political life.

When Jesus is arrested, he goes compliantly and tells Peter to put away his sword. In the Matthew version of this story, Jesus indicates that he is capable of invoking God's power but deliberately chooses not to. Jesus is thus not supposed to be powerless. If we look to him as a model of virtue, this is an important fact. The powerless have no choice but to submit and surrender. But Jesus has a choice, and his choice is peace, love, and forgiveness. It is important to note here that Jesus' model is thus tied to speculation about Jesus' divine powers. And thus it may be that Jesus cannot be used as a model for human life. But Jesus does explicitly state that the peacemakers are to be blessed and that we should love our enemies and turn the other cheek when struck.

In the Luke version of the arrest story, Jesus goes so far as to heal the assailant whose ear is cut off by Jesus' defenders. This story is unique to Luke (as are the parable of the Good Samaritan and Jesus' final forgiving word, as discussed in the preceding chapter). In Mark, Matthew, and John, the ear is cut off but not healed. However, in Matthew and John, Jesus does tell Peter to put his sword away after the incident. The common theme is nonresistance. Luke goes further in showing Jesus actually reaching out to and healing his enemy. The idea of sheathing one's sword and healing one's injured enemies would be an odd one for warrior heroes like Achilles and Joshua. But these ideas make sense in the context of virtues such as mercy, love, and forgiveness. It is no surprise that one who would heal an enemy would also plead for God to forgive those same enemies.

Jesus' peaceful life and death show us a character who turns away from the wars of this world in order to love and heal his neighbors and his enemies. Despite this the subsequent history of Christianity is one of violence, hatred, and brutality. This might just be blatant hypocrisy on the part of Christians, and Jesus does remind us that hypocrisy is a common human failing. But some of those who developed a more violent and less loving version of Christianity did attempt to justify violence by appeal to the Bible. Some may have thought that Jesus advocated nonresistance because he was in fact powerless: that he would have fought if he could. Others may have thought that Jesus did not mean for human beings to take his model seriously, since he was divine and not really human. But such interpretations ignore the crucial fact that Jesus explicitly advocated peacemaking, love of enemies, tolerance, and forgiveness.

Jesus' most important and radical sayings about nonresistance and love are found in Matthew's Sermon on the Mount (and Luke's Sermon on the Plain): "Do not resist one who is evil" and "love your enemies and pray for those who persecute you" (Matthew 5:39, 5:44; Luke 6:27–30). Such loving and pacific messages are reiterated in other places. In Hebrews (12:14), Paul exhorts: "Strive for peace with all men, and for the holiness without which no one will see the Lord." Paul famously writes of love as the key to ethics, since love is related to the other virtues: "Love is patient and kind; love is not jealous or boastful; it is not arrogant or rude. Love does not insist on its own way; it is not irritable or resentful; it does not rejoice at wrong but rejoices in the right. Love bears all things, believes all things, hopes all things, endures all things" (1 Corinthians 13:4–7). Similarly, the first letter of John is an extended reflection on love that connects the virtue of love to both of the great commandments: love God and love your neighbor. John writes: "We love because he first loved us. If any one says, 'I love God,' and hates his brother, he is a liar; for he who does not love his brother whom he has seen, cannot love God whom he has not seen. And this commandment we have from him, that he who loves God should love his brother also" (1 John 4:19–21). Thus it is fairly obvious that Jesus did advocate love and peace for human beings.

THE PROBLEM OF APOCALYPTIC VIOLENCE

All of this is wonderful and elevating. But ambiguities remain. Jesus also says, "I have not come to bring peace, but a sword" (Matthew 10:34). And Jesus uses a whip—at least in John's version of this story (John 2:15)—to drive the money-changers and their animals out of the temple. Jesus offers us a vision of tolerance and forgiveness in his claim: "Judge not, and you will not be judged; condemn not and you will not be condemned; forgive and you will be forgiven" (Luke 6:37). But Jesus also makes it clear that there will be a final judgment and punishment for those who do not have the proper faith. Indeed, those who are not among the faithful will suffer wrath and vengeance when the "son of man" returns "in a cloud with power and great glory" (Luke 21:27). What is remarkable is that this passage occurs in Luke, which we might think of as the most forgiving and loving of the Gospels.

The ambivalence found here is exacerbated when we consider the Bible in its entirety. As discussed in the previous chapter, the Old Testament tells a long history of warfare, cruelty, and atrocity carried out in the name of God. Some argue that this tribal brutality was radically overturned by Jesus and his pacifistic message. Stanley Hauerwas writes, "Jesus challenged both the militaristic and ritualistic notions of what God's kingdom required—the former by denying the right of violence even if attacked and the latter by his steadfast refusal to be separated from those 'outside.' "[1] This view is a compelling reading of the general spirit of the Gospels. However, it requires substantial interpretive effort that must ignore the brutal imagery of the apocalyptic passages that include a final revelation of the "war in heaven" (Revelation 12:7) that will be completed at the end of time.

Christians have rejected peace and love for millennia. One might claim that Christian pacifism and love must make concessions when Christians dwell in the real world. This is what John Howard Yoder calls, a "Constantinian heresy," by which he means the sorts of compromises that Christians make when they gain political power.[2] Yoder follows Tolstoy, Martin Luther King Jr., and others in emphasizing the central value of pacifism in Jesus' message. But Jesus' ideal of nonresistance is intimately tied to the eschatological claim that God's kingdom is not a kingdom of this world. For Yoder, the Constantinian compromise represents a denial of Jesus' virtues in favor of a "pagan" emphasis on politics and happiness in this world. Some call this realism. And we see realism, most famously, in Machiavelli's claim that the prince must not be too committed to the Christian idea of virtue and self-sacrifice. Realism and pagan virtues continue to be intimately connected to political power. A current example of this is found in Robert Kaplan's recent book *Warrior Politics*, the subtitle of which makes this clear: "Why Leadership Demands a Pagan Ethos."[3] But one need not go so far as Kaplan in advocating a return to Machiavelli and Sun-Tzu. A lesser compromise with realism can be found in the Christian "just war" theory, which is a tradition of thinking about appropriate limits for the use of political violence.

Christian violence may in part be inspired by the brutal imagery of the Old Testament, which remains present in the apocalyptic vision of Christianity. Revelation quotes Jeremiah, for example, in claiming, "If anyone slays with the sword, with the sword they must be slain" (Revelation 13:10; Jeremiah 5:2). One might interpret this passage as a lesson to encourage us to "beat our swords into plowshares" (Isaiah 2:4). But this won't happen until after the final apocalyptic battle. In the meantime, Christians may have to compromise with the reality of fighting evil—despite the fact that Jesus appears to have commanded otherwise.

There are really two messages present in the New Testament: a call for Jesus' followers not to resist evil and a promise that purifying violence will be employed by God in the end of time. Violent imagery borrowed from the Old Testament is put directly into Jesus' mouth in the Gospels. Jesus says of those who reject the apostles, "Truly, I say to you, it shall be more tolerable on the day of judgment for the land of Sodom and Gomorrah than for that town" (Matthew 10:15). To understand this, recall that God had utterly destroyed Sodom and Gomorrah with fire and brimstone. This punishment and the idea of a vengeful and destructive God cannot easily be expunged from the Christian texts. In Luke, Jesus refers directly to the destruction of Sodom. In an apocalyptic prophecy,

Jesus tells his disciples that the day is coming when God will separate the holy from the unholy. "But on the day when Lot went out from Sodom, fire and sulphur rained from heaven and destroyed them all—so will it be on the day when the Son of man is revealed" (Luke 17:29–30). It is true that Jesus does not claim that his disciples are to do the destroying themselves. But God's judgment will have destructive power. It is easy to see how such passages could lead Christians beyond the pacifism that seems to be the heart of Jesus' story.

One could argue that Jesus' ideas and his model are incomplete and insufficient for those of us who must live in the "real" world. Christian pacifists such as Tolstoy or Yoder may reply that such a claim begs the question of what the "real" world actually is. From this perspective, Jesus calls us to create a new world by refusing to compromise with evil. The real world, from this perspective, is one where we do not resist evil. But this approach requires a substantial leap of faith that even many devout Christians are unwilling to take. Indeed, Christians who reject this pacifistic ideal use human reason to articulate the more developed view of the just war theory. From this perspective, if we want advice about how to live, we need more than what Jesus can tell us. Catholic thinkers follow Aquinas in making use of reason to discern the "natural law." The problem is that natural law seems to push us beyond the pacifistic ideal of Jesus' life. After all, natural law appears to show—as Aquinas notes—that we are entitled to use violence to defend ourselves when attacked. Here we see the conflict between what reason tells us and what Jesus' model shows.

JESUS AND POLITICS

A further problem occurs in considering what Jesus would have thought about political power. Jesus does not provide us with a theory of politics, nor does he show us how a ruler should rule. This problem has been freely admitted by defenders of the Christian idea of just war, who acknowledge that early Christian pacifism evolved into the just war idea in light of changing political realities. It was Augustine, not Jesus, who—after Christians had acquired political power—argued for the idea of a Christian just war. Augustine based his idea on love of the neighbor: we may use force to defend our neighbors from harm. But this represents an interpretation of Jesus' message that is not directly supported by Jesus himself.

Jesus' radical idea of nonresistance to evil makes it clear that Jesus wants nothing to do with political power, which is all about using violence to control violence. The apolitical nature of Jesus' message may be the most crucial point for understanding Jesus' ideas about tolerance and peace. Jesus' eschatological vision points beyond politics toward the religious kingdom of God. One should render unto Caesar what belongs to Caesar—but the things that belong to God are Jesus' real interest. Indeed, when Pilate asks Jesus whether he is the king of the Jews, Jesus replies with the following: "My kingship is not of this world; if my kingship were of this world, my servants would fight, that I might not be handed over to the Jews; but my kingship is not from this world" (John 18:36). This shows us the difficulty that those who wield political power will have in appropriating and applying Jesus' message. Jesus says that the true kingdom is not of this world and that his true followers will thus not fight in this world.

Jesus is, quite frankly, an insufficient guide for politics. We see this problem in Paul's letter to the Romans, which was probably written in 58 or 59 C.E., prior to the Gospels. In Romans 12, Paul explains the ideals of peace and love in language that is quite similar to that found in the Sermon on the Mount. Indeed, he claims that Christians should "bless those who persecute you . . . repay no one evil for evil . . . and live peaceably with all" (Romans 12:14–18). The rationale that is given for this is apocalyptic: judgment, wrath, and vengeance belong to God. What is interesting in Romans, however, is that the next chapter defends the idea that political authorities can use violence in God's name: "He [the political authority] does not bear the sword in vain; he is the servant of God to execute his wrath on the wrongdoer" (Romans 13:4). The ambiguity here verges on contradiction: Christians are supposed to refrain from violence and defer to God's apocalyptic vengeance, but the state can employ violence in God's name.

To understand this problem, it is important to remember that Jesus and the early Christians were part of a small and alienated political faction. Indeed, the facts of Jesus' life and death show us this in stark detail. As a Jew, he was subject to Roman rule. But he was also a member of a small sect of radical reformers within Judaism. In short, Jesus had neither political nor religious authority. His view is that of a powerless outsider.

One could understand his calls for peace and tolerance, then, to be a sort of morality of weakness—what Nietzsche called a "slave-morality." Weak minorities call out for toleration because, in fact, they need to be tolerated by those in power. They advocate peace because violence is ineffective against a ruthless dominant power. A cynic such as Nietzsche would say that Jesus' worldview developed out of disempowerment.

The Gospel texts were written as the Romans brutally suppressed the Jewish uprising that resulted in the destruction of the temple in Jerusalem. Jews became aware of the fact that violent rebellion had only resulted in more misery and indeed in a total assault on their religious culture. The Christian solution was to turn away from war and adopt a nonviolent approach to life. From this perspective, one turns the other cheek because one is powerless to do anything else. And from this perspective, it makes sense that the oppressed group will call itself blessed, as Jesus does in the beatitudes when he blesses the meek, the merciful, and the peacemakers. Of course, one might also claim in response to this cynical view that Jesus is not reacting to a lack of power but, rather, that he is clarifying the basis of an ethic of love and peace. One need not be a slave to acknowledge the truth of the claim that power corrupts because power and violence are evil.

The difficulty of following Jesus as a model of virtue is found in the demands of nonviolence. Jesus deliberately submits to the tyrants who eventually kill him and who continue to oppress his people. He does not fight back. If we follow Jesus' model, we might end up submitting to the likes of Hitler and Osama bin Laden. Indeed, the Romans were conquerors and brutal rulers who deserved to be resisted. But Jesus nowhere authorizes us to resist such evil tyrants. His life and death show us that he will not take up the sword even to fight against tyranny. One wonders whether this model is acceptable in a world in which terrorists possess weapons of mass destruction with which they could kill millions of innocents.

Some Christians respond to this by turning to apocalyptic pronouncements about the way that God uses violence to complete the final eschatological battle. Indeed, some evangelicals appeared to greet the horrors of September 11 with eschatological glee. Jerry Falwell and Pat Robertson claimed that the terrorist strikes were God's wrath for sin. Some have also seen recent events in the Middle East—from the founding of Israel to the invasion of Iraq—as signs of the end times. Most of this appears to be a misreading of texts such as Revelation, which were addressed to the theological and political problems of the dominance of the Roman Empire. But the difficulty of this approach runs deeper. It shows us the continued presence in Christianity of the idea of a wrathful God using violence to purge the world of sin. The difficulty is that this apocalyptic vision runs counter to Jesus' avowed doctrine of forgiveness and nonresistance.

When Christians gained power, they compromised with power and became more willing to employ violence both in the context of war and in pursuit of ideological purity. Later Christians developed Christianity from a position of power that Jesus never intimated they would have. Nor, in fact, did he recommend that they should adopt such positions of power. Cruel intolerance and crusading war are the prerogative of those who possess political power. Jesus and his immediate followers did not have this option, nor did they appear to want it. Instead, Jesus cultivates resignation in the face of power and criticizes the hubris of the powerful, while also expressing apocalyptic expectations about divine retribution. Jesus' criticism of power is not constructive: it does not specify how Christian rulers are supposed to rule in this world when they find themselves in power. And the fact that his advocacy of nonresistance is articulated from within a larger apocalyptic worldview makes it difficult to know whether pacifism can be divorced from apocalyptic expectation.

AMBIGUITY AND THE PROBLEM OF FAITH

Christians who advocate the idea of just war may try to downplay the idea of nonresistant pacifism that is found in Jesus' life and teaching. Peace-loving Christians may, likewise, try to ignore the warlike passages found in New Testament apocalyptic. But I think we must admit that the Christian texts are decidedly ambivalent. And this is why we must go beyond Christianity toward a more fully developed humanistic approach to ethics.

Some humanists find it hard to see the peace-loving message of Christianity. In *The End of Faith*, Sam Harris echoes Bertrand Russell and other critics of Christianity in claiming that religious faith is the primary source of intolerance, hatred, and war in the world. But Harris forgets that religious faith can also be a great source for peace and love. The difficulty is that a faith that is based entirely on ancient scriptures will always be insufficient as a guide for life. These scriptures are fragmentary records of conversations that occurred in the distant past. Thus the scriptural legacy must be supplemented by humanistic reflection on ethics that is willing to criticize and reinterpret some of the content of the scriptural tradition.

The difficulty of the ambivalent legacy of Christianity has provoked deep thinkers to propose revisions and interpretations that go beyond the letter of the text. Many have noted that Jesus' message of "turning the other cheek" is mixed with the imagery of violence. In an imaginary dialogue with Jesus, Voltaire asked Jesus about the claim that he had come to bring a sword. According to Voltaire, Jesus replied: "It is a copyist's error. I told them that I brought peace and not a sword." One wishes that this were true and that this typographical error would have been caught in the first millennium: it would have saved us centuries of wars fought in the name of Jesus.

Tolstoy also recounts the difficulty he had in coming to terms with Christianity. One of his problems was that Christian nations were decidedly warlike. The state demands service that includes the duty to kill enemies. This runs counter to the Christian idea of "loving the enemy." Tolstoy realized how easy it was to fall into hypocrisy, especially when social and political forces continually conspire to keep the military machine well oiled with human blood. But then Tolstoy returned to the scriptures and came to the conclusion that Jesus' basic message was "resist not evil." According to Tolstoy, then, the warlike spirit of later Christianity runs counter to the nonresistant pacifism of the Gospels.

Such conclusions require us, however, to revise or ignore significant portions of the Bible. And for us to fully adopt a pacifist morality, we have to significantly revise our preconceptions about morality itself. Indeed, a humanist approach may never be able to support the sort of absolute pacifism that Jesus appears in places to advocate. Jesus' story shows us that pacifism leads to a miserable death. And he is unwilling to raise a sword against the evil tyrants who persecute him and his people. This absolute nonresistance is accepted by Jesus and acceptable for some Christians because of the possibility of resurrection. In this sense, Christian ethics is inextricably tied to Christian theology: without a theology that rewards self-sacrifice, absolute pacifism makes little sense. It is true, then, that Jesus points in the direction of a radical revision of our moral preconceptions. However, it remains an open question as to whether this revision makes sense without its connection to Christian theology. And, as we've been noting here, moral theologians are themselves divided on the question of just how radical Jesus' new vision of morality actually is.

CONCLUSION

Despite ambiguities, the predominant values for Jesus were peace and love. I am sympathetic to these Christian values. But my worry is that the Christian texts do not provide a consistent enough argument for these virtues. Indeed, a fully developed argument is lacking.

One wishes, for example, that Jesus had more clearly and systematically articulated his reasons for advocating the idea of loving enemies. Martin Luther King Jr. offered such a defense, for example, in his discussion of how nonviolence and love are connected to the idea that all life is interrelated and all men are brothers. King explains the Christian idea of agape, or love, as follows: "Agape means a recognition of the fact that all life is interrelated. All humanity is involved in a single process, all men are brothers. To the degree that I harm my brother, no matter what he is doing to me, to that extent I am harming myself. . . . Because men are brothers. If you harm me, you harm yourself."[4] But King's interpretation goes beyond Jesus and is connected to further reflection on politics and community. Jesus never states his view so directly, and he does not show us how to actualize this ideal in coordinated nonviolent action.

Another problem is that Jesus' disavowal of politics seems naïve and self-defeating, especially if we are agnostic about Christian eschatology. The appeal to eschatological faith is insufficient for those of us committed to the use of reason, just as it is insufficient in today's pluralistic global culture. And Jesus' silence on the question of how political power should be employed needs to be supplemented with a more detailed theory of political life.

We should consider a few further objections to Jesus' view here, in order to show what is missing from Jesus' original idea when it is viewed from the standpoint of human reason. One problem is that the Christian idea of love demands more than seems appropriate from the standpoint of justice. Freud claimed, for example, that the idea of loving enemies was absurd. Love should be given to those who deserve it, but according to Freud, enemies do not deserve to be loved. Indeed, enemies deserve to be fought and evil should be resisted, especially if we want to live in the "real" world. Moreover, the idea of loving the enemy seems to degrade the idea of love and do an injustice to those who actually deserve our love. Indeed, we see this clearly in Jesus' claims about conflict and dissension within the family, which, by the way, is the context of the passage in which Jesus says he comes to "bring a sword" (Matthew 10:34). For Jesus, agapic love means that we should leave behind the particular love of the family and develop a more universal love that culminates in the dissolution of the family. This does an obvious injustice to the normal idea of the family and the importance of concrete duties to those with whom we are most intimate.

One answer given to this objection is that Jesus' idea of love is so expansive as to be almost beyond comprehension. John Shelby Spong puts it this way: "Love has no chosen people, for that implies that some are unchosen. Love bears no malice, seeks no revenge, guards no doorway. A life defined by love will not seek to protect itself or to justify itself. It will be content simply to be itself and to give itself away with abandon."[5] Spong equates this pervasive love with the holy and with God. The difficulty of this idea is that it is so expansive as to be vacuous. In other words, it makes it impossible to judge and evaluate among and between ideas, actions, and persons.

A love this broad appears to encompass everything, and it can result in the perverse idea that "anything goes," since everything can be worthy of love. Indeed, this seems to be the radical idea of tolerance that is advocated by Jesus: we are not to judge others, but simply to love them and forgive them for their faults. This creates a problem for ethics in the real world, since in the real world, we must make and enforce judgments about what is good and evil. The expansive idea of love refuses to make these judgments—or simply leaves them to God. While one may admire the openness and compassion expressed in the idea of love, it provides little guidance for how to proceed in a life that demands judgment. In short, Christian agape cannot be the basis of a political system that must make judgments and use coercive force to enact them.

Let's be even more explicit. It might be the case that pacifism is, in Sam Harris' words, "flagrantly immoral" because it is "a willingness to die, and to let others die, at the pleasure of the world's thugs."[6] Indeed, this does seem to be something like what Jesus had in mind: he goes willingly to his death and he acknowledges that his disciples will share a similar fate. When Jesus says in Matthew that he comes to bring war, he follows this with a further explanation: his goal is not really war; it is the cross. Followers of Jesus must "take up the cross" and follow Jesus: "He who finds his life will lose it, and he who loses his life for my sake will find it" (Matthew 10:39). From a certain perspective, this can appear to be immoral. Absolute pacifism is so otherworldly that it can end up denying the value of life in this world. This passage seems to indicate that Jesus' followers should give up their lives in Jesus' name—a path that has been taken by many Christian martyrs. And one could take this to mean that Christians should just resign themselves to death and do nothing to prevent it. As Pierre Bayle put it in the seventeenth century, Christians will not make good soldiers. "The best that could be expected would be that they would not be afraid to die for their country and their God." The problem is that Christians are supposed to "abstain from every semblance of violence." Bayle admits that Christianity might be amenable to what he calls "defensive war." Indeed, this is the basic idea that later Christians developed under the idea of a just war, which is a war fought in defense of the innocent. But the conundrum articulated by Tolstoy remains: how can a Christian willingly serve in a war when Jesus counsels us not to return evil for evil.

I have argued elsewhere against absolute pacifism and have defended a less absolute version of pacifism—one that is linked to the just war theory.[7] My argument against absolute pacifism is that it relies on eschatological faith. My version of a more practical form of pacifism follows from skepticism about political power and its abuses. From this perspective, one of the limits to Jesus' message is his apparent acquiescence to established political power. It is remarkable that Jesus does not denounce his enemies or the political power structure as they execute him. Indeed, he forgives them! Here we see, in stark relief, the problem of the sort of resignation that results from an absolute sort of pacifism. When one turns one's gaze toward the next world and resigns oneself to death, pacifism becomes a sort of quietism that is ineffective at creating positive social change.

Of course, pacifists are careful to point out that pacifism is not always the same thing as passive-ism. One can be a pacifist and an active and energetic force for social change. But the problem remains for Christians: can one move beyond Jesus' model of passive resignation, or is Jesus' model really a model that leaves us dying on the cross without hope for justice in this world? Despite this problem, absolute pacifism remains inspiring because it so radically transforms our values. It is not surprising that some might see it as immoral. It runs counter to the warrior virtues of heroes like Achilles and Joshua. And it overturns the traditional structure of vengeance and retribution.

Jesus tells us, "You have heard it said, 'An eye for an eye and a tooth for a tooth.' But I say to you, Do not resist one who is evil. But if any one strikes you on the right cheek, turn to him the other also" (Matthew 5:38–39). This idea of not resisting evil is based on a radical reestimation of what is of value. If this life and its goods are of such fleeting value that they are not worth defending, then our view of ourselves is radically transformed. It is easy to see how this idea can lead to a life of service dedicated to social justice, charity, and love. This ideal and the understanding of Jesus' life as a model of service remain inspirational.

Despite this, we should not deny the ambiguities that are found in the Christian texts and in the subsequent history of Christian cruelty, intolerance, and war. Indeed, if the otherworldly demands of Christianity make it seem an impossible idea, Christians may find it easier to make compromises with power and violence in this world. This criticism might begin from the idea that Jesus alone is the perfect model of love and nonresistance. Since the rest of us cannot hope to attain to perfection, we might as well negotiate with the evil of the real world.

A more fully developed humanistic ethic would thus also state why violence, cruelty, and intolerance are wrong *in this world* for reasons that are accepted by all humans, even those who are agnostic about the claims of Christian eschatology. And it would articulate a reasonable ethic of political power. Unfortunately, this more fully developed theory cannot be found in the original model provided by Jesus.

NOTES

1. Stanley Hauerwas, *The Peaceable Kingdom* (Notre Dame: University of Notre Dame Press, 1983), 85.

2. John Howard Yoder, *The Original Revolution* (Scottdale, PA: Herald, 2003).

3. Robert D. Kaplan, *Warrior Politics* (New York: Random House, 2002).

4. Martin Luther King Jr., "Pilgrimage to Nonviolence," in *Testament of Hope* (New York: HarperCollins, 1986).

5. John Shelby Spong, *A New Christianity for a New World* (San Francisco: Harper San Francisco, 2002), 140.

6. Sam Harris, *The End of Faith* (New York: Norton, 2004), 199.

7. Andrew Fiala, *Practical Pacifism* (New York: Algora, 2004).

6

JESUS AND THE SANCTITY
OF LIFE: ABORTION

It is not the will of my Father who is in heaven that one of
these little ones should perish.

—Matthew 18:14

This chapter begins a group of chapters in which I will consider several topics of contemporary ethical concern. The first three focus on the so-called life issues: abortion, euthanasia, and the death penalty. The thesis of these chapters is that it is difficult to answer the question "What would Jesus do?" about these complicated issues. I make this claim in opposition to those who assert that the Christian scriptures provide us with a definite set of doctrines about these issues. While the passage from Matthew cited above might appear on a bumper sticker opposing abortion, the topics I will consider here are more complex than bumper-sticker mottoes would admit. Indeed, these issues continue to be of concern because of their complexity. It is not useful to simply retreat to the claim that Jesus provides all of the answers to these questions. Such an appeal to authority inhibits good judgment by preventing us from understanding the complexities of the issues. Bumper-sticker theology is no substitute for the hard work of careful thinking.

The most obvious argument in support of the claim that even Christians need to continue to ruminate carefully on these issues is the fact that Christians themselves disagree about these topics. But my argument in these chapters is not primarily focused on diversity within the Christian community. Rather, my goal is to clarify the sorts of questions that would have to be answered in order to decide any of these issues.

We do not have enough information about Jesus—as he is represented in the Gospels—to say exactly what Jesus would have thought about issues like abortion, euthanasia, and the death penalty. Jesus does not address these issues directly. And even when we can find some relevant pronouncement, we need to be sensitive to the context in which these pronouncements were made, just as we need to be aware of the political, social, and technological changes that give rise to ethical issues in the contemporary world. When we interpret biblical texts, we are applying reason in a way that takes us beyond the idea of divine command ethics. Critical thinking is required to figure out how God's commandments are to be applied.

My conclusion is skeptical: we do not have enough evidence to say what Jesus' opinions about these topics would be. I should admit that I am sympathetic to the idea of a "consistent ethic of life," which was promoted by Pope John Paul II, and to the general idea that we should develop reverence for life as advocated by Christians such as Albert Schweitzer and Karl Barth. But this general idea about the sanctity of life does not lead to definitive conclusions about these issues. One might, for example, be in favor of the death penalty for murder because it forcefully shows how much we value innocent life: we value life so much that we are willing to kill murderers to defend it. Again, it is difficult to draw such a conclusion from the biblical texts. Nor did John Paul II support such a conclusion. The difficulty of this issue—as with the others we will consider here—is that Jesus says nothing specifically about the death penalty. Nor could Jesus have been aware of the changed political context of the contemporary world, in which the death penalty is rarely used, in which it is carried out as "humanely" as possible (via lethal injection), and in which we take precautions to ensure that only the guilty are executed. The same sorts of reservations will lead to skeptical conclusions about all of the issues discussed here. Jesus said nothing about abortion. Nor did he say anything about euthanasia. We might attempt to apply the general idea of the Golden Rule and Jesus' virtues in thinking about these issues. But the following chapters will indicate the difficulty of deciding how to apply Jesus' basic ethical ideas in these complicated cases of contemporary concern.

QUESTIONS ABOUT ABORTION

Abortion is the voluntary act of terminating a pregnancy. Christian churches in the United States have different views on this topic. The Catholic Church is opposed to abortion—except in cases when the life of the mother is in jeopardy. Indeed, John Paul II argued that abortion, like euthanasia and the death penalty, is part of a "culture of death" that violates the spirit of the Gospels. But the Presbyterian Church is a bit more liberal in its understanding of abortion. The Presbyterian Church is quite honest in its recognition of the difficulty of making decisions about abortion. Indeed, it states explicitly: "There are no biblical texts that speak expressly to the topic of abortion."[1] The Bible gives some general ideas about the sanctity of life, and Jesus does express love for children. But the Bible gives very little guidance for resolving the complicated questions that arise when considering abortion.

There are at least four general sorts of questions to consider when thinking about abortion.

1. What is the ontological and moral status of the fetus? The ontological question asks what sort of being a fetus is; the moral question asks what sort of value it has. So we must ask questions such as: Is the fetus a person? Or does the fetus deserve consideration as what philosopher's call a "moral patient," a being that has rights, is worthy of respect, or should be considered as an object of moral concern? Related to this is the question of when during the course of a pregnancy the fetus achieves this status.

2. What is the relationship between the fetus and the mother? Is the fetus a mere appendage of the mother? Does the mother have the right to do whatever she wants with her fetus? Or, if we accept that the fetus is an independent person, can the mother's rights trump whatever rights the fetus might have? Related to this are questions about the rights and interests of others who are related to the mother and the fetus, such as the father of the fetus and the immediate family of the mother.

3. Does society have a duty or right to regulate abortion? Does the state have a right to interfere in this issue, or is it a private matter, solely the concern of the mother? Included here are questions about the proper limits of state power, questions about the relationship between law and religion, and questions about social regulation of reproduction and sexuality. We might also consider the question of the rights of women in general.

4. What is the context in which abortion is considered? For example, has the woman been raped? Or is the mother's life or reproductive health in danger? We might also want to consider whether the fetus is expected to develop into a normal and healthy child. And we

might want to consider the total health of the family into which the fetus is to be born: its economic status, the needs of other children who are already alive, and the special needs of the mother or other relatives. In general the question is how the total life situation of the mother, the fetus, and the rest of the family relate to our conclusions about the morality of abortion in particular cases.

It is important to note that the Gospels do not provide us with definitive answers to these questions. Thus it is quite difficult to say what Jesus would have thought about abortion.

Many think that abortion is ultimately a religious question, in part because it is assumed that religion alone gives us an idea of the *sacred* value of life. And religions have long attempted to answer questions about what Paul Ramsey calls "the edges of life," the origin and end of life.[2] Pope John Paul II unites his criticism of abortion and euthanasia under a religious principle that he calls "the gospel of life." The basic idea is that no human being has the right to destroy innocent human life. According to this view, God alone is the "lord of life" who decides when we come into existence and when we die. This view of obedience to God's creative power encompasses the entirety of the procreative process from the sexual drive to birth and death. For humans to interfere in the natural generative process is to go against the will of God. Abortion is considered an "unspeakable crime" that is described by John Paul as follows:

> The one eliminated [in abortion] is a human being at the very beginning of life. No one more absolutely innocent could be imagined. In no way could this human being ever be considered an aggressor, much less an unjust aggressor! He or she is weak, defenseless, even to the point of lacking that minimal form of defense consisting in the poignant power of a newborn baby's cries and tears. The unborn child is totally entrusted to the protection and care of the woman carrying him or her in the womb.[3]

This is an important and powerful point: if we interpret the Golden Rule as requiring us to care for the weak, the innocent, and the defenseless, then we should care for the fetus. However, the abortion debate remains unresolved precisely because it is not clear that those basic moral ideas—caring for the weak, avoiding harm to the innocent, and defending the defenseless—apply to the fetus. It might be that the fetus at an early stage of development is not yet worthy of this sort of moral consideration.

As noted, there are complicated questions to be asked about the ontological and moral status of the fetus. One typical answer to these questions is to claim that the fetus has a soul. The question about whether the fetus has a soul hinges on what we mean by "having a soul" and on what we think about who or what has a soul. Do all biological beings have souls, or only those with a certain sort of DNA? Is a certain level of brain development or cognitive ability a prerequisite for having a soul? Is having a soul an all or nothing status, or are there degrees of having a soul? And how are we to consider beings who have the potential to develop a soul (or in the case of euthanasia, beings who have lost this capacity because of brain injury)?

Views about the moral status of the fetus have shifted over the years. Aristotle maintained that abortion was acceptable when it was performed "before perception and life arises."[4] Aristotle leaves it open as to when this point is reached. But ancient Stoic philosophers held that abortion was acceptable prior to birth because it was birth that "animated" or ensouled the child. This idea was based on the idea that the soul was a sort of air or breath that entered into the child when it began to breathe air.[5] Thomas Aquinas and other medieval Christians thought that "quickening"—when the mother felt the fetus move inside her—marked the moment of ensoulment. But even within the Catholic tradition, thinking about ensoulment has shifted. In the nineteenth century, under Pope Pius IX—who also defended the idea of the immaculate conception of the Virgin Mary—the new idea was that ensoulment happened at conception.[6]

THE BIBLE AND THE FETUS

One would think that we should be able to resolve the question of when the soul enters the body by looking to the revealed word of God in the Bible. One wishes that God had given us a clear answer about this. Unfortunately, the biblical texts that are used in support of the idea that life begins with conception are few, and they often have very little to do with abortion. Some of the passages that are routinely cited by those who build a biblical case against abortion include Psalms 22:9–10 or 139:13–16, Jeremiah 1:5, and Luke 1. The difficulty of these verses is that they employ poetic language in contexts that do not directly apply to the abortion debate: they speak of life in the womb but do not answer the question of ensoulment or provide any indication of how to answer the question of the ontological or moral status of the fetus.

In the passage from Luke, for example, Mary, the mother of Jesus, and Elizabeth, the mother of John the Baptist, have both miraculously conceived children: Mary is a virgin and Elizabeth is old and barren. Elizabeth's pregnancy had been announced by an angel to her husband Zechariah. This announcement included the following claim: "And he will be filled with the Holy Spirit even from his mother's womb" (Luke 1:15). Mary and Elizabeth meet together when Elizabeth is in the sixth month of her pregnancy. She says to Mary, "When the voice of your greeting came to my ears, the babe in my womb leaped for joy" (Luke 1:44). The gist of this passage is that John the Baptist was conscious of the presence of Jesus while both of them were still in their mothers' wombs. The problem is that these are quite special cases where God has supposedly directly intervened to create miraculous children in a barren woman and in a virgin. It is not clear that this has anything to do with ordinary pregnancy. And the fact that it happens during the sixth month of pregnancy does not tell us whether the fetus is ensouled in the early stages of pregnancy.

But let's be honest about this passage. It is an imaginative reconstruction designed to give credibility to the claims that were made about Jesus' divinity. One may reasonably ask, how would the author of this passage know any of this, and is it true? One might attempt to "confirm" the story by looking to the other Gospels. Mark, which is generally considered the oldest and most accurate biography of Jesus, contains no mention of the virgin birth. Nor does John. And although Matthew mentions the idea of the virgin birth being announced to Joseph in a dream, it contains no mention of the scene between Elizabeth and Mary.

Even if we accept the idea that John and Jesus were possessed of the holy spirit when within the womb, it is not clear exactly when during the course of the pregnancy this is supposed to happen. It is not a rare occurrence for an expectant mother to feel the fetus move during the sixth month. But most contemporary abortion discussion focuses on the first trimester only. Even if we accept that a fetus can know what is going on outside the womb by the sixth month, the crucial question still remains the status of the fetus from conception to the sixth month. Indeed, one may further suggest that fetal movement even in the sixth month has little to do with the presence of a conscious soul but might be the result of reflex action and the stimulation of the fetus as a result of changes in the mother's blood chemistry. This passage from Luke thus gives us no guidance for thinking about abortion. Moreover, the passage is not something attributed to Jesus anyway: Jesus did not tell the story, nor did he authorize it. So, in other words, we still don't know what Jesus would have thought about abortion.

Of course, Jesus did avow that God loves children. He teaches his disciples by referring to a child in their midst, saying, "It is not the will of my Father who is in heaven that one of these little ones should perish" (Matthew 18:14). The total context of this passage shows that it is about not corrupting the youth, not causing "one of these little ones who believe in me to sin" (Matthew 18:5). But the reference is to living children. It is not about fetuses. A further set of passages gives us a different view of what Jesus may have thought about life in the womb. In his apocalyptic message in Luke, Jesus repeatedly mentions that the apocalypse will show no mercy even to infants and life within the womb. "For these are days of vengeance, to fulfill all that is written. Alas for those who are with child and for those who give suck in those days" (Luke 21:22–23). If we read this as a prediction of the atrocities that will be done prior to Jesus' triumphant return, it is clear that God will have no pity, even on these unborn children, or at least he will do nothing to prevent their suffering. Later, as Jesus is being led to his death, he prophesies further woe and directs his remarks to the "daughters of Jerusalem" who weep for him. He says, "Blessed are the barren, and the wombs that never bore, and the breasts that never gave suck" (Luke 23:29). Again, these claims are a prediction of future doom. But these passages may lead one to the conclusion that it is better to abort a baby than to let the child grow to suffer under the eschatological catastrophe. I am not saying that this is exactly what Jesus has in mind. However, these passages show us the difficulty of saying anything definitive about what Jesus would say about the sanctity of life in the womb.

A passage from Deuteronomy (30:19) that is cited on bumper stickers and billboards in favor of the pro-life argument is the idea that we should "choose life." However, the passage in question is focused on the problem of idolatry: the point of the passage is that to choose life, one must choose God. Here is the whole passage: "I have set before you life and death, blessing and curse; therefore *choose life*, that you and your descendants may live, loving the Lord your God, obeying his voice, and cleaving to him; for that means life to you and the length of days." The passage has nothing whatsoever to do with abortion or euthanasia. Indeed, the definition of life that is given here is a metaphor. Life means to love God. It has nothing to do with biological life. Rather, the idea is that to truly live, one must love God.

There is one passage in the Old Testament that does seem to pertain directly to ending the life of an unborn child. But it does not make it a substantial crime. "When men strive together, and hurt a woman with child, so that there is a miscarriage, and yet no harm follows, the one who hurt her shall be fined, according as the women's husband shall lay upon him; and he shall pay as the judges determine. If any harm follows, then you shall give life for life, eye for eye, tooth for tooth, hand for hand, foot for foot, burn for burn, wound for wound, stripe for stripe" (Exodus 21:22–25). This passage characterizes the harm of such an induced miscarriage as the violence that is inflicted upon the expectant mother. But the amount of damage is determined by the husband and not by the woman. This shows us the extent of the ancient patriarchal system. The question of whether harm is done directly to the fetus is not considered—the harm here is harm to the woman, not harm to the fetus. One reason for this might be that an early miscarriage—one that occurred before the fetus was ensouled—was not considered to be a harm.[7]

There has been lively debate about this passage. I do not claim that the interpretation that I present here is definitive. Rather, I want to emphasize the fact that this passage is open to interpretation. Moreover, my general point is that this ambiguous passage and the few other scattered references to life in the womb cannot really direct us toward a conclusion about abortion. There may be good reasons to be against abortion. But these ancient texts do not provide such reasons. Nor do they prove that a Christian should be opposed to abortion.

A further problem arises when we consider the use of these ancient texts as a source of moral insight into abortion in light of the development of new technologies that allow safe medical abortion. Abortion was not uncommon in the ancient world. Plato acknowledges in the *Theatetus* that midwives could cause a miscarriage with "drugs and incantations," and in the *Republic* he hints that the eugenic project might require abortion and infanticide.[8] Moreover, Hippocrates' oath includes an explicit refusal "to give a woman a pessary (a vaginal suppository) to produce abortion."[9] But ancient abortion was not nearly as safe for the mother as it currently is. It often involved violent shaking of the mother, the ingestion of poisons, or the insertion of foreign objects into the uterus that could lead to infection. The issue of abortion is changed now that medical technology makes it safer. Indeed, new issues are raised by new medicines such as the birth control pill, the "morning after pill," and RU-486, which can prevent a pregnancy from progressing.

THE WOMAN QUESTION

Another crucial issue to consider here is the status of women. For thousands of years, women and women's sexuality have been subordinate to men. The sexual revolution of the last fifty years was facilitated by modern technology, especially the birth control pill, which gave women control over their reproductive lives. It is important to note that the passage in Exodus discussed above assumes that the value of the woman and her offspring is intimately connected to the man. Our more advanced view of women's rights must not be overlooked in the abortion debate, especially when we consider abortion in cases when the life of the mother is in jeopardy or when she has been raped.

Jesus appears to have held women in high esteem. Indeed, it is women—including Mary Magdalene—who discover the empty tomb, and women share in the revelation of the risen Christ. But it is significant that there were no women among the twelve disciples. Jesus was still a product of his culture, which was patriarchal. From the perspective of women's rights, it is thus impossible to say what Jesus would have thought about women having control of their bodies, their sexuality, and their reproductive capacities. It is important to note, of course, that women's rights issues do not lead to unambiguous conclusions when thinking about abortion. After all, female as well as male fetuses are aborted. Indeed, in some cultures, female fetuses are aborted at higher rates because female children are considered less valuable.

The most important issue remains the ontological and moral status of the fetus. But Jesus really has nothing to tell us about this issue, which is why we need to go beyond Jesus and use reason to think critically about this complicated issue. Some might argue that Jesus' idea of love and his self-sacrificial model may show women that they should be willing to sacrifice themselves for nine months to support an unborn child. This is a matter of interpreting the Golden Rule to include the unborn child as a neighbor who deserves love. As John Noonan claims in arguing against abortion, "the fetus as human was a neighbor; his life had parity with one's own."[10] Even a defender of abortion such as Judith Jarvis Thomson claims that a woman might have an obligation to be a "minimally decent Samaritan" and sustain a pregnancy when there is no risk and only slight inconvenience. But Thomson rejects full-blown Good Samaritanism: a woman is not required to sacrifice herself for the fetus. Indeed, Thomson notes that there are circumstances in which abortion is the compassionate choice. But this depends on the circumstances. While Thomson is wary of advocating abortions for minor inconveniences, she concludes that "a sick and desperately frightened fourteen-year-old schoolgirl, pregnant due to rape, may of course choose abortion, and any law which rules this out is an insane law."[11]

How should the Golden Rule apply to the schoolgirl in this case? Might Christian compassion lead us to think that this abused girl deserves the remedy of abortion? We simply do not know what Jesus would say about this case.

A general point to be made here is that the Golden Rule provides us with little guidance in cases in which there are conflicts of rights. Although loving your neighbor is a good principle, sometimes we need more concrete guidance about how to apply this principle. Along these lines, R. M. Hare applies the Golden Rule in an argument against abortion: "If we are glad that nobody terminated the pregnancy that resulted in our birth, then we are enjoined not, ceteris paribus, to terminate any pregnancy which will result in the birth of a person having a life like ours."[12] The difficulty here is the "ceteris paribus" (or "all things being equal") clause. This approach leads to a general conclusion that most pregnancies should be allowed to proceed because they will produce individuals who will be glad to be born.

However, this approach leaves open the possibility of imagining cases in which it would have been better not to have been born. Peter Singer uses this sort of reasoning to argue in favor of abortion in the case of deformed fetuses and in favor of euthanasia for severely handicapped children. While Singer is notorious among those who advocate the culture of life, similar attitudes are expressed even in the Judeo-Christian tradition. In the Old Testament, Job curses the day that he was born: "Let the day perish wherein I was born, and the night which said 'a man-child is conceived.' Let that night be darkness!" (Job 3:3). There are parallels here with Jesus' warning, in Luke, of eschatological doom; it is possible to imagine that it is better not to be born. From this perspective, the Golden Rule may in fact argue in favor of abortion. Of course, the moral of the story of Job is that one must suffer patiently and without complaint because God's ways are incomprehensible. But this message seems to run counter to the idea, as expressed by Jesus, that we should work to end suffering.

CONCLUSION

The Bible does not provide us with definitive answers to the questions with which we began. Jesus does not say that the fetus is a neighbor whom we must love. Nor does he say how such love might manifest itself, or whether in some rare circumstances it would be better not to have been born. Neither does Jesus tell us how to deal with tragic con-

flicts in which the life of the mother is in jeopardy or in which pregnancy is the result of the deliberate violation of her body. And Jesus does
not tell us how to deal with the reproductive technologies of modern
medicine. He does not speak about abortion. But nor does he speak of
birth control methods, artificial insemination, or much else that is related
to sexual and reproductive health.

Some Christians might claim that in the absence of direct scriptural
guidance, we should resort to a general sense of piety and use prayer
to reach conclusions. But such an approach will be burdened by the
difficult fact that the prayers of different people will lead to different
conclusions. At this point we might reach a pro-choice conclusion and
claim that individuals should be allowed to choose their answers according to the best dictates of their consciences. But even this position is at
best a pragmatic compromise. To decide for oneself whether abortion is
the right choice, we need answers to the complicated set of ethical and
ontological questions with which this discussion began. To reach conclusions, we need to go beyond the Bible and use reason to think our way
through these tough questions.

NOTES

1. "Presbyterian 101: A Guide to the Facts about the PCUSA," www.pcusa.org.

2. Paul Ramsey, *Ethics at the Edges of Life* (New Haven: Yale University Press,
1978).

3. Pope John Paul II, *Evangelium Vitae* (Vatican Library, 1995).

4. Aristotle, *Politics* (Chicago: University of Chicago Press, 1984), 1335b.

5. See Konstantinos Kapparis, *Abortion in the Ancient World* (London: Duck-
worth, 2002), 43.

6. See Ronald Dworkin's discussion in chapter 2 of *Life's Dominion* (New York:
Knopf, 1993).

7. See discussion in Kapparis, *Abortion in the Ancient World*, 47.

8. Plato, *Theatetus*, 149d, and *Republic*, 461c, in *Plato's Collected Dialogues*, ed.
Hamilton and Cairns, Bollingen Series (Princeton, NJ: Princeton University Press,
1961).

9. Hippocrates, "The Oath," from *Internet Classics Archive*, http://classics.mit.edu.

10. John T. Noonan, "An Almost Absolute Value in History," reprinted in *Applying Ethics*, ed. Olen, Van Camp, and Barry (Belmont, CA: Thomson Wadsworth,
2005), 132.

11. Judith Jarvis Thomson, "A Defense of Abortion," in *Applying Ethics*, 142.

12. R. M. Hare, "Abortion and the Golden Rule," *Philosophy and Public Affairs*
4:3 (1975): 208.

7

JESUS AND CARE: EUTHANASIA

Come, O blessed of my Father, inherit the kingdom prepared
for you from the foundation of the world; for I was hungry
and you gave me food, I was thirsty and you gave me drink,
I was a stranger and you welcomed me, I was naked and you
clothed me, I was sick and you visited me, I was in prison and
you came to me.

—Matthew 25:34–46

Euthanasia literally means a good or happy death. The idea behind
euthanasia is that killing or letting die can be an act of compassion,
benevolence, and love when we end life in order to end suffering. The
idea that we might express love by killing someone or allowing them
to die may seem to run counter to the idea that life is sacred and that
we have a special obligation to care for the sick. From a perspective that
emphasizes the sanctity of life, one might argue that mercy requires us to
make a dying person comfortable, but that it can never be right to kill
the person or help him or her die.

Jesus says nothing directly about euthanasia. Jesus defends the general idea of caring for others in the Golden Rule. And he advocates
virtues such as love, forgiveness, and mercy. But he does not address the
question of how best to care for a man who is suffering from pain without hope of improvement or a woman whose brain injuries leave her in
a dependent and nonconscious state. Nor does Jesus tell us whether we
should respect the wishes of those who want to die and have asked us
to help them die with dignity. And he tells us nothing about the professional responsibilities of doctors and nurses. Jesus had the power to heal
the sick. But this does not tell us what the rest of us should do to care

for the sick and dying who cannot be healed: we need to know how to extend care through the long process of dying.

The U.S. Supreme Court has upheld Oregon's "death with dignity" law, which in some cases allows terminally ill patients to obtain lethal medications from their doctors. But overshadowing this landmark case during 2005 was the tragic case of Terri Schiavo. Schiavo's cognitive functions were severely impaired, and her husband argued that she would have wanted to be allowed to die by removing her from artificial support and withholding food and water. At issue in this case was the question of what Schiavo would have wanted, as well as the question of who had the right to decide for her, given that she was incapacitated.

Some religious voices took a vigorously pro-life stance in the Schiavo case, maintaining that mercy required that Schiavo be given food and water. One of the biblical verses used to support this view was the passage from Matthew quoted at the outset of this chapter. The argument was made that Jesus would have given food and drink to Schiavo out of a sense of compassion, love, and mercy—and indeed, that this sort of Good Samaritanism is required by the Golden Rule. The difficulty of euthanasia, however, is that it is not clear how love of the neighbor should be expressed. What if the one who is thirsty also does not want to drink because he wants to die? What if someone who is suffering would prefer to be put out of her misery? What if someone asks us for help in dying? Or what if a "person" lacks higher cognitive function and would be unable to sustain her life without extraordinary medical intervention? Jesus provides little concrete guidance for answering such questions.

As with abortion, there are a variety of systematic questions that must be carefully considered in order to come to reasonable conclusions about euthanasia.

1. What exactly do we mean by euthanasia? There are a variety of practices included here. Voluntary euthanasia occurs when the one who is dying consents. Involuntary euthanasia occurs when consent is not given. Active euthanasia occurs when deliberate steps are taken to end a person's life. Passive euthanasia occurs when one is simply "allowed to die." Physician-assisted suicide is a related concept that involves ending one's own life with the assistance of a physician who prescribes medications or procedures that will bring about death. The Oregon law makes physician-assisted suicide allowable in certain closely regulated circumstances. Clarity about these definitions is necessary so that we know what we are talking about.

2. As with abortion, the question of who or what is a person or moral patient is involved here. Is someone in a coma or persistent vegetative state a person? Do infants with undeveloped cognitive functions deserve the same sort of moral concern as adults? What criteria apply here: higher-order consciousness, mere animal sentience, motility, or simple bodily integrity?

3. Even after we answer the question of who or what is a person, the question remains open as to what we ought to do to a person who wants to die or who is suffering greatly and without hope for recovery. Should we allow such people to die? Should we take extraordinary steps to prolong their life? Or should we help them to die quickly and painlessly? At issue here is the value of autonomy and consent. If a person gives (or has given in the past) consent to be allowed to die or to be painlessly killed, is this consent sufficient to allow for euthanasia?

4. We also need to ask the political question of whether the state should be involved in regulating how and when people die. Indeed, we should bear in mind that euthanasia may become part of a eugenic project that results in forced euthanasia. So the question becomes both whether the state should allow euthanasia and whether the state should be in the business of sanctioning or even recommending it. The same sorts of questions apply at the level of doctors and hospitals: do we want our health-care providers to be involved in the business of helping people to die (or in extreme cases, killing people)?

A CONSISTENT ETHIC OF LIFE

As with abortion, the idea of a "gospel of life" or a "consistent ethic of life" might help us answer these questions. The Protestant ethicist Paul Ramsey puts it this way: "The immorality of choosing death as an end is founded upon our religious faith that life is a gift. . . . To choose death as an end is to throw the gift back in the face of the giver; it would be to defeat his gift-giving."[1] This is quite similar to the basic view outlined by Pope John Paul II in *Evangelium Vitae*, where the pope adds a critique of modern liberal culture: the modern emphasis on autonomy extends in a sinful direction when autonomy is understood as our capacity to determine when and how we die. Such decisions are God's and not our own. The pope worries, furthermore, that euthanasia is part of the "culture of death," which is "marked by an attitude of excessive preoccupation with efficiency and which sees the growing number of elderly and disabled people as intolerable and too burdensome."[2] The pope concludes that "euthanasia is a grave violation of the law of God, since it is the deliberate and morally unacceptable killing of a human person. This doctrine is based upon the natural law and upon the written word of God."[3]

It might be that the natural law leads us to condemn euthanasia. Natural law arguments would appeal to reasons that should be acceptable to reasonable persons. Indeed, some of these arguments might focus on claims about the sacred value of life and the redemptive power of suffering. Other arguments may direct us against suicide. Kant, for example, argued that suicide was wrong because it was not possible to universally legislate suicide; this is true even though suicide may appear to bring about greater satisfaction than continued life. Christianity is not alone in rejecting euthanasia. The Hippocratic Oath requires that a doctor "give no deadly medicine to any one if asked, nor suggest any such counsel."

But the ancients were not unanimously opposed to the idea of ending one's own life. We know that Socrates willingly drank the hemlock, in part because he had led a full life and was convinced that a man, such as himself, who had led a good life would be rewarded in the afterlife. Although this example is a bit out of place—since Socrates was *forced* to take the poison—it is useful as an example because Socrates reconciles himself to death based on the fact that he is already an old man. Plato seems to have thought that once a certain old age was reached, it would be a blessing to die well. He writes in the *Timaeus* (81e): "That sort of death which comes with old age and fulfills the debt of nature is the easiest of deaths, and is accompanied with pleasure rather than with pain." The problem is that modern medical technology makes it difficult to say exactly how and when a death is in accord with nature in this way. Our medical technology allows us to prolong life in ways that may in fact be contrary to nature. Indeed, this presents us with difficult decisions that Jesus and the ancients did not have to face.

John Paul II claims, however, that the written word of God tells us that euthanasia is wrong. Unfortunately, as with abortion, the Bible is virtually silent on this topic, perhaps because—like abortion—it was a topic that was of little interest to ancient people. The Old Testament does give us a couple of examples of what might be called "mercy killing." In Judges 9, Abimelech, in the midst of battle, asks to be killed by a sword after a woman has crushed his skull with a millstone. And in 2 Samuel 1, Saul is killed out of mercy by an Amalekite. King David seems to condemn this killing—but it should be remembered that Saul was a king. The difficulty of these passages is that they are about warriors in battle and give us no guidance for the tragic cases of ordinary life. How are we to apply these examples to the contemporary case of an old man with bone cancer who wants to end his misery and "die with dignity"? How are we to apply these examples to contemporary cases of people who are "brain dead" but sustained by medical technology? It is not clear that these few examples from the Old Testament are relevant to the cases that concern us most.

Moreover, the Old Testament needs to be read in light of Jesus' call for mercy, forgiveness, compassion, and love. The question Christians ask is "What would Jesus do?" But someone in Jesus' time would never have thought of a circumstance in which a brain-dead patient is kept alive by machinery—such technology was beyond the imaginative powers of the ancients. Nonetheless, one might think that we can derive a general view of euthanasia from Jesus' general attitude toward death and sickness. But there is ambiguity in Jesus' view of dying. He does bring a few people back from the dead, implying perhaps that it is good to keep people alive and resuscitate the dead. One should consider in this context the story, which appears in all three of the synoptic Gospels, of the twelve-year-old girl—Jairus' daughter—who is "not dead but sleeping" and whom Jesus commands to arise. And one would have to consider the story of Lazarus, which appears using the name of Lazarus only in John. These stories show Jesus bringing the dead back to life.

It is instructive to consider why—within the structure of the Gospel narratives—Jesus raises the dead. One could argue that he does not resurrect the dead because he wants the dead to live. Rather, he resuscitates them because he wants to demonstrate his power. In going to raise Lazarus, for example, Jesus tells his disciples that he is going to do it "so that you may believe" (John 11:15). And when he raises Lazarus, he says, "I have said this on account of the people standing by, that they may believe that thou didst send me" (John 11:42). The public demonstration of power that occurs in this story is quite different from the story of healing Jairus' daughter. In two of the synoptic Gospels, the story ends with Jesus telling her parents to tell no one what had happened (Mark 5:43; Luke 8:56).

Another reason Jesus raises the dead is to ease the suffering of the mourning survivors. John tells us that Jesus loved Lazarus and Lazarus' sisters Mary and Martha (John 11:5). And when Jesus sees Mary and her relatives crying over Lazarus' death, Jesus weeps too. It is clear that his love and compassion for Mary motivates him to bring Lazarus back from the grave. What is significant in both of these cases of Jesus' healing power is that the "patients" are not left in vegetative states; nor are they dependent upon life-support machinery; nor are they left in excruciating pain. Rather, Jesus restores them to robust life, and the grief of their relatives is relieved. But what if such restoration is not possible, as in the case of Terri Schiavo? Our medical technology does not always restore robust life; rather, we often keep people alive but in a state of diminished capacity and dependency that often causes even more grief. How would Jesus show compassion for those who love patients who are kept minimally alive by contemporary medical technology?

DEATH AND SELF-DETERMINATION

One crucial point is that Jesus nowhere says that death is a horrible thing to be avoided at any cost. In general, Jesus does not seem to view death as something to be feared, in part because he promises the power to overcome death. Jesus says that we should not worry about taking extraordinary steps to preserve life. He says, "Do not be anxious about your life" and "do not be anxious about tomorrow, for tomorrow will be anxious for itself" (Matthew 6:25, 34). This might seem to be a reference to the resigned acknowledgment in Ecclesiastes that there is "a time to be born, and a time to die" (3:2). The author of Ecclesiastes goes on to claim that "there is nothing better for them [i.e., for humans] than to be happy and enjoy themselves as long as they live" (3:12). But when the possibilities for happiness are diminished and only a long twilight of suffering remains before death, it might be acceptable to simply acquiesce to death. At least, Jesus seems to counsel that we should have no anxiety about dying.

One might argue that love of life and courage in the face of death make it acceptable to hasten death, so that suffering may be overcome and the soul may be released from its tribulations. John Lachs puts it this way: "Continued physical existence is of no benefit to an individual in intractable pain or to people who are done with life. No serious religious person and no one who loves life can maintain that the continued travail of our biological organism is worth its cost in human suffering. The body, after all, is not the human being; we love and celebrate its intelligent motion, not is cells and chemistry."[4] Although Jesus thinks that resurrection was possible, he actually refused to speculate on the difference between soul and body. In Matthew 22:29–32 (Mark 12:19–27; Luke 20:27–38),

Jesus implies that the resurrected soul would be wholly different from the body of the living, and he claims that God is a God of the living and not a God of the dead. But unfortunately, passages such as these do not really help us answer the question about whether we should keep dying bodies alive or help ease them into death.

Perhaps the most important point to consider with regard to death and dying is Jesus' own submission to death on the cross. This episode shows us that death is not the worst thing that can happen. In preparation for his death, Jesus says: "Unless a grain of wheat falls into the earth and dies, it remains alone; but if it dies, it bears much fruit. He who loves his life loses it, and he who hates his life in this world will keep it for eternal life" (John 12:24–25). As Jesus courageously and patiently submits to his own final ordeal, it is clear that he, at least, welcomes the death of the physical body because it prepares the way for eternal life.

This view of courageous submission to death is intimately connected to the theological claim that death is overcome through Christ. Paul claims that it is Jesus' sacrifice that allows Christians to say, "O death, where is thy victory? O death, where is thy sting?" (1 Corinthians 15:55). But claims such as this are connected to a larger story in which death is understood metaphorically as sin and distance from God. As Paul explains, "The sting of death is sin" (1 Corinthians 15:56). The larger story goes back to Genesis and the idea that death came into the world with Adam's original sin (cf. Romans 5:12–14). Thus, when Christians (and Jews) speak of "choosing life" (as discussed with regard to Deuteronomy above), this has a connection with claims about obedience to God. The twist for Christians is that obedience to God can only be fulfilled, given our sinful nature, through faith in Jesus' sacrifice and the possibility of forgiveness of sin. It is this blood sacrifice that makes it possible for us to remain with God (and thus with life) despite our disobedience and even through the ordeal of our physical deaths.

We have strayed quite far from the topic of euthanasia. The difficulty is that Christian reflections on death are linked to these complex and debatable theological claims. But the question remains: what would Jesus have thought about euthanasia? The honest answer is: we don't know. The difficulties we confront in trying to use the passages considered above to interpret what Jesus would think about euthanasia should be obvious. Jesus resuscitation of Jairus' daughter and his resurrection of Lazarus are rare occurrences that are tied to the larger endeavor in the Gospels of establishing Jesus' power. Jesus' own death is an extraordinary and seemingly necessary theological event that cannot be used as an example in a discussion of euthanasia. And it should be obvious that Jesus' healing actions are quite different from the "miracles" of modern science. Indeed, Jesus' view of disease is one in which it is caused by demons: his approach to healing is to cast out the demons who cause disease. Modern medicine's basic understanding of disease is radically different from Jesus'. The capacity of modern medicine to prolong life is also radically different. And it is this capacity that presents us with a new set of problems, about which Jesus provides little guidance. To be honest, we should admit that Jesus says nothing about what to do about removing a feeding tube from a woman who has been in a persistent vegetative state for years. Nor does he tell us what to think about a law such as Oregon's that allows terminally ill patients to obtain lethal medications from licensed physicians.

One might argue that the Golden Rule and Jesus' idea of compassionate concern for the well-being of the neighbor can be a guide here. But the idea of "doing unto others as we would have done to ourselves" results in divergent conclusions about euthanasia. One might argue that since we value life, the Golden Rule tells us that we should be allowed every chance to live. But this is complicated by cases in which life itself becomes unbearable because of suffering, or in cases in which it is difficult to say that anything resembling human life remains (as in the case of certain profound brain injuries). One way of applying the Golden Rule is to ask the patient herself what she wants to have done in such cases. On this interpretation of the Golden Rule, consent is key: we should allow patients to die (and perhaps assist them in dying) according to their wishes. When explicit consent is lacking, we could decide such cases by imagining what a patient would consent to, if she had the capacity to answer such a question. The difficulty is that in some cases (e.g., Terri Schiavo), there are disputes about what the patient would want.

But consent itself is disputable as a key to morality for some Christians. Pope John Paul II claims that it is wrong to consent to death and that suicide is an immoral "rejection of God's absolute sovereignty over life and death."[5] John Paul II condemns what he calls the "Promethean attitude" that leads people to think they can control everything, even their own deaths.[6] From the pope's perspective, life and death are not in our control. Nor should they be, because God is ultimately the sovereign of life and death.

Linked to this is a claim about the importance of suffering. John Paul II claims that "suffering, while still an evil and a trial in itself, can always become a source of good."[7] The idea is that God gives us suffering for some purpose, that suffering is bearable with the help of God's grace, and that suffering puts us in touch with the redemptive model of Jesus' crucifixion. As Paul puts it, "We rejoice in our sufferings, knowing that suffering produces endurance, and endurance produces character, and character produces hope, and hope does not disappoint us, because God's love has been poured into our hearts through the Holy Spirit which has been given to us" (Romans 5:3–5). There is something to commend such a view even to agnostics: suffering can indeed help to create virtue. However, there may be limits to the amount of suffering that is productive. Some forms of suffering may produce character, but other forms of suffering are gratuitous and may even be destructive of virtue. Some types of suffering actually erode virtue by reducing the sufferer to a state of weakness, misery, and dependence. To allow this to happen may itself be a form of cruelty. One might think that in such circumstances, it would be allowable for people to choose to end their lives.

Modern science has increasingly put life and death into human hands in a way that would have been unimaginable for the ancients. The difficulty of modern science is, however, that it encourages doctors and caregivers to "play God." In Daniel Callahan's words, euthanasia is "self-determination run amok."[8] This problem is exacerbated by the fact that medical technology allows us to prolong life in unprecedented ways. And the question of what sorts of medical intervention are appropriate for the old and incapacitated has become a routine one that is now regulated through the use of living wills and advance directives. However, as the President's Council on Bioethics has warned, we should be careful about thinking that the old are no longer worthy of living simply because they are old: "We must erect firm and permanent safeguards against certain inhuman 'solutions' to the challenges of caring for the dependent elderly— such as active euthanasia or the promotion of assisted suicide, solutions that define a category of persons as 'life unworthy of life' or as persons deserving of abandonment and beyond the scope of our care."[9]

The idea of the council is that dependency, dementia, and other sorts of reduced capacity do not provide reasons for euthanasia. The council is also wary of our growing reliance on advance directives and living wills. Of course, on the other hand, the Golden Rule does seem to imply that we should take a patient's desires into account, as expressed in such documents. Love of the neighbor may in fact require that we respect her wishes, even in her choice of end of life care, including her wishes about how and when she wants to die.

Finally, it is important to consider the difference between passive and active euthanasia. It might be, as James Rachels has influentially argued, that sometimes it is better to actively kill a person than to let him die in a slow process that produces more suffering than actively killing him would.[10] Simply letting a suffering patient die without actively hastening his death in some circumstances may be viewed as an act of needless cruelty, and the Golden Rule may require that we employ active euthanasia. This is the idea of mercy killing, where we kill another in order to benefit him. Of course, this idea is contentious because we tend to think that it is worse to actively do something than it is to passively allow something to happen. The President's Council on Bioethics has argued against any use of active euthanasia: "It is self-contradictory to propose to 'care' for any patient by making him dead; and it is hard to think wholeheartedly about best care if one morally eligible option is to ease the suffering person out of existence."[11]

Jesus does care for the sick. He heals, and he gives his disciples the power to "heal every disease and infirmity" (Matthew 10:1). But he does not consider the subtle distinction between acting and nonacting. Nor does he tell those of us without miraculous power what we should do about the suffering of those we cannot heal.

CONCLUSION

The point here is that Jesus is not an adequate guide for thinking about such complex questions. Jesus does advocate mercy, care, and love. But he has nothing to tell us about "mercy killing." Although Jesus had the power to restore the dead to life, we mortals who lack such power are in a different situation when we must consider whether actively killing someone may in fact help to ease that person's suffering. To make decisions about such a complex matter requires careful reflection on a number of issues that Jesus simply does not address: the nature of personhood, the importance of autonomy and consent, the extent to which suffering is virtuous, and the legal question of whether the state should support or allow euthanasia.

NOTES

1. Paul Ramsey, *Ethics at the Edges of Life* (New Haven: Yale University Press, 1978), 146.
2. Pope John Paul II, *Evangelium Vitae* (Vatican Library, 1995), para. 64.
3. Pope John Paul II, *Evangelium Vitae*, para. 65.

4. John Lachs, *In Love with Life* (Nashville: Vanderbilt University Press, 1998), 122.

5. Pope John Paul II, *Evangelium Vitae*, para. 66.

6. Pope John Paul II, *Evangelium Vitae*, para. 15.

7. Pope John Paul II, *Evangelium Vitae*, para. 67.

8. Daniel Callahan, "When Self-Determination Runs Amok," in *Social and Professional Ethics*, ed. William H. Shaw (Belmont, CA: Thomson Wadsworth, 2005), 92. See John Lachs' reply, "When Abstract Moralizing Runs Amok," in John Lachs, *The Relevance of Philosophy to Life* (Nashville: Vanderbilt University Press, 1995), chap. 19.

9. President's Council on Bioethics, *Taking Care: Ethical Care Giving in Our Aging Society*, September 2005, 47, www.bioethics.gov.

10. James Rachels, "Active and Passive Euthanasia," *New England Journal of Medicine* 292 (January 1975): 78–80.

11. President's Council on Bioethics, *Taking Care*, 130.

8

FORGIVENESS AND MERCY:
THE DEATH PENALTY

Be merciful, even as your Father is merciful.

—Luke 6:36

Jesus advocates mercy and forgiveness. Mercy is a virtue that is linked to other virtues such as compassion, but mercy is essentially a virtue for the powerful. When someone is "at your mercy," you have power over that person; the idea of mercy is that this power should not be abused. It would seem that Jesus' ideal of mercy would lead him to reject the death penalty. Unfortunately, Jesus never says this directly.

STOIC AND HEBREW IDEAS

Jesus is not alone among the ancients in counseling mercy. Ancient Stoic philosophers such as Cicero, Seneca, and Marcus Aurelius also advise the powerful to restrain themselves and practice mercy, tolerance, and forbearance. According to Seneca, mercy is a royal virtue. Seneca discusses his thoughts about mercy or clemency in a letter to the emperor Nero, written at about the same time that the Gospels were being formulated.[1] According to Seneca, any person can break the law to take a life, but only the emperor can break the law to save a life. To show mercy is a noble act that expresses strength, patience, and other godlike virtues. This is also pragmatic advice for the powerful. Clemency helps rulers to display power and retain it. But the Stoic view is that mercy is also essential to a life of virtue. The goal of Stoicism is to develop the self, and one way to do this is to focus primarily on one's own life and virtue. Tolerance and mercy are virtues that remind us that judging and punishing the actions of others is not our primary concern. This is not to say that there is no right or wrong; rather, the point is that the actions of others are beyond our control. As the Emperor Marcus Aurelius reminds us with regard to those who do wrong: "Teach them better, if you can; if not, remember that kindliness has been given you for moments such as these."[2] This does not mean that punishment is not deserved, but that punishments should be meted out with a spirit of tolerance and mercy.

Some Stoic elements can be found in Jesus' thought. But Jesus' view remains thoroughly grounded in the Hebrew tradition. Jesus modifies this tradition by defending a new idea of God as merciful, loving, and forgiving: God's benevolent concern for human flourishing is connected with his recognition of our faults and forgiveness of our sins. Furthermore, Jesus thinks that we should model our behavior on God's mercy, love, and forgiveness. Since we need God's merciful love, we should also be merciful and loving toward other human beings. All of this is summed up in the lines that follow Jesus' call for mercy in Luke (6:37): "Judge not, and you will not be judged; condemn not, and you will not be condemned; forgive and you will be forgiven."

The demand that is made here is directed at individuals and not at those who exercise political power. Christian proponents of the death penalty will argue that political power is entitled to judge, condemn, and even punish with death, since the virtues required of rulers are different from those of ordinary individuals. In Romans 13, Paul argues that authorities can use violence in God's name: the political authority "does not bear the sword in vain; he is the servant of God to execute his wrath on the wrongdoer" (13:4). It seems that there is one law for individuals and another for political authorities. But Jesus does consider the way in which individuals participate in acts of punishment as members of a group. When a woman is to be stoned for committing adultery, Jesus says, "Let him who is without sin among you be the first to throw a stone at her" (John 8:7). The difficulty introduced here is that the members of the community, including presumably the political authorities, are individuals who should focus on their own virtue and avoid condemning others. The ambiguity here verges on contradiction: Christians are supposed to refrain from violence, and they are to forgive and be reluctant to condemn others, but the state can employ violence in God's name. This is further complicated by the fact that Jesus willingly submits to the death penalty.

One response might be to emphasize that the passage from John is considered by scholars to be a later addition to the text. Since John is the last written and least historically accurate account of Jesus' ideas, this passage should be taken with a grain of salt. On the other hand, Paul is our earliest source for Christian teaching, and his letter to the Romans predates the Gospels.

This textual analysis is of little help in deciding whether Jesus would support the death penalty in its current usage. The death penalty as currently practiced is quite different from capital punishment as practiced in the Bible. Jesus' was crucified, which is a form of torture that causes physical pain while also putting the executed body on public display. And Jesus' crime was supposed to be blasphemy—for claiming to be the Christ. Jesus was crucified along with thieves. And in his world, adulterers were executed as well. But the death penalty is used today only for murder and treason. We do not execute blasphemers and thieves. And we no longer crucify or stone criminals. We have found a more humane method of capital punishment: lethal injection (although the humaneness of this procedure has come under fire recently; in California, the case of Michael Morales has raised the question of whether lethal injection is really a painless way to die). Moreover, executions occur in a controlled and protected environment after extensive trials and appeals. And executed bodies are not put on display. We have made progress toward a more humane application of the death penalty. The question is whether further progress should include its eventual abolition.

One might turn to the Bible to find advice for thinking about this question. But the Bible contains contradictory advice, as noted above. And the contradictions are exacerbated by the difference between the Old and New Testaments. Jesus' ideas about a loving and merciful God are stated in contrast to a view that holds that God is stern and unsympathetic. The God of Moses was not known for mercy. Indeed, Moses' God commands bloodshed, war, slaughter, and sacrifice. But Jesus says in several places that God "desires mercy, and not sacrifice" (Matthew 9:13, 12:7). Jesus' idea is part of an ongoing argument within ancient Judaism about the nature of God and the requirements of ethics. The incipient Christian idea can be derived, for example, from Psalm 103, where God is said to be merciful and gracious, full of steadfast love. This idea is picked up by Hosea, Micah, and others, even though these prophets still speak of God's anger and vengeance. The psalmist does acknowledge that God can be angry in his pursuit of justice, but this psalm says that God will not remain angry forever, and that God will forgive our sins. This is summed up in the idea that "as a father pities his children, so the Lord pities those who fear him" (Psalm 103:13).

The gist of this brief review of the Hebrew tradition is that there are two rival views of God: one that is vengeful and one that is merciful. Jesus seems to view God as merciful, but the Christian texts also contain images of vengeance and—as in Romans 13—allow for the state to execute God's wrath.

THINKING CRITICALLY ABOUT THE DEATH PENALTY

The big question to be considered here is whether one should show mercy in punishing the guilty, especially with regard to the death penalty. One reading of mercy would say that benevolence requires forgiveness and forbearance, and thus that punishments should be made less severe. Indeed, this has been the general way in which the system of punishment has developed in the West. The U.S. Constitution prohibits the use of "cruel and unusual punishments." And the death penalty—together with its gallows, guillotines, and electric chairs—has gradually faded away. On the other hand, one might argue not only that the death penalty is required by justice but also that it shows proper love and compassion for the victims of crime and their surviving family members. Moreover, one might argue that if the death penalty deters crime, it benefits potential victims.

In the nineteenth century, the Utilitarian philosopher John Stuart Mill argued that the death penalty for murder was the most merciful punishment for murder that it was possible to use. And although he was in favor of abolishing the death penalty for lesser crimes, he argued that it would be wrong to do away with the death penalty for murder, because the death penalty for murder expressed the idea that life is of ultimate value. Murder is the ultimate crime against life, and so it deserves to be punished by death. Mill recognized that a system of punishment should be designed to prevent and deter crime. Not only does the death penalty prevent a murderer from murdering again, but it also terrifies the imaginations of potential criminals and so deters murder. Moreover, Mill argued that the death penalty was less cruel than torture or other punishments that would have a significant deterrent effect. For Mill, even though the death penalty is falsely imagined by most to be the worst punishment possible, there are penalties worse than death, and execution can be a mercy.

One wonders what Jesus would have made of such an argument? As mentioned in the previous chapter, Jesus did not think that death was the worst possible outcome. Indeed, the basic idea of Christianity is that there is life beyond death. Nonetheless, Jesus' principles of nonresistance to evil, love of enemies, and forgiveness of sin do seem to argue against the death penalty. Again, the thesis of this chapter is that there is no clear answer to be found to the question of what Jesus would think about the death penalty.

As with the other applied topics we have discussed, there are many questions to consider when thinking about the death penalty.

1. Is the death penalty required by justice? Is justice really a retributive balance system that takes a life for a life and an eye for an eye? If we show mercy or forgive crime, have we done something unjust by not bringing the scales back into balance? Or are there values that go beyond this strictly retributive scale of justice, such as love, mercy, and forgiveness?

2. Does the death penalty serve to deter crime? Utilitarians, like Mill, would argue that it does. But there is an unresolved debate about this question. The U.S. Conference of Catholic Bishops has argued that there is no conclusive evidence that the death penalty deters crime.[3] Moreover, the further question is whether deterrence matters at all. It is important to note that Jesus nowhere discusses deterrence or other Utilitarian approaches to either punishment or forgiveness.

3. Does it matter that occasionally innocent people will be wrongly executed, or that the death penalty may be used against juveniles or those who are mentally incompetent? In the last several years, numerous people convicted of murder have later been exonerated. And the Supreme Court has ruled that juveniles and the mentally retarded cannot be executed. With regard to exoneration, one might argue that the use of DNA evidence should be able to fix the problem. But there is still the problem of police incompetence or malice. One wonders if the system can ever be perfected so that we can ensure that only the guilty are executed. Is it simply easier to abolish the death penalty completely?

4. What are we to do about racial, economic, or other bias in the way the death penalty is applied? Poor nonwhites tend to be executed at higher rates than those who are white and affluent. At issue here is the question of fairness and equality in applying the death penalty. There is also the question of whether the system can ever be fixed to make it more equitable.

5. What are our ethical obligations to all of those who are involved in the process of criminal justice? This would include our obligations to the victims of crime and their families, our obligations to the guards and medical professionals who are in charge of executions, and our obligations to the family and loved ones of those who are to be executed.

There is no clear answer to these questions in terms of what Jesus would do. On the one hand, the Old Testament seems to require the death penalty for numerous transgressions. For example, in Leviticus 20, death is the punishment for adultery, incest, homosexuality, bestiality, and sorcery. Thus one might argue—as John Howard Yoder does—that the idea of "a life for a life and an eye for an eye" as articulated, for example, at Exodus 21:24 represents an attempt to *restrain* the use of the death penalty so that it was not applied to such a broad range of crimes. Rather than unleashing the full fury of vengeance, justice appears to require that the avenging act should be limited by such a system of equivalence.

At any rate, the death penalty was used since the time of Moses. And it was in use through the time that Jesus himself was executed. Indeed, Jesus' submission to execution may provide an oblique authorization of the death penalty: he never questioned capital punishment on his way to the cross. It is only in the modern world that we witness those who advocate abolition of the death penalty. Such thoughts were simply not on the table in the ancient world.

But one may argue that Jesus did explicitly call the law of Exodus into question. In the Sermon on the Mount, Jesus says: "You have heard that it was said, 'An eye for an eye and a tooth for a tooth.' But I say to you, Do not resist one who is evil. But if anyone strikes you on the right cheek, turn to him the other also" (Matthew 5:38–39). This seems to be a clear rebuttal of the Mosaic Law. And Jesus also advocates in this sermon love of enemies, forgiveness, and mercy.

One could argue that Jesus' idea represents a further refinement of the Old Testament attempt to restrain vengeance. But again, this is not entirely clear. One may also argue against the death penalty as the Protestant theologian Karl Barth does. Barth argues that rejection of the death penalty follows from the idea of the sanctity of life as well as from an emphasis on the Christian virtues of humility and forgiveness. Humility leads us to question whether human beings are wise enough to administer the death penalty. And the Christian idea of forgiveness follows from the idea that Jesus' sacrifice was the last necessary act of expiation for sin: the execution of Jesus represented an eschatological overcoming of vengeance. While Barth does acknowledge some rare cases in which the death penalty may be acceptable, he concludes with a sense of outrage about the extent to which Christians approve the death penalty. "If the command to protect life is accepted and asserted in some sense in a national community, then it is impossible to maintain capital punishment as an element in its normal and continuing order. It is an astonishing and disturbing fact that for nineteen hundred years there has been a Christian Church, and for four hundred years a Protestant, which has not only failed to champion this insight but has continually opposed it."[4]

Like Barth, Pope John Paul II takes the commandment "thou shall not kill" to lead to a near absolute prohibition on the death penalty. The prohibition on killing leads to the requirement not to kill the innocent— as in the prohibition on abortion. But with regard to criminals, the basic idea is that nonlethal means of defending the innocent against aggressors should be employed. "The nature and extent of the punishment must be carefully evaluated and decided upon, and ought not go to the extreme of executing the offender except in cases of absolute necessity: in other words, when it would not be possible otherwise to defend society. Today however, as a result of steady improvements in the organization of the penal system, such cases are very rare, if not practically non-existent."[5]

John Paul II's view is that we should not kill even murderers, because decisions about life and death belong to God. This is the idea behind a "consistent ethic of life." This view of the death penalty is strengthened by considering other Christian values such as forgiveness. John Paul II's view has been taken to heart by the U.S. Conference of Catholic Bishops, which has renewed the call for the abolition of the death penalty in the United States. And it has provided a focal point for debates about Christian punishment in general. Critics worry that the pope's view resulted from a sort of sentimental humanism. But Stanley Hauerwas has suggested in support of abolition that the key to Christian punishment is the goal of reconciliation that is facilitated by forgiveness and mercy.[6]

In opposition to such a perspective, some argue that to abolish the death penalty would be to ignore the essential difference between killing the innocent and killing the guilty. For example, Supreme Court Justice Antonin Scalia—who is Catholic—recently rejected the pope's ideas about applying the gospel of life to the death penalty. "The more Christian a country is the less likely it is to regard the death penalty as immoral. . . . I attribute this to the fact that, for the believing Christian, death is no big deal. Intentionally killing an innocent person is a big deal."[7] The first part of this claim is obviously false: the death penalty has gradually been eradicated in the Christian West, while it remains in use, along with other forms of corporal punishment, in Islamic nations that base their law on a more literal reading of the ancient idea of "an eye for an eye." But he may be onto something when he claims that Christians must take murder seriously. Scalia argues that the death penalty has been a long-standing part of Western culture and that the pope was imprudent to sweep aside the traditional idea that the state has a right to use the ultimate punishment against murder. This shows us the general problem discussed throughout the present book, that there are disagreements even *within* Christianity about these issues.

In defending the death penalty, Scalia claims that Christians generally believe that punishment is deserved because they believe in free will. He implies that Christians reject the "liberal" idea that the criminal's environment is partially to blame for his acts. Rather, for Scalia, crime is a result of the sinful possibilities inherent in the idea of free will. Since the criminal chooses his crime, he fully deserves the punishment.

When one takes such a perspective to its logical outcome, it eliminates one of the arguments that might be given for mercy, since mercy often looks to mitigating circumstances. But if we take the notion of radical free will seriously, there can be no mitigating circumstances, since the individual always had the clear choice either to do right or to do wrong. Moreover, accord to this perspective, the criminal's subsequent behavior—including repentance or rehabilitation—simply does not matter. We saw this attitude in California with Governor Arnold Schwarzenegger's refusal of clemency in 2005 for Tookie Williams, a gangster and murderer who had apparently changed his ways and had been advocating against the gangster lifestyle. The strict crime and punishment approach holds that a deed once done must be punished. From this standpoint, mercy and forgiveness make little sense, since they are outside the scope of retribution. One way of putting this is to argue that human beings must accomplish justice, while it is up to God to have mercy on the soul of executed criminals. This attitude is not, however, supported by reference to Jesus. Jesus did claim that human beings should show mercy and express forgiveness, and he did not advocate a strict regime of retribution.

It is important to note that an argument that emphasizes radical free will and responsibility is not concerned with the question of whether the death penalty has a deterrent effect. Those who argue for deterrence assume that a system of punishment plays a causal role in behavior. But defenders of radical free will deny such social determinism and thus also ignore the question of deterrence. In defense of the idea of radical free will, one might consider the example of Jesus. Jesus knew that his actions would lead to his execution. But he went forward with his activities anyway. Thus the death penalty was not able to deter Jesus. Nor was the possibility of torture and death able to deter the early Christians who followed Jesus into martyrdom. This discussion should at least make us cautious in claiming that the death penalty has deterrent power, especially when considering those who believe—as suicidal terrorists apparently do—that death is nothing to be feared and that suffering will be rewarded.

A further issue with regard to the death penalty is the question of political power and its connection to the ideas of mercy, forbearance, forgiveness, and nonresistance to evil. It is difficult to establish a final Christian view about this, as we noted in our previous discussion of pacifism. The most important piece of evidence for Christians in this discussion should be the fact that Jesus acquiesces to the death penalty and to political authority in general: he nowhere argues that his own execution, or that execution in general, is wrong. And, as noted above, Paul argues in his letter to the Romans that political power can be used to exact God's will.

One might try to make sense of this discussion by articulating a division of labor with regard to crime and punishment. On the one hand, the state's duty is to carry out justice along retributive lines; its further duty is to protect the innocent by establishing preventive and deterrent punishments. On the other hand, the duty of love and forgiveness may be a duty for individuals and not for the state. In this sense perhaps the traditional idea of retaliation is to be employed by the state, while the new model of Christian mercy is to be adopted by private individuals. Said differently in the language of Augustine, in the city of man, political authorities should not be soft on crime, but those who aspire to dwell in the city of God should work to develop love, forgiveness, and mercy. The difficulty of this bifurcated view is that it is not clearly based on Jesus' words, which proclaim the new virtues of mercy, forgiveness, and love to be universally valid for all of us right now.

CONCLUSION

As with the other issues we have discussed in this book, the conclusion of the present chapter is that the biblical texts do not provide definitive guidance for deciding what Jesus would think about the death penalty.

This is especially true when considering the death penalty as it is used in the contemporary world. Jesus was not familiar with a world where the death penalty was used only for murder, and used rarely at that—or where lethal injection was a replacement for crucifixion. His was not a world in which a massive prison industry houses criminals who used guns to commit crimes. More importantly, his was not a world in which criminals were entitled to a fair trial, to representation by adequate counsel, and to an appeals process based on publicly proclaimed constitutional principles.

As with the other issues we are discussing here, the general conclusion is that what is required is further reflection that is willing to go beyond the Bible. Jesus may be turned to as an inspirational model for values such as mercy, forgiveness, and love. And it is clear that he thought we should move beyond the strict equivalence of the law of retaliation as found in Exodus. But his model is insufficient as a guide for thinking about the death penalty in the contemporary world. What is needed is not a return to Jesus but, rather, the application of reason and a commitment to the hard work of philosophical reflection.

NOTES

1. Seneca, "On Clemency," in *The Stoic Philosophy of Seneca*, ed. and trans. Moses Hadas (New York: Doubleday Anchor, 1958).

2. Marcus Aurelius, *Meditations*, trans. Maxwell Staniforth (Baltimore: Penguin, 1969), 9.11, 141.

3. U.S. Conference of Catholic Bishops, "A Culture of Life and the Death Penalty," December 2005, 8, www.usccb.org.

4. Karl Barth, *Church Dogmatics* (T. T. Clark, 1936–1997), III:4, 445.

5. Pope John Paul II, *Evangelium Vitae*, para. 56.

6. Stanley Hauerwas, *Performing the Faith* (Grand Rapids: Brazos, 2004), chap. 8.

7. Antonin Scalia, "God's Justice and Ours," *First Things* 123 (May 2002): 17–21.

9

SEXUALITY AND THE FAMILY

> You have heard that it was said, "You shall not commit adultery." But I say to you that everyone who looks at a woman lustfully has already committed adultery with her in his heart. If your right eye causes you to sin, pluck it out and throw it away; it is better that you lose one of your members than that your whole body be thrown into hell.
>
> —Matthew 5:27–29

In the previous chapters, I considered issues that could be related together under the general topic of the sanctity of life. In the present chapter and the next, I will consider topics loosely organized under the principle of social morality. I call these topics social because they are, for the most part, about how we organize ourselves and behave in groups. I will discuss what Jesus says about sexuality and the family in this chapter and what he says about slavery and social welfare in the next one. Jesus' conclusions about these topics are not entirely clear. Jesus' two main commandments are: love God and love your neighbor as yourself. We can derive some basic conclusions from these commandments. However, Jesus does not address these topics in a systematic fashion, and some of what he does say runs counter to our current system of values.

SEXUAL ETHICS

Jesus' condemnation of "adultery in the heart" as indicated in the passage above should lead one to reject much of contemporary society. Pornography and the sex industry facilitate adultery in the heart. We see lax sexual morality in premarital sex and easy divorce. And we are more permissive about homosexuality. Loose sexual morals can be linked to problems such as rape, venereal disease, and pedophilia.

The most important fact about Jesus and sexuality is that in the Gospels, Jesus never has any sort of sexual relations. If we were to follow Jesus' model, we would not have sex at all, nor would we allow ourselves to be stimulated by sexual desire. We should bear this in mind when thinking about the question of what Jesus would do with regard to sexuality.

For Jesus and Paul—as for Plato and other ancient thinkers—sexual desire needs to be strictly controlled. Unbridled sexuality leads to what Augustine called "the filth of concupiscence" and "the hell of lustfulness."[1] The need to control sexual desire may result in self-mutilation—as mentioned in the passage quoted at the outset of this chapter. The idea of plucking out one's eye might be a metaphor, but a similar passage about self-mutilation in the name of purity shows up in Mark (9:43–48), although in Mark it is not so closely tied to the problem of adultery. The idea of "adultery in the heart" does not show up in any of the other Gospels. Nonetheless, Jesus takes the pursuit of sexual purity seriously and aligns himself with similar concerns that were expressed in the Hebrew scriptures of Deuteronomy and Leviticus.

One of the key issues here is, as Paul explains in 1 Corinthians 6, that the body is a member of Christ or a temple of the holy spirit. When the body is joined together in an impure way with an impure object, the body—the temple of God—is defiled. Thus Paul explicitly condemns sex with prostitutes because it joins the body to an impure body. In the first letter to the Corinthians, Paul speaks extensively of sexuality, marriage, and love. While Paul states in 1 Corinthians 13 that love is patient, kind, and generous, he also states in 1 Corinthians 6 that adulterers and "sexual perverts" will not inherit the kingdom of heaven. The word Paul uses in this passage, *arsenokoitois* (literally lying or having sex with men), also appears in 1 Timothy 10, where "sodomy" (as it is translated here) is associated with murder, kidnapping, perjury, and other crimes. One should note that Paul most likely did not write the letter to Timothy or the other "pastoral epistles" (to Timothy and to Titus). But at any rate, this does show us condemnation of homosexuality in the early Christian community.

Western societies are much more open about sexuality than they once were, and much less concerned with purity and sexual self-control. This increased openness may seem to result in increased happiness, as we are better able to enjoy sexual pleasure in the absence of a repressive sexual purity code. Critics worry, however, that our new openness has helped to break down the traditional idea of the family. Such criticisms are also linked to criticism of feminism. The liberation of women is also held to be responsible for the breakdown of the patriarchal family. The "sexual revolution" was tied to the liberation of women, especially the autonomy that women experienced with the development of the birth control pill, which allowed women to control their reproductive lives. But critics point out that along with this came the legalization of abortion, the spread of pornography, and an apparent increase in promiscuity and homosexuality. Robert Bork, who was once nominated to the U.S. Supreme Court, claims that "radical feminism is the most destructive and fanatical movement to come down to us from the Sixties."[2] According to Bork, radical feminism is committed to the view that sexuality and gender are socially constructed. And thus Bork links feminism to the view that "heterosexuality, being socially constructed, is no more 'natural' or desirable than homosexuality."[3] The solution to this problem is to return to the natural order of gender distinctions and natural (i.e., heterosexual) sexuality. But such a return would promise increased repression for women, homosexuals, and indeed for adults who enjoy consensual sex outside of marriage.

The question of whether homosexuality is permissible marks a crucial religious dividing line. The Episcopal Church, U.S.A., has been struggling with this question and appears ready to divide over the question of whether the church should have ordained Gene Robinson, an openly gay man, as bishop of New Hampshire. Some conservatives maintain that if homosexuality were normalized by allowing gay priests or same-sex marriage, this would represent the beginning of the end of civilization, since traditional marriage and the traditional family structure are the cornerstones of civilization. But others argue that acceptance of homosexuality is required by the idea of respecting individual differences. Episcopalian Bishop John Shelby Spong has argued, "For homosexual people, their only 'sin' seems to be that they were born with a sexual orientation different from that of the majority. Yet we know that orientation to be perfectly normal. . . . Sexual orientation is not a moral choice."[4]

It is true that there are passages in the Bible that condemn homosexuality, but it is also important to note that Jesus never says anything at all about homosexuality. The Old Testament condemns homosexuality explicitly in the following places: Deuteronomy 23:17–18; Leviticus

18:22; and Leviticus 20:13. Paul also condemns it: 1 Corinthians 6:9–10; Timothy 1:9–10; and Romans 1:26–27. But it is not clear what Jesus himself thought about the Old Testament rules of sexual ethics. In some places, his desire for purity seems quite severe and restrictive; in other places, he seems more lenient and forgiving. Jesus quite frankly provides us with an insufficient model for thinking about homosexuality or about sexual ethics in general.

One of the difficulties for using the Bible to think about sexual ethics is that the Old Testament contains an ethics of sex and system of punishments that we have soundly rejected. In Leviticus 20, for example, the condemnation of homosexuality occurs within the context of a condemnation of adultery, and the punishment for both adultery and homosexuality is death. But we do not kill either adulterers or homosexuals. In the Old Testament, we also witness polygamy. And some contemporary Christians—some fundamentalist Mormons, for example—still practice polygamy based on claims that go back to these Old Testament models. Moreover, the Old Testament (and the New as well) is not friendly to the idea of equality for women. The traditional family of the Bible is thoroughly patriarchal.

Moreover, if we were to return to biblical ideas about sexual morality, we would have to revise our permissive attitude toward divorce. The American tradition that celebrates individual rights views marriage as a contract that is freely entered into by both parties and can be freely ended by them. This idea runs counter to Jesus' ideas about divorce and marriage. Jesus prohibits divorce in all three of the synoptic Gospels. This is one of the clearest things he says about family life and sexual ethics. And Jesus states explicitly (Matthew 19:8–9) that although Moses allowed for more permissive attitudes about divorce, Jesus will only allow it in case of adultery. Thus Jesus shows that his views about family life differ from those of the Old Testament.

The ethics of sexuality usually begins by answering the basic question "What is sex for?" But other questions must be asked. How does human sexuality relate to other aspects of the human person: is it a primary psychological force, or simply one small part of the human experience? Are our sexual desires innate or learned? Are gender roles defined by nature or by society? And a further question is whether society has the right to dictate rules of sexual conduct, or whether sexuality is a private matter best governed by contractual principles such as the idea of mutual consent. Jesus gives us no explicit answers to these questions. This is part of the reason that sexual morality provokes so much debate by Christians: the answers to these essential questions cannot be found directly in the words of Jesus (although Paul is a bit more explicit about sexual ethics).

It is important to note that Jesus does not offer us psychological or social theories of sexuality or gender. Without such a psychosocial theory, it is difficult to derive useful conclusions about the moral issues related to sex and gender. This is true because of the basic principle that "ought implies can." What this means is that if we ought to do something, we should actually be able to do it. Moral imperatives—such as that we should completely eradicate sexual desire—that are impossible to enact should be rejected as absurd. If we ought to be monogamous, then we should be able to control our desires and avoid adultery. Likewise, if homosexuality is wrong, then homosexuals should be able to control themselves and resist their homosexual desires. But we need more information than what Jesus provides to decide whether, for example, homosexual desires can be overcome or whether such desires are natural and can only be "overcome" by inflicting psychological damage.

Jesus does think that sexual desire can and should be controlled, even though he realizes how difficult this can be. This is the gist of the passage about plucking out the eye that leads to adultery in the heart. We have free will and we can control our desires, even though such control can be painful and can require a sort of self-mutilation. Again it is important to note that this assumes a theory about sexual desire: that it is not essential to the self. Rather, when we cut off the offensive organ that creates improper sexual desire, we are actually eliminating something that is impure and not part of the true self that God wants us to be. It should be obvious that this idea runs counter to much of what current psychology tells us about the importance of integrating sexual desire into a healthy life.

There are several contemporary ways of understanding sexuality and answering the question of what sex is for. On the one hand, biologically speaking, sexuality is simply about how we use our genitalia. A biological understanding of sex will also focus on how we pass on our genetic information and create new life. Another perspective, articulated most famously by Michel Foucault, is that sexuality is part of a larger structure of organized pleasures: here sexuality is about pleasure and about the individual and social decisions that are made about pleasure. This view is connected to the claim that sexuality is about structural relationships and group dynamics that are organized primarily by gender. And feminists and post-structuralists such as Judith Butler have emphasized—as Robert Bork has noted—that gender and sexuality are socially constructed.

Sexual ethics should be located within the framework of more general moral principles. One might think, for example, that the Golden Rule would be sufficient to regulate sexuality. The principle of loving your neighbor as yourself should apply in sexual contexts: we should respect our sexual partners and satisfy their desires, just as they should respect us and satisfy our desires. The Golden Rule approach might provide us with arguments in favor of monogamy and fidelity, since faithful monogamous relationships are useful for developing the sort of reciprocity and trust that is desired here. But such an application of the Golden Rule does not necessarily follow, as it is possible to imagine consensual and respecting relationships that involve multiple partners.

One significant problem found in both the Greek and Hebrew traditions is that sexuality seems to require special regulation, in part because sexual desire is so strong that it appears to distract us from the true good, which is God. Augustine, for example, struggled against sexual desire. He thought—in a way similar to Plato—that there were two wills struggling within the self: a carnal lusting will and a spiritual will. The key was to avoid bad habits of sexual desire and to develop virtues that allowed the spiritual will to triumph. This problem informs Paul's discussion of homosexuality. Paul writes that God created a natural order, but that idolatry led people away from this natural order, and that such bad faith is tied to the commission of unnatural sexual acts (Romans 1:24–27). Although there is no similar condemnation of unnatural sexuality articulated by Jesus, Jesus did think that sexual desire needed to be strictly controlled.

Such an approach is quite different from the general ethical view of hedonism and some versions of Utilitarianism. Hedonists claim that pleasure—including sexual pleasure—is the key to happiness. The goal is to regulate behavior in order to maximize pleasure and minimize pain. One might argue that one of the best ways to maximize pleasure is through fidelity and monogamy. However, this requires further argument. Such argument is lacking in Jesus, in part because he is simply not concerned with maximizing pleasure.

Instead of emphasizing pleasure, Christian ethics has argued that sexuality is primarily about procreation and love. According to the Vatican's Statement on Sexual Ethics, "every genital act must be within the framework of marriage."[5] Adultery, homosexuality, masturbation, and oral and anal sex are wrong because they use the genitals improperly. This doctrine is derived from a theory about the proper or natural function of the genitalia: God made the genitals for reproductive purposes, and sexual pleasure is intended to get us to use our genitals for such purposes. This naturalistic approach is grounded in a long tradition following Aquinas that holds that natural sexual desire is a desire to reproduce. The difficulty of this idea is that sexual desire is usually more immediate: it is often a desire for sexual pleasure itself and not a desire to reproduce. Again, Jesus tells us nothing about the psychological and biological mechanisms that underlie sexual desire.

We see the importance of reproduction in the stories of Abraham and his offspring, the founding fathers of God's chosen people. But these stories are also about the control of sexuality. We see this especially in the importance of circumcision. Abraham circumcises himself (at age ninety-nine!) when he makes his covenant with Yahweh. In this act, the genitals are dedicated to God as a sign of the covenant, which included the promise that God would make Abraham the father of a multitude. Circumcision indicates the privileged status of the male gender. This gender hierarchy is supposed to be based on the God-created "natural" distinction between the genders: God created Eve to be Adam's companion and helper. And only men can achieve the privileged status of fulfilling the covenant with God. Jesus relies on this naturalistic approach when he states that the genders are made distinct and that marriage is the proper relation in which "the two shall become one flesh" (Mark 10:8). And Paul relies on this idea when explaining why women should remain subordinate to men.

The practice of circumcision was so essential as a sign of the covenant that before Joshua led his troops in their genocidal campaign against the inhabitants of Canaan, the entire army paused while the Israelites circumcised all of the males of the generations that were born while they wandered in the wilderness. And Luke (2:21) tells us that Jesus was circumcised as well. This is important for establishing his credibility within the Hebrew context. But it is also the only reference we have to Jesus as a sexual being (or at least a being with a sexual or gendered body).

In the context of a tradition that emphasized fatherhood and procreation, it is remarkable that Jesus had no sexual relations: he was celibate. There is no real evidence in the Gospels to support the claims of those interpreters who suggest that Jesus had relations with Mary Magdalene or that he had a homoerotic relationship with the beloved disciple who wrote the Gospel of John. Jesus was primarily interested in sexual purity culminating in abstinence. In one interesting passage, Jesus goes so far as to advocate celibacy in the radical form of castration. He says that "there are eunuchs who have been so from birth, and there are eunuchs who have been made eunuchs by men, and there are eunuchs who have made themselves eunuchs for the sake of the kingdom of heaven" (Matthew 19:12–13). While not directly requiring self-mutilation in the name of sexual purity, Jesus' own life and self-sacrificial death is an example of this sort of sacrifice of the body. It should be clear, at any rate, that Jesus is not interested in the pursuit of sexual pleasure. Instead he advocated asceticism and self-denial, as Paul does when Paul claims that it is preferable not to have sex at all (1 Corinthians 7:1).

If we admit, as Jesus does, that not everyone is able to become a eunuch, we wonder how we are to deal with sexual desire. Jesus did not leave us with a comprehensive or sufficiently detailed statement about sexual topics. It might appear that we could derive Jesus' views about these topics from the general sexual ethic of the Hebrews as found in the ancient texts. However, these texts are somewhat ambiguous: Deuteronomy and Leviticus focus on sexual control, while the Song of Solomon celebrates sensuality. And even Paul admits that although celibacy is the ideal, since sexual desire is a satanic temptation, it is better to marry and regulate sexual desire than to "be aflame with passion" (1 Corinthians 7:9).

At any rate, Jesus deliberately calls some of the sexual morality of the Old Testament into question. Jesus is quite clear about divorce, for example: Jesus is less permissive about divorce than Moses was. But there is some ambiguity even here. In Mark, there is a categorical prohibition against divorce; in Matthew, divorce is permitted in cases of adultery. Ambiguity also remains when considering Jesus' view of adultery. The traditional punishment for adultery was stoning to death (see Deuteronomy 17 or 22). But Jesus overturns this punishment in the famous passage in John (8:7) where he says, "Let he who is without sin cast the first stone." I mentioned this passage toward the end of the previous chapter and noted that it only occurs in John and may be a later editorial insertion. So it is difficult to say what Jesus would say about adultery and its regulation. On the one hand, in Matthew 5:28 he condemns adultery of the heart and the wandering eye and avows that it will be punished in hell. But he refuses to condemn the adulteress, saying in conclusion to her: "Neither do I condemn you; go and do not sin again" (John 8:11). It is not clear, then, how Jesus thinks society should regulate sexuality. While Jesus suggests that in pursuit of sexual purity we should be willing to mutilate ourselves, he also refuses to condemn others who have broken the sexual code.

JESUS AND THE PATRIARCHAL FAMILY

At issue when thinking about adultery is the purity of the procreative act. The word "adultery" in English is related to the concept of making impure—to adulterate is to alter, to make impure, or to defile. What is made impure in adultery is the lineage of the offspring. In Hebrew society, blood relationships were essential tools of social organization (as they are today in our own society). Sexuality had to be controlled so that familial relationships were clear. We can see the importance of this fact in considering the role of genealogy in the biblical texts. The Hebrews were descendants of Abraham and Jacob. Priestly power was established through the line of Aaron. And Jesus' own bloodline on his father's side was traced back to David and to Adam. Adultery confounds these lineages by confusing patrimony.

Adultery and sexual purity have much to do with family identity. Indeed much of the contemporary Christian concern with sexuality has to do with family values. But it is not so clear what Jesus' view of the family was.

In certain key passages Jesus declares war on what we might consider traditional family values. Jesus says in Matthew: "He who loves father or mother more than me is not worthy of me; and he who loves son or daughter more than me is not worthy of me" (10:37). This idea is also expressed in Luke in two places. First, Jesus says: "I came to cast fire upon the earth; and would that it were already kindled. . . . Do you think that I have come to give peace on earth? No, I tell you, but rather division; for henceforth in one house there will be five divided, three against two and two against three; they will be divided, father against son and son against father" (Luke 12:49–53). He also says: "If anyone comes to me and does not hate his own father and mother and wife and children and brothers and sisters, yes, and even his own life, he cannot be my disciple" (Luke 14:26). This passage is explained later by the idea that one must renounce everything—including one's family—to be a disciple of Jesus. We see a similar spirit evoked in the story in Luke in which the young Jesus turns up missing: his frantic parents find him in the temple, which Jesus maintains is his real "Father's" house. In these passages, piety and faith are more important than loyalty to the family and the bloodline.

Jesus enacts this apparent anti-family message in the episode in which his own family asks to speak with him (Matthew 12:46 ff.). Jesus responds with the question "Who is my mother and who are my brothers?" And he turns away from his immediate family and opens his arms toward his disciples. The context for this episode is set in Mark 3, where we learn that the audience in Jesus' hometown thought that Jesus was crazy and that he was possessed by Beelzebub, the prince of demons. Jesus' family, it seems, wanted to take him home, comfort him, and defend him from the accusations of the local religious authorities. It is then that Jesus turns away from his family and embraces his disciples.

This context tells us quite a bit about what Jesus has in mind. His radical vision is greeted with incredulity by most. Indeed, his own family doubts that he is sane. But Jesus' faith in his vision leads him to turn against his family in order to create a new community. The same model applies to all who would be disciples of Jesus: to be a true disciple, one may have to reject those—including one's own parents—who do not support the demands of Christian discipleship.

It is important to bear in mind that the claim that one should hate mother and father runs counter to the fifth commandment, which demands that we honor our mothers and fathers. Of course, the Ten Commandments are only part of a larger moral edifice. Indeed, the Old Testament has an even more severe statement of the need to put piety above family. In Deuteronomy (13:6–9) we read: "If your brother, the son of your mother, or your son, or your daughter, or the wife of your bosom, or your friend who is as your own soul entices you, saying 'Let us go and serve other gods'. . . you shall not yield to him or listen to him, nor shall your eye pity him, nor shall you spare him, nor shall you conceal him, but you shall kill him; your hand shall be the first against him to put him to death."

Jesus' discussion of "war" in the family should be interpreted with this passage in mind. It is difficult, however, to bring such a passage together with Jesus' other pacific ideals. This passage makes it clear that real violence toward family members in the name of piety is in fact a possibility. "Family values" are, at any rate, secondary to the demands of piety and religious purity.

Ideals about sexual and religious purity are part of the structure of a patriarchal family and social system in which women are considered inferior and impure. The ancient Hebrew tradition held that menstrual blood was impure and that Eve was created subordinate to Adam. Paul picks this idea up in 1 Corinthians (11:8–9): "For man was not made from woman, but woman from man. Neither was man created for woman, but woman for man." Paul goes on in 1 Corinthians 14 to say: "As in all the churches of the saints, the women should keep silence in the churches. For they are not permitted to speak, but should be subordinate, as even the law says. If there is anything they desire to know, let them ask their husbands at home. For it is shameful for a woman to speak in church" (14:34–35). Some argue that Paul outlines this view only to reject it. One might offer in support of this view the letter to the Galatians where Paul undermines social distinctions based on race or gender: "There is neither Jew nor Greek, there is neither slave nor free, there is neither male nor female; for you are all one in Christ Jesus" (Galatians 3:28). But Paul also states, in his first letter to Timothy, that the submissiveness of women is linked directly to the fact that Eve deceived Adam. "Let a woman learn in silence with all submissiveness. I permit no woman to teach or to have authority over men; she is to keep silent. For Adam was formed first, then Eve; and Adam was not deceived, but the woman was deceived and became a transgressor" (1 Timothy 2:11–14). Women are to keep silent so that they do not cause men to fall again. We see the idea also expressed in 1 Peter 3. Peter calls for submissiveness based on another Old Testament model, that of Sarah's obedience to Abraham.

REREADING THE OLD TESTAMENT

Peter's reference to Sarah is interesting, for in the story of Abraham and Sarah we see some interesting sexual practices. Sarai—Sarah's name before she and Abram made a covenant with God—is barren. Recognizing this failure on her part, she gives Abram—Abraham's name before his conversion—her maid, Hagar, to satisfy his sexual and procreative desires. Moreover, as Abraham and Sarah travel about, they pretend they are merely brother and sister, and Abraham allows Sarah to be ravaged by local kings, including the pharaoh of Egypt. The book of Genesis includes a variety of other interesting sexual practices.

Lot, who is blessed by God and is eventually rescued from the destruction of Sodom, offers the sexual favors of his virgin daughters to an angry mob in order to protect the angels of the Lord. Some argue that Lot was protecting these angels from the sexual advances of the mob (men interested in "Sodom-izing" these angels). This is tied to the fact that sodomy was used in the ancient world as a tool of power. A conquering tribe would sexually dominate both the women and men of the defeated group. The prohibition on sodomy may have been focused more on preventing this sort of oppressive use of sexuality than on prohibiting relationships between consenting adults. But to continue the story, when Lot escapes from the destruction of Sodom, his disobedient wife is killed by God. When Lot and his daughters are hiding in the desert, his daughters desire to procreate. Since they are alone with Lot, they make him drunk and have sex with him so that they might become pregnant.

The difficulty of such ancient stories is that they seem to allow adultery, polygamy, incest, and other sexual practices. How can we use these stories in thinking about our own views of sexual morality? But both Paul and Peter referred to these Genesis stories in arriving at their own understanding of sexual morality. And Jesus directs us back to Genesis for the view that men and women are created distinct and intended by God for each other.

On the other hand, we might argue that we need to interpret such passages carefully and not take them literally. Paul himself argues for an allegorical reading of the Old Testament in Galatians 4:21. He uses an allegorical reading of the story of Abraham in which the slave Hagar is interpreted as Mount Sinai, bearing children for slavery, while Sarah is interpreted as a free woman who bears children of the promise (which Paul intends to mean children of Christ). This opens the question of how we are to interpret the sexual morality we find in the New Testament and throughout the Bible. What is to be taken literally, and what is to be regarded as allegory?

We might think that the ambiguous sexual morality found in the Genesis stories was cleared up by the codification of the law under Moses. Thus in Deuteronomy and Leviticus we see a more rigorous approach to sexual morality. But this rigor seems to go too far in the other direction in pursuit of cleanliness and purity. In Leviticus 15, discharges of semen and of menstrual blood require cleaning and purification. If men and women have sex, they are both to be considered unclean until the end of the day. Leviticus 18 sets up a series of sexual prohibitions, including the prohibition against seeing one's relatives "naked," a euphemism for incest. It also prohibits sex with menstruating women, sex between males, and sex between humans and animals. Leviticus 19 prohibits sex between a man and a female slave. And it also prohibits selling your daughter for a harlot. Leviticus 20 goes farther and mandates the death penalty for most of these crimes: for adultery, incest, homosexuality, and bestiality. And Leviticus 20 mandates that one who has sex with a menstruating woman should be exiled.

These passages require substantial interpretation if we are to implement them today. We do not execute adulterers and homosexuals. And we do not require menstruating women to be secluded for seven days. Nor do we condone slavery. Those who appeal to Deuteronomy or Leviticus in order to put forward the idea that homosexuality is prohibited are usually selecting a couple of phrases from among the whole. If such literalists suggest that we return entirely to the morality of the Old Testament, we should reject this as a return to an era of strict patriarchy and the routine use of cruel and unusual punishment. This runs counter to the way in which Jesus refuses to stone the adulteress. But we should note that Jesus still warns that adulterers will be thrown into hell. The point here is that such punishments are left for God and are not the prerogative of human beings.

CONCLUSION

We should note, again, that Jesus says nothing directly about homosexuality or other sexual topics such as birth control or masturbation. And he says very little about women. In the passage from the Sermon on the Mount cited above with regard to adultery, the focus is on men. It is the male's responsibility not to commit adultery either in fact or in the heart. This might mean that Jesus does not recognize that women have the same sort of sexual appetite as men. At least it is clear that Jesus' primary address in the Sermon on the Mount is men (and not women). Of course, there are women in the New Testament. Jesus heals women, and women attend Jesus at his crucifixion. But Jesus does not directly address the question of the role of women in society. He does not answer the question of whether women should have political equality. He provides little direct guidance for contemporary women's issues.

Jesus does think that God created two distinct genders. And, as noted above, he links this natural gender distinction to marriage and the natural way in which "two become one flesh." Some argue that this leads to a prohibition on homosexuality, which is an unnatural union. But it is important to recall that Jesus never directly says anything about homosexuality.

In conclusion, we might return to Jesus' virtues and to the commandments to love God and love your neighbor. One of the problems of sexuality is that it tends to produce an idolatrous sort of hedonism: pursuit of pleasure can lead away from God. Jesus' model fits well within an ascetic tradition that aims to sublimate sexuality in order to lift one's attention toward God. But the Golden Rule would seem to encourage us to help make our neighbor's happy. We might think that this would lead us to respect our neighbor's pursuit of sexual happiness—so long as this pursuit does not hurt others or undermine the social fabric. This is the idea of contemporary liberal societies, which aim for tolerance with regard to sexual practices. Jesus does seem to advocate a certain sort of tolerance even though he maintains a fairly stringent and traditional idea of sex and gender. This contradiction is not easily resolved within the Christian framework. To resolve it properly, we need a fuller defense of individual liberty, a more comprehensive account of sexuality, and a less patriarchal view of women. In other words, we need to go beyond the Bible and develop a more comprehensive and rational theory of sexual ethics.

NOTES

1. Augustine, *Confessions* (London: Collier Macmillan, 1961), book 3, 36.

2. Robert Bork, *Slouching toward Gomorrah* (New York: HarperCollins, 1996), 194.

3. Bork, *Slouching toward Gomorrah*, 197.

4. John Shelby Spong, *The Sins of Scripture* (New York: HarperCollins, 2005), 125.

5. Vatican, *Persona Humana*, para. 7, in *Analyzing Moral Issues*, ed. Judith Boss (New York: McGraw-Hill, 2005), 366.

10

SLAVERY AND SOCIAL WELFARE

But many that are first will be last, and the last first.

—Matthew 19:30

In thinking about social justice, it is essential to develop ideas about the proper relation between the individual and the community. A number of questions need to be answered. Do individuals have rights? What is the relation between the welfare of the individual and the good of the community? Are social roles fixed and unchanging, or can there be social mobility? Should society be organized hierarchically? And so on. These ideas have been developed in the last few centuries in the direction of liberalism. The basic principles of liberalism include the idea that individuals have rights, that society has some obligation to provide for the general welfare, that closed hierarchies are unjust, and that individuals should have some say over how they are governed. Unfortunately, with the crucial exception of caring for the poor, these ideas are not easily found in the biblical sources. While Jesus does advocate concern for the poor, this alone does little to ameliorate the fact that the worldview of Jesus and the early Christians was one of hierarchical organization, fixed social roles, and slavery. It is true that Jesus' vision of a "brokerless kingdom" or a "kingdom of nobodies," to use terms borrowed from John Dominic Crossan, is radically at odds with a world in which there is poverty, oppression, hierarchy, and slavery: in the kingdom as Jesus imagines it, the first shall be last and the last shall be first. But it is also true that Jesus does not condemn slavery. And his simplistic solution to poverty—personal charity—does not help us resolve the political and economic problems of redistributing wealth.

SLAVERY

In the New Testament, slavery is discussed together with the virtue of obedience. Paul says that slaves should "obey in everything those who are your earthly masters, not with eye service as men-pleasers, but in singleness of heart, fearing the Lord" (Colossians 3:22). This is not only a defense of slavery. It is also connected to Paul's theological principles. Paul says that masters should treat their slaves justly and fairly because they "also have a Master in heaven" (Colossians 4:1). This analogy between God's rule and the rule of masters on earth is similar to some of what we considered in chapter 8 under the idea of mercy. God is a merciful master who, although he has absolute power, shows mercy on those who are faithful and obedient.

One of the requirements of obedience is exclusivity. Jesus says that one should only serve one master: "No one can serve two masters; for either he will hate the one and love the other, or he will be devoted to the one and despise the other." Jesus uses this principle to condemn idolatry, especially the idolatry of money. This passage continues: "You cannot serve God and mammon" (Matthew 6:24; Luke 16:13). These passages make sense in a culture in which there are earthly masters who deserve faithful and exclusive obedience. Without this basis in earthly master–slave relationships, the theological analogy makes little sense.

It is difficult for us in the twenty-first century to fully understand the importance of exclusivity and obedience. Our social relationships are structured on freedom. We can change jobs if we get fed up with our bosses; and we can sue if we are abused or harassed at work. In other words, we have rights, and these rights provide protections against the arbitrary will of our superiors. But in the ancient world, there was no concept of rights in this sense. Rather, masters were called upon to be merciful and slaves were commanded to be obedient and to patiently suffer.

Slavery is a fact in the Old Testament. Abraham had slaves. Joseph was sold into slavery. And the Hebrews did not reject slavery after escaping from bondage in Egypt. Indeed, just after proclaiming the Ten Commandments, Moses expounds laws for regulating slavery (Exodus 21). The New Testament also condones slavery: "Let all who are under the yoke of slavery regard their masters as worthy of all honor, so that the name of God and the teaching may not be defamed" (1 Timothy 6:1). Jesus says nothing against slavery. He tells his disciples, "Whoever would be first among you must be your slave" (Matthew 20:27; Mark 10:44). This passage could be read as an ironic revaluation that has little to do with slavery: it says that the best leader must serve his followers. This may be true. But Jesus nowhere says that slaves should be freed. Rather, he promises recompense in "the new world" (Matthew 19:28) where the first will be last and the last will be first (Matthew 19:30, 20:16). Such claims would have appealed to the oppressed and enslaved as a promise for deliverance in the kingdom of God. Perhaps this shows us that Jesus recognized that slaves want to be free. But Jesus does not tell us whether or how the longing for freedom should be actualized in this world.

The truth is that the Bible simply assumes slavery as an accepted mode of social existence. The ambiguities of biblical accounts of slavery have been used in various ways in subsequent discussions of slavery. In 1775 Thomas Paine noted the paradox of Christian slave-holding and slave-trading by referring us back to the Golden Rule. "Christians are taught to account all men their neighbors; and love their neighbors as themselves; and do to all men as they would be done by; to do good to all men; and Man-stealing is ranked with enormous crimes." But Paine notes with outrage that some Christians "allege the Sacred Scriptures to favor this wicked practice."[1] Abraham Lincoln noted in his second inaugural speech (1865), to cite another example, that both sides in the debate over slavery "read the same Bible, and pray to the same God; and each invokes his aid against the other." Abolitionists could articulate anti-slavery arguments based on the Bible as Paine did, but advocates of slavery could also invoke biblical passages to support their position as well, especially passages from the Old Testament and from Paul's letters.

The abolition of slavery had more to do with the advance of liberal humanist philosophy and the idea of human rights than with the ethics of Jesus. Rousseau, Paine, and other Enlightenment philosophers are more significant for thinking about the abolition of slavery than Jesus was. For thousands of years Christians supported slavery, and Christian economies benefited from chattel slavery and indentured labor. This was tied to views about hierarchy, heredity, and race. Just as royalty was thought to be superior to peasants, so Africans, Asians, and Jews were thought to be inferior to Europeans. Indeed, some interpret the mark that was placed on Cain—the first murderer—as a racial stigma; dark skinned peoples were thought to be the descendants of Cain. The supposed inferiority of certain types of people justified their enslavement or exclusion from society. And in the case of some ethnic groups, it was thought to justify their extermination.

The official abolition of slavery is undoubtedly a sign that human beings are making progress in history. But we should not ignore the fact

that many human beings are still held in de facto slavery despite its il-
legality. And slaves are exploited not only economically but often also
sexually and psychologically. Indeed, one of the main sorts of slavery that
exists today is sexual slavery where the bodies of women and children
are bought and sold for the sexual use of predatory men.

It is important to note that although Jesus condemns oppression,
Jesus nowhere explicitly condemns slavery. Some argue that Paul calls
slavery into question in Galatians 3:28: "There is neither Jew nor Greek,
there is neither slave nor free, there is neither male nor female; for you
are all one in Christ Jesus." But the focus here is that God has no regard
for social and class distinctions. These social distinctions are assumed to
exist, but there is a spiritual transformation that allows all who are bap-
tized to be sons of God. In his letter to the Colossians, as quoted in the
epigram above, Paul explicitly requires obedience from slaves and fairness from masters. And he links this to the obedience of wives to their
husbands. A similar statement also shows up in his letter to the Ephesians,
where Paul concludes: "Whatever good any one does, he will receive the
same again from the Lord, whether he is slave or free" (Ephesians 6:8).

Jesus himself provides no clear guidance on the question of slavery.
Any idea we might derive about this is the result of substantial interpretive effort. The difficulty is that while Jesus does condemn oppression
and injustice, this does not include a condemnation of slavery. In part
this is the result of the ancient idea that slavery is simply an economic
relation that can be distinguished from oppression and exploitation. It
is this idea that allows for the idea of a benevolent and merciful slave
master.

Jesus maligns those on the top of the social hierarchy because he
tends to think that the pursuit of prestige and wealth leads to a sort of
idolatry that distracts us from the true good. This idea is clearly linked
to the first commandment: love God. One might think, with this in
mind, that Jesus' claim that we cannot serve two masters would lead
to the abolition of slavery. The rich man serves mammon, but the slave
serves his earthly master. So we might expect Jesus to say that slaves
must be released from bondage so that they might properly serve God.
But Jesus does not say this. And Paul claims—in Colossians 3:22, quoted
above—that slaves should obediently serve their earthly masters, for such
service is pleasing to God.

One might think that the second of Jesus' two great commandments—to love your neighbor as yourself—would be used by Jesus to
call slavery into question. Thomas Paine thought that the commandment

should be applied in this way. But it is remarkable that Jesus does not say this. The right to life, liberty, and the pursuit of happiness are key ideas of modern political thought. But these ideas are not directly articulated by Jesus. Indeed, Jesus nowhere defends the idea of a right to individual liberty that is a necessary feature of those condemnations of slavery that have developed in the modern world.

One possible interpretation of this fact is that Jesus' focus is simply not on this world. But to claim that Jesus is entirely focused on the next world is to ignore claims about social justice that show up in the Sermon on the Mount and elsewhere. A better explanation is that Jesus is primarily interested in consequences and virtues and not rights. With regard to virtue, some of our virtues are defined by our social roles. In the ancient world, social roles were located within a hierarchical social organization. A slave's virtue is obedience and a master's virtue is to treat his slave well; a woman's virtue is to remain silent in church, while a man's virtue is to treat his wife with respect. From this perspective, slavery is not viewed as a negative thing unless the master treats the slave poorly. Aristotle went so far as to claim that certain persons are naturally predisposed to be slaves. Jesus does not advocate this view—but it was prevalent in the ancient world. With regard to consequences, Jesus repeatedly expresses his desire that the hungry be fed and that the naked be clothed (see Matthew 25:25–46). The immediate consequence of directly caring for those in need is his primary focus.

Larger social problems like the abolition of slavery and of class and racial distinctions are beyond the scope of what Jesus discusses. One reason for this is that Jesus has an apocalyptic expectation of a radical transformation in which the first will be last and the last first. The best that Jesus offers is a call for humility that one supposes is directed at the high and mighty. He says in a version of the "first will be last" motif that "everyone who exalts himself will be humbled and he who humbles himself will be exalted" (Luke 14:11; Matthew 23:12). But this is not a call for social reform. Rather it is a call for personal humility tied together with the promise that in the kingdom of God the hierarchy will be reordered in this way.

Jesus' goal is not to transform this social order through political reform. Rather, he envisions a total revolution that points beyond the current social organization toward a religious transformation. Prior to this eschatological upheaval, he does focus our attention on the social obligation to help those individuals who are suffering. This obviously follows from the principle of loving one's neighbor. But this principle is complicated in its application. Love of one's neighbor does not include freeing that neighbor from bondage. Nor does Jesus care about democratic social reform. Indeed, he is committed to a hierarchical universe in which God rules.

POVERTY

While Jesus is silent about the evil of slavery, he did explicitly and repeatedly maintain that we have an obligation to care for the poor. And he seems to advocate a sort of communism that was adopted by early Christian communities, who organized themselves as communes of shared resources. Jim Wallis notes that "one of every sixteen verses in the New Testament is about the poor or the subject of money. In the first three Gospels it is one out of every ten verses, and in the book of Luke it is one in seven!"[2] Poverty and its alleviation are a special focus for Jesus. He wants us to care for the poor as well as for the maimed, the lame, and the blind (Luke 14:13). This obligation is directly derived from the commandment to love your neighbor as yourself.

The question of how best to care for the poor is, however, a difficult one. As mentioned in chapter 3, there are complicated issues involved in thinking about how best to alleviate poverty. First, we have to understand why it is a problem. Second, we have to think about who is responsible for it. And third, we have to imagine effective ways to overcome it.

But prior to this we have to define the problem. Some may claim that in the United States, poverty is not really a problem at all. The median family income in the United States is about $45,000 and the average family income is around $90,000 per year. From this perspective, we have a wealthy society. But 17 percent of the population falls below the poverty line, which is around $19,000 for a family of four. This seems to be a negative fact: nearly one-fifth of Americans are, according to this definition, poor. On the other hand, one might claim that our societal wealth as a whole is, in fact, transferred to these impoverished individuals and families: we have public schools and institutions of public health, which effectively raise the standard of living and provide opportunity for even the poorest Americans. In addition to these public redistributions of wealth, we have other, more direct aid to the poor—both from government programs and from private charity.

But perhaps the real problem of poverty today is found beyond the borders of the United States. In affluent countries, poverty is a relative matter: the poor simply have less than the norm. But there is another order of poverty in the world. Robert McNamara has described this as "absolute poverty" or "life at the very margin of existence."[3] According to a recent UNICEF report, more than 10 million children under the age of five die each year from preventable causes such as malnutrition, unsafe water, and the lack of basic health care.[4] And nearly half of the world's population lives on less than two dollars a day, while more than 1 billion human beings live on less than one dollar a day. So, even if we might want to claim that poverty is not a problem in the United States, it seems difficult to deny that deplorable poverty exists throughout the world.

It might seem odd to have to ask the question of why poverty is in fact an evil. But some may argue that being poor is not so bad. Those who make such sanguine claims usually do not have in mind the grinding poverty that afflicts those outside the United States. It should be obvious that this sort of abject poverty is a problem simply because it is a threat to health. Extreme poverty leads to negative health effects, including high infant mortality rates and decreased life expectancy. This is a result of inadequate health care, poor diet, and polluted environments. When health is in jeopardy, the idea of the sanctity of life seems to require a response. Indeed, if we care about life, we should do what we can to alleviate poverty. The parable of the Good Samaritan shows us this, as does the story of the rich man who was condemned to Hades because he failed to feed the poor man at his gate (Luke 16).

Poverty is a problem because it undermines self-esteem. This is one of Jesus' primary focuses. Jesus' blessing of the poor in the Sermon on the Mount and his claim that the last shall be first are attempts to increase the self-esteem of the poor and oppressed. The poor should not despair because of their poverty. Their poverty is not a sign that God does not love them. Indeed, Jesus promises that God does love them and will reward them in due course.

As for who is responsible for poverty, the question is usually whether it is the poor themselves who are responsible or the rich who hoard wealth and exploit the poor. Defenders of free-market capitalism tend to think that the responsibility for poverty rests on the poor themselves. Capitalism provides the freedom to work and multiple opportunities to make money. Those who remain poor, from this perspective, have simply failed to cultivate the virtues necessary for success in the capitalist economy. Max Weber pointed out that this idea was rooted in a form of Christian theology that held that wealth was a sign of God's grace.

Communism, in opposition to this, holds that the poor are kept poor by those who run the system. The poor are a mobile supply of labor that is exploited by the capitalists and manipulated into serving the interests of those who own the means of production.

These two ideas of who is responsible for poverty are linked to ideas about its solution. Capitalism claims that it is up to the poor to free themselves from poverty, and that direct handouts to the poor do not work because they do not help the poor to develop the virtues that are necessary for success in the capitalist system. Indeed, welfare assistance can serve further to undermine the self-esteem of the poor both by focusing attention on their failures and by making them dependent on those who give the assistance. Communism, in opposition to this, holds that what is needed is a revolution in the free-market system that will allow for communal ownership of social property and an equal distribution of social wealth. Here, the solution is to create a system in which basic human needs are fulfilled. As Marx puts it: "To each according to his needs." The difficulty of this proposal, according to defenders of capitalism, is that it creates dependence and undermines self-esteem. And such a system would also undermine productivity by creating disincentives for innovation and hard work. According to the capitalist critique, a communist organization of society would create greater and more pervasive poverty in the long run.

There are clearly complex issues to be considered in thinking about poverty. But Jesus' answer is lacking in complexity. His solution is simple: give to the poor. In Luke (6:30–31), Jesus says: "Give to every one who begs from you; and of him who takes away your goods do not ask them again. And as you wish that men would do to you, do so to them." This ideal of pure Christian altruism thus appears to reward theft. And it runs counter to the competitive and individualistic ethic of modern capitalism grounded in the idea of private property. A capitalist would wonder how Jesus proposes to get people to work for a living, if begging and thievery are allowed. But Jesus is not concerned with the question of work. He himself never works. Nor does he advocate learning a trade and earning a living. In fact, in the famous "lilies of the field" passage (Matthew 6:25 ff.), Jesus tells us not to worry about work because God will provide. Jesus explicitly tells his followers not to worry about where food, drink, and clothing will come from: "Seek first righteousness, and all these things shall be yours as well" (Matthew 6:33). And this is why Jesus also tells his followers to sell all they own and give alms to the poor (Luke 12:33; Matthew 19:21): the poor would be sustained by such donations. But Jesus does not explain how this whole system is supposed to function if everyone follows his advice and no one is left worrying about how to produce food, drink, and clothing.

Not only does Jesus not advocate work, but he also condemns those who have wealth. In Matthew, after Jesus says that we should sell what we possess and give to the poor, he immediately claims that it is easier for a camel to go through the eye of a needle than for a rich man to enter heaven (Matthew 19:24). Jesus also routinely expresses contempt and antagonism for those who work for a living. In the parable of the laborers in the vineyard (Matthew 20), Jesus states that workers who work the whole day long will not be rewarded at a higher rate than those who only labor for an hour. And in the parable of the prodigal son (Luke 15), Jesus argues that a father will love his son even if his son is idle and squanders his inheritance. Now, such parables are intended to show that all are welcome in God's kingdom and that God forgives sins. But they also serve to show that work is not needed to get ahead, because everyone will be rewarded equally.

Jesus' concern with alleviating poverty expresses a general sort of altruism that is focused on the immediate needs of the poor. While Jesus does not directly answer the question of how far we should extend our altruistic concern for the poor, it is quite clear that within the immediate neighborhood, Jesus intends us to do as much as we can to help the poor.

As discussed in chapter 3, such an idea has been expressed in the contemporary world in an influential article on global poverty by Peter Singer. Singer has proposed that morality requires the affluent to give to the poor up to the point of "marginal utility"—up to the point at which the affluent themselves become poor.[5] Jesus would seem to concur. And he may even demand more: Jesus' example of self-sacrifice might be the primary model. At the very least, Jesus' message in Luke points us to the conclusion that we are indeed required to follow Singer's advice: we are to give whatever is needed to alleviate suffering, including the very shirts off our backs.

This approach is based on the idea of loving one's neighbor. But the difficulty of this idea is that Jesus does not look deeper into the social and political questions of how best to alleviate poverty in the long run. Indeed, it should be obvious that Jesus' goal is not the long run: his goal is to alleviate suffering here and now. Moreover, given the eschatological tone of the Gospels, it is not clear that ideas about the "long run" as we conceive it apply.

Jesus' ideas about giving to the poor were part of a long Hebrew tradition of thinking about social welfare. This tradition begins in Leviticus 25, where Moses defines the seventh year as a Sabbath year: a year of rest and recuperation for the people and the land. And then he proclaims that after the seventh year of seven years (that is, every fifty years), there shall be a Jubilee year. In this year slaves shall be released, the poor shall be helped, and debts shall be forgiven. In Deuteronomy, this year of release is supposed to occur every seven years. In this year, "if there is among you a poor man, one of your brethren, in any of your towns within your land which the Lord your God give you, you shall not harden your heart or shut your hand against your poor brother, but you shall open your hand to him, and lend him sufficient for his need, whatever it may be" (Deuteronomy 15:7–8).

This passage focuses on charity within the community. But Jesus broadens this and requires charity for all. The Good Samaritan is a model for charity between members of rival groups. Jesus' ideas are thus part of a long Hebrew tradition of social justice. Jesus seeks to renew and extend this idea. The primary concern in this tradition is helping others here and now. Questions of long-term success are subsidiary to the question of alleviating present suffering.

It should be noted, of course, that the economy of the ancient world was different from our own. Jesus' world consisted primarily of a local agricultural economy, although there were large cities and trade between cities. One significant difference between the economy of Jesus' time and our own is that usury—the practice of loaning money for interest—was prohibited. Clearly the practice of charging interest is one of the ways in which the rich get richer while the poor remain poor. Ezekiel noted this when he defined a righteous man as one who "does not oppress any one but restores to the debtor his pledge, commits no robbery, gives his bread to the hungry and covers the naked with a garment, does not lend at interest or take any increase" (Ezekiel 18:7–8). But our economy runs on loaning money for interest. One wonders what Jesus would think about this, as well as the disparities of wealth that correspond to the difference between those who have money to loan and those who borrow.

Jesus does emphasize the importance of forgiving debts, as for example in Matthew 18:23–35. And the idea of forgiving debt is found in Matthew's version of the Lord's Prayer (6:12). God will forgive our debts when we forgive those who owe us a debt. This idea may be a more metaphorical sense of debt that equates debts with sin. But in the story in Matthew 18 where Jesus shows how we should forgive debts, it is literally cashed out in monetary terms. And this idea of forgiveness of debt fits with Jesus' other messages that condemn the rich and discourage hard labor. This idea develops into the communism of the apostles, who "had all things in common, and sold their possessions and goods and distributed them to all, as any had need" (Acts 2:44–45, 4:32–35). This communist ideal seems to be the direction toward which Jesus' ideas point.

CONCLUSION

In the present chapter, we have seen that there are substantial ambiguities in Jesus' views on social morality. Social philosophers, ethical thinkers, and economists since Jesus' time have worked hard to understand the topics discussed here. While we might argue that progress has been made with regard to the abolition of slavery, this does not appear to be Jesus' primary concern. At the same time, our economic system continues to create disparities of wealth that run counter to Jesus' egalitarian and communistic ideal. Acceptable approaches to slavery and poverty require complex and systematic ideas about human nature, human rights, and the economy. Jesus provides no such systematic approach. Jesus' idea of loving one's neighbor seems to be a useful first step in thinking about these issues. But this idea needs much further development.

One undeveloped theme in the present chapter is the degree to which political institutions should implement social morality. Should there be *laws* against slavery? And should there be a system of mandatory taxation that redistributes wealth from the rich to the poor? These institutional and political questions will form the basis of the next chapter.

NOTES

1. Thomas Paine, "African Slavery in America," in *The Portable Enlightenment Reader*, ed. Isaac Kramnick (New York: Penguin, 1995), 646–47.

2. Jim Wallis, *God's Politics* (San Francisco: Harper San Francisco, 2005), 212.

3. Quoted in Peter Singer, *Practical Ethics* (Cambridge: Cambridge University Press, 1993), 218–19.

4. Quoted in Peter Singer, *One World* (New Haven: Yale University Press, 2002), 151.

5. Peter Singer, "Famine, Affluence, and Morality," in *Practical Ethics*.

11

THE PROBLEM OF POLITICS

Render to Caesar the things that are Caesar's, and to God the
things that are God's.

— Mark 12:17; Matthew 22:21; Luke 20:25

One of the recurring questions of the last several chapters is the question of the proper relationship between morality and politics. Jesus
leaves us with no clear answer to this question. He does not tell us how
political power should be instituted or whether political power should
be used to make people moral. Jesus peacefully submitted to political
power when the authorities came to take him away. And he claimed that
we should render unto Caesar that which belongs to Caesar. This claim
is offered as a response to some Pharisees who were trying to trip him
up. This passage seems to imply acquiescence to the political status quo.
But there is some irony in the passage, since Jesus may be telling those
who collaborate with the Roman occupation to give up collaborating
and return to God. But the idea of focusing on what belongs to God is
not all that helpful in thinking about politics.

Christians diverge substantially over political questions. Tolstoy connected Jesus' pacifist message to a sort of anarchism, but others follow
Augustine in arguing that a strong central power is needed to help create order. If political life is thought to be a kind of organized violence,
then it is not clear whether Jesus, the pacifist, can ever wholeheartedly
support the idea of the state. But on the other hand, the state might be
a necessary component of the idea of loving one's neighbor, insofar as
the state provides goods for all.

Some contemporary American Christians think that the United
States is a Christian nation and that we should institute Christian laws

125

about abortion, euthanasia, the death penalty, and homosexuality. Some go so far as to argue in favor of school prayer and the public display of religious messages. Others argue against the presence of religion in public life. One of the recent examples of this problem was the question of whether the Pledge of Allegiance should include the phrase "one nation under God." Opponents of the presence of religion in public life continue to challenge the conjunction of politics and religion.

Jesus provides us with little concrete guidance about these complex issues. And he tells us very little about whether the state has an obligation to defend moral judgments or promote religion. Moreover, Jesus is not a defender of patriotism and particularism of the sort that is implicit in the claim that the United States is a nation under God. In the modern world, we have come to accept the idea that states should be tolerant of alternative answers to complex questions about morality and religion. This idea is known as liberalism. Some might argue that liberalism can be traced back to Jesus and his advocacy of tolerance. But the more basic question is what Jesus thought about political power.

ETHICS, POLITICS, AND LAW

In general, the Gospels present us with a negative view of political power. The villains in the Gospels are the politically powerful, including Herod and Pilate. One reason for this is the fact that in the first century, the Jews were oppressed by the Romans. Those Jews who did have political power were viewed by many as traitors. For the authors of the Gospels, the good guys were the rebels and the bad guys were those in power. We see this point of view reflected in the Matthew and Luke story of how Jesus is tempted in the wilderness with the devil's offer of political power. Jesus responded to this temptation by quoting scripture: "You shall worship the Lord your God and him only shall you serve" (Matthew 4:10; Deuteronomy 6:13). This story occurs at the beginning of both Matthew and Luke, and it sets the stage for the idea that to obtain political power one must make a pact with the devil, as Judas does in his betrayal of Jesus.

The moral and religious law, as Jesus understood it, was distinct from the positive law of the land, in part because the Jews lived under Roman rule. But more importantly, Jesus seems to think that the two basic moral commandments—love God and love your neighbor—are so clear and all-encompassing that we really need very few positive laws to govern us. Jesus was interested in basic moral principles; he was not interested in their specific legal application or in the complexity of positive law. Indeed, Jesus' critique of the Pharisees was that they were so interested in the details of law that they had forgotten its spirit. In Matthew and Luke, Jesus castigates the Pharisees for adhering to the minutiae of the law while neglecting primary values such as justice, mercy, faith, and the love of God (Matthew 23:23; Luke 11:42).

Jesus' primary interests were religious and moral, not political. The kingdom of God, as Jesus understood it, was already present and had little to do with political power. One served God by serving others. But this service did not require legal sanction. Nor did it require a complex legal code. One could practice ethics and piety on one's own, without state support.

The virtues advocated and exemplified by Jesus—peacefulness, toleration, forgiveness, and love—are primarily virtues for private individuals. Moreover, such virtues can seem to be liabilities for political power. A state is by definition the entity that possesses a monopoly of force in a geographic region. It must use this force to protect its inhabitants from foreign and domestic enemies. Pacifism, tolerance, forgiveness, and love seem to be virtues that are unsuited to the exigencies of political life. The anti-Christian nature of political power is seen clearly, for example, in Machiavelli's claim that to retain power a prince had to reject Christian virtues.

Jesus' life story shows us the danger of confronting established authorities with moral and religious criticism: they will kill you. But this also reminds us that there is supposed to be another realm of value that goes beyond the value of life and power in this world. While Jesus is the "king of kings," his kingdom is not of this world. This is why he willingly submits to his own execution rather than stage a political revolt. But this is also why Jesus is a poor model for those of us who are interested in democracy and human rights. Jesus was not a defender of democracy; and although he emphasized love for persons, he had no idea of human rights as establishing a zone of autonomy that should be protected from the power of the state.

It should not be surprising that politics in the Christian world was, for centuries, undemocratic and illiberal. Democracy, the idea of human rights, and the notion that church and state should be separated are modern ideas that blossomed in the Enlightenment. Indeed, Christian authorities—especially the Catholic Church—resisted liberalization. It was not until the twentieth century that the Catholic Church became interested in democracy and human rights. Even a defender of liberal politics such as the Catholic philosopher Jacques Maritain emphasized spiritual transcendence, while also recognizing the importance of developing a just social order. For Maritain, the "human person is both part of the body politic and superior to it through what is supra-temporal, or eternal, in him, to his spiritual interests and his final destination."[1] The point is that spiritual values transcend the values of political life. The state should deal justly with its citizens, but the citizens are directed beyond political life toward transcendent value. At best, then, even a proponent of liberal ideas such as Maritain reaches ambivalent conclusions about political life.

While some contemporary Christians, such as George W. Bush, appear to think that liberal democracy is God's will for mankind, this is a new development in the long history of Christian thought. God's will was traditionally linked to central monarchic power, since, as Robert Kraynak argues in *Christian Faith and Modern Democracy*, Christianity is based on a hierarchically ordered view of the universe. Dante, for example, argues in his essay "On World Government" that a single world government under a single monarch is required, because God is the one and only ruler of the universe and government should be instituted in imitation of this model. Dante further argues that God willed the conjunction of Jesus and the Roman Empire that we see in Luke's account of the birth of Jesus. In Luke 2, the edict of Caesar Augustus to "enroll the world" is the catalyst that leads to Jesus' birth. According to Dante, this shows that God viewed the Pax Romana as exemplary and ultimately wants there to be a conjunction of worldly and spiritual power that will create lasting peace. Such an interpretation sheds an interesting light on the conjunction of God and Caesar that we find in Jesus' claim about rendering unto Caesar. According to Dante, God was using Caesar to carry out his eschatological plan.

Modern liberals tend to think that hierarchically organized political power is authoritarian, intolerant, and oppressive. Those who defend hierarchy hold that truth and goodness are best instituted by those at the top of the social hierarchy. Plato, for example, flirted with the idea that philosopher-kings should use their wisdom to control the state. Christian hierarchies are grounded in the idea that truth is revealed through Jesus, his apostles, and those who possess authority from God, including popes and kings, and who thus ought to rule over those who do not have direct access to truth and virtue. One key passage supporting this view is John 14:6: "I am the way, the truth, and the life; no one comes to the Father but by me." A hierarchical interpretation of this passage would claim that the truth is not available to everyone, except through the mediation of Christian authority. Such a claim can easily be developed into an argument for theocracy and religious intolerance.

The conflict between democratic and nondemocratic interpretations of Christianity opens onto a related question about whether Christianity is "of this world" or apart from it. Augustine focused on this question in his *City of God*, where he distinguished between the city of man and the city of God. In the city of man, human beings turn away from God and love themselves only; in the city of God, human beings piously worship God. Augustine prophesies eternal punishment for citizens of the city of man. Indeed, the really important "political" struggle is the apocalyptic struggle between the two cities. Augustine derives this view in part from the apocalyptic Revelation of John, which culminates in the creation of a new earth and a new Jerusalem: "Then I saw a new heaven and a new earth; for the first heaven and the first earth had passed way and the sea was no more. And I saw the holy city, new Jerusalem coming down out of heaven from God" (Revelation 21:1–2). This apocalyptic vision involves massive destruction, war, and turmoil. This perspective is not unique to the book of Revelation. Jesus foretells of "war and rumors of war" in which "nations will rise against nation, and kingdom against kingdom" (Mark 13:7–8). And he prophesies of a time when the son of man will come in a cloud with power and great glory (Luke 21:27).

This messianic ideal is ambiguous. On the one hand, there is an emphasis in the New Testament texts on an eschatological sort of politics: the goal is a political arrangement that promises the end of politics with the triumphal entrance of God as ruler on earth. In this sense, politics is about preparing the way for the kingdom of God. With this goal in mind, it is no wonder that Christians have engaged in crusades, inquisitions, and other violence that seeks to transform the world according to the prophetic ideal. And it is not surprising that some Christians continue to be motivated by end-times prophecy to engage political life from the standpoint of apocalyptic thinking.

On the other hand, since the city of God is not of this world, perhaps we should simply render unto Caesar what is due to Caesar while turning our attention entirely to the spiritual realm. Thus, another way to interpret the messianic promise is to view it as a reminder that we ought to focus our energy on God as a transcendent spiritual being who pulls us beyond ordinary life. This is a method of renunciation that points beyond politics. Political life—from this perspective—is full of temptations and spiritual dead-ends, and the goods obtained from political life are transient and illusory.

This distinction between the two realms of value is represented quite clearly in the passage from Mark, referred to above, that one should "render to Caesar the things that are Caesar's, and to God the things that are God's" (Mark 12:17). Jesus explicitly advocates complying with legal obligations. Unlike Thoreau, who maintained that he would not give his tax money to support injustice, Jesus acquiesced to taxation and to political authority in general. One reason for this is that Jesus and his followers seemed to think that the kingdom of God was near at hand. Rather than disturbing the political boat, the idea was to go along with political authority while focusing on spiritual things. Again, the idea of an imminent apocalypse is ambiguous. On the one hand, in death the righteous will soon enough be united with God, just as Jesus himself was carried up into heaven after his death. On the other hand, Jesus claimed that "there are some standing here who will not taste death before they see the kingdom of God" (Luke 9:27) and "this generation will not pass away till all has taken place" (Luke 21:22).

This idea of compliance is also supported by Paul. In Romans 13, Paul writes, "Let every person be subject to the governing authorities. For there is no authority except from God, and those that exist have been instituted by God. Therefore he who resists the authorities resists what God has appointed, and those who resist will incur judgment" (13:1–2). Paul goes on to say that we should "pay taxes, for the authorities are ministers of God, attending to this very thing. Pay all of them their dues, taxes to whom taxes are due, reverence to whom reverence is due, respect to whom respect is due, honor to whom honor is due" (Romans 13:6–7). This idea is linked subsequently to the idea that "salvation is near" (Romans 13:11). The general idea is that God has a plan, that the political authorities are part of this plan, and that this plan will be enacted soon. The difficulty of this passage is that Paul counsels a sort of detachment from this world in the previous chapter of Romans: "Do not be conformed to this world but be transformed by the renewal of your mind, that you may prove what is the will of God, what is good and acceptable and perfect" (Romans 12:2). And in this chapter, Paul replays the basic ideas of the Sermon on the Mount, including the idea of not returning evil for evil (Romans 12:17). The best policy is obedience and prayer and peaceful compliance with the political authorities.

This same idea is reiterated in the first letter of Peter (attributed to the apostle Peter but most likely written decades after the apostle's death).

Peter writes: "Be subject for the Lord's sake to every human institution, whether it be to the emperor as supreme, or to governors as sent by him to punish those who do wrong and to praise those who do right. For it is God's will that by doing right you should put to silence the ignorance of foolish men. Live as free men, yet without using your freedom as a pretext for evil; but live as servants of God. Honor all men. Love the brotherhood. Fear God. Honor the emperor" (1 Peter 2:13–17).

What is truly remarkable in this passage is that Peter twice tells us to obey the emperor. Peter follows this with an exhortation to what is known as the "household duty code." The basic idea here is for Christians to follow accepted social customs so that they do not provoke the reproach of non-Christians and local authorities. Peter tells us that slaves should obey their masters and that women should obey their husbands—the same ideas found in Paul's letters to the Colossians and the Ephesians. But Peter also links this to Jesus' moral example and to the doctrine of not returning evil for evil as articulated in the Sermon on the Mount. Peter says that when Jesus was reviled, "he did not revile in return; when he suffered, he did not threaten; but he trusted to him who judges justly" (1 Peter 2:23). Christians are to submit to political authorities—even to the emperor. And they should expect to be persecuted, just as Jesus was persecuted. But they should also look beyond the goods of this world and have hope for redemption, because "the end of all things is at hand" (1 Peter 4:7).

The context of these ideas about obedience and political conformity has much to do with political reality during the first century. It would have been clear to Jesus and his followers that revolts and agitation simply caused the Roman state to become more oppressive. Jesus himself was executed for his social agitation, which, by the way, was less overtly revolutionary than the insurgent activities of some of his more "zealous" contemporaries. Paul wrote his letter to the Romans in 58 C.E. This was just a few years prior to the Jewish revolt that culminated in the destruction of Jerusalem and its temple. Peter's letter is probably written in the 80s or 90s—after the destruction of the temple. Jesus and his followers appeared to take a middle course between open revolt against Rome and collusion with Roman authority. One should render to Caesar what was Caesar's, one should honor the emperor, without losing sight of the true good, which is God and not Caesar. This middle course was thus linked to a new theological idea that looked beyond the world of politics toward another realm of value with the hope of an apocalyptic transformation that would cleanse the world.

NATURAL LAW AND POLITICAL LIFE

If human beings had followed Jesus, Paul, and Peter's advice, we may never have progressed toward liberal democracy. Jesus and Paul both advocated that we pay our taxes, but the American revolution was motivated by the motto "no taxation without representation." The hierarchical political society to which early Christians recommended submission was overthrown during the last few centuries in the name of human rights and democracy. While Paul advocated submission, Locke advocated a right to revolt when the government no longer fulfilled its fiduciary obligation to defend our rights. While Peter advocated honoring the emperor, Jefferson wrote that we have a right and a duty to throw off oppressive government. While Jesus peacefully submitted to his own demise, revolutionaries in the last few centuries have fought and killed in the name of liberty. The new idea that it was acceptable to resist authority and fight for liberty culminated in the American Declaration of Independence. And the basic rights outlined in the American founding documents eventually led to the abolition of slavery and political equality for women. But these new ideas can find no support in biblical texts, despite the fact that Locke and others appeal to the idea that the creator endows us with inalienable rights.

The Old Testament clearly shows us a society based on kingship, priestly hierarchy, patriarchy, class identity, ethnic warfare, and slavery. The idea that the creator advocates liberal democracy is not to be found there. Nor is it found in the New Testament. The New Testament does no better in terms of these issues, despite the more egalitarian spirit of Jesus' ideas about caring for the poor. Indeed, the ideal of the "new Jerusalem" is one of God's rule as a king on a throne and as the focal point of worship. The new Jerusalem is not a city of liberty and individuality; rather, it is focused on purity that is obtained by the exclusion and extermination of the impure.

When Locke, Jefferson, and others appeal to the "creator," they do not have in mind an exclusive and hierarchical God. Nor is the enlightened republic a perfect religious state in which there is conformity and uniformity of worship. Rather, the God of the Enlightenment represents an idea of God that has been reformed and recreated according to human ideas about justice, including ideas about human rights and toleration. Indeed, while Locke quotes selectively from the Bible to make his case in his *Second Treatise on Government*, his primary focus is "natural law" and not revelation. Natural law is the law of nature made available to reason or known through conscience. Locke and others had to appeal to natural law to make their arguments in favor of democracy because this case cannot be grounded in the Bible. At the very least, the natural law allows us to discover ways of governing ourselves that are suitable for a human world this side of the apocalypse.

The natural law approach can be supported by appealing to the New Testament. Even Paul admits that the law should be known by those who have not encountered the Gospels: "When Gentiles who have not the law do by nature what the law requires, they are a law to themselves, even though they do not have the law. They show that what the law requires is written on their hearts, while their conscience also bears witness and their conflicting thoughts accuse or perhaps excuse them" (Romans 2:14–15). Peter reaffirms this in Acts (10:34–35): "God shows no partiality, but in every nation anyone who fears him and does what is right is acceptable to him."

Peter implies that one can be righteous without being Christian or being part of a Christian nation. This important fact should be kept in mind when thinking about those in our contemporary society who call for a return to Christian values. Often this call for a return aims beyond the idea of natural law toward something like Dante's ideal of Christian monarchy. But it is not clear that it is necessary to have a Christian nation in order to be moral. Almost all of the authors of the New Testament claim that private individuals can be moral and can find God without any help from political authority: Jesus was born, after all, in a non-Christian nation under the rule of the pagan Augustus. We should thus be careful when we hear claims about the need for a return to Christian politics. This can mean a return to the idea that the state is being used by God to carry out an eschatological plan. But it is not clear that Jesus himself ever calls upon any political authority to take up such a crusading task.

CONCLUSION

So, what are we to make of Jesus' views about politics? D. J. Harrington rightly concludes on a skeptical note that "the New Testament provides no uniform doctrine of 'church and state.' "[2] He notes that there are three diverse ideas about the church–state relationship in the New Testament: caution (as expressed in the passage about rendering to Caesar), cooperation (as expressed by Paul in Romans), and resistance (as expressed in Revelation). Harrington also notes that we must then look beyond the Bible to natural law, as I've suggested above. One should note, however, that natural law can be used to criticize the Bible. Why should we accept what Jesus says, for example, about "rendering to Caesar what is Caesar's"? Isn't it possible, as Thoreau argued, that Jesus was simply wrong about this? Christian scholars try to avoid such conclusions by arguing that one needs a hermeneutic principle that can allow for a relativized application of basic principles: Jesus was responding as best he could within his historical context. But we still do not know how Jesus would have responded to changed context, including a context in which Christian ideas are now viewed as central.

The most difficult problem to be faced in trying to think about the relation between church and state is that Jesus is, quite literally, nearly silent on the issue. Indeed, the most remarkable aspect of Jesus' biography is his behavior when he is confronted by Pilate. This episode is repeated in all four Gospels. And it shows us Jesus in direct relation to political power. Jesus is questioned by Pilate, who asks him if he is "king of the Jews." In Mark, Matthew, and Luke, Jesus responds to Pilate's question by saying, "You have said so." And then Jesus remains silent. We may have become so used to this story that we do not find this fact remarkable. However, in another narrative this would have been an opportunity for a discourse on political power, a defense of liberty, a condemnation of power, or a call for rebellion. When Socrates is accused, Plato provides an elaborate defense speech, culminating in his condemnation of the city of Athens. Jesus, however, remains silent. We do not know exactly what he thinks of the political power that condemns him. Nor do we know what he wants us to think about his execution or about the power that kills him.

In John, Jesus goes further and replies: "My kingship is not of this world; if my kingship were of this world, my servants would fight, that I might not be handed over to the Jews; but my kingship is not from the world" (John 18:36). This reply is, at least, more instructive than silence. But it directs us toward compliance and cooperation with authority. Followers of Jesus should acknowledge that Jesus' kingdom is not of this world, and they should not take up arms to fight in his defense. Again, the difficulty of this conclusion is that it provides us with no reason to struggle against oppression or injustice. Nor does it give us a reason to fight in defense of religion. Indeed, the model left us by Jesus is one of obedience to political authority, even unto death.

When we understand this aspect of Jesus' story, it becomes difficult to decide what Jesus would say about the relation between ethics and politics. Even if we could clearly establish what Jesus' conclusions would be about issues such as abortion or euthanasia, it is not clear whether Jesus would want the state to enforce these conclusions. In our own society, freedom of choice, conscience, and religion are time-honored principles. It is not clear what Jesus would think about this. The conclusion here is that Jesus said nothing about a time when he or his followers would obtain political power, so Jesus did not leave us with answers about what to do once power is obtained. Obviously, the powerful should continue to be virtuous, and they should continue to uphold the two basic moral commandments—love God and love your neighbor. But it remains unclear how to apply these commandments to the concrete question of enacting legislation on moral issues.

NOTES

1. Jacques Maritain, *Man and the State* (Chicago: University of Chicago Press, 1951), 148.
2. D. J. Harrington and James Keenan, *Jesus and Virtue Ethics* (Lanham, MD: Sheed and Ward, 2002), 111.

12

JESUS AND THE ENLIGHTENMENT

> Ever since the creation of the world, God's invisible nature,
> namely his eternal power and deity, has been clearly perceived
> in the nature of things that have been made.
>
> —Romans 1:20

In the previous group of chapters, I have noted some of the difficulties of looking to Jesus for advice about ethical life. While Jesus can provide an inspiring model, he takes us only so far. We need to go beyond Jesus and develop a more robust and systematic approach to ethics. The history of Western culture shows the continuing attempt to come to grips with the basic ethical ideals postulated by Jesus, but it also involves going beyond Jesus. One way this happens is through the natural law tradition that looks to the moral message that we find in the nature of the God-created world. The basic faith of this approach is that human beings can discover God and morality through what Aquinas calls the "light of natural reason." As Paul says (Romans 2:15), the law is "written on our hearts."

After the Renaissance, there was a gradual split between Christianity and ethical philosophy. This split developed as philosophers turned directly to the question of ethics in search of general moral principles. One of the reasons for this new modern focus was the awareness that Jesus provided a limited model of the ethical life. This idea really develops in earnest during the era known as the Enlightenment (roughly the eighteenth century). Philosophers of the Enlightenment generally agreed that Jesus was a moral exemplar. But they maintained that progress toward enlightenment required going beyond Jesus.

The philosophers of the Enlightenment are foundational for contemporary thinking about ethics, politics, and religion. When we teach philosophical ethics today, we have to consider Immanuel Kant (1724–1804) and John Stuart Mill (1806–1873), who each had an interesting relationship to Christianity. When we consider political theory, we have to consider John Locke (1632–1704), Thomas Jefferson (1743–1826), and others who developed the Christian tradition in modern ways. This chapter will discuss these thinkers as well as René Descartes (1596–1650) and Jean-Jacques Rousseau (1712–1778).

DEISM AND ETHICS

Philosophers of the Enlightenment attempted to reconstruct religion along rational lines. This reconstruction included two key elements: a critique of the miraculous from the perspective of empirical science and a renewed commitment to rational ethics. In both cases one might argue that the attempt was made to naturalize Jesus. Jesus was viewed as a natural man, rather than as a supernatural being. The name "son of God" and stories of the virgin birth were understood as literary signs of honor and respect. Stories of his miracles were criticized as either the result of hyperbolic attempts to establish Jesus' nobility or as the mistaken reports of the uneducated and credulous. And his ethical vision was shown to be a part of a perennial ethical philosophy that can be known by human reason.

One of the focal points of this reconstruction of religion was an effort to understand the historical Jesus. This analysis resulted in a deliberate attempt to compare Jesus with Socrates. One basis for this comparison is found in the Gospel of John. The prologue to John begins with the claim that "in the beginning was the Word and the word was with God and the Word was God" (John 1:1). John goes on to discuss the enlightenment that results from the word made flesh: "The true light that enlightens every man was coming into the world" (John 1:9). The Greek word for "reason" or "word" is *logos*. John equates the light that enlightens with *logos*, while also making it clear that this light is Jesus. However, since the Renaissance, as Western thinkers became reinterested in pagan sources, Socrates was held up as the exemplar of reason and the ethical life. Thus the comparison between Jesus and Socrates is natural for thinkers in the Christian tradition. But Jesus and Socrates provide quite different models of the good life. Jesus spoke with the passion—some might say the fanaticism—of a religious zealot, but Socrates was more modest and less fanatical. As we shall see, Enlightenment philosophers had revisionist views about Jesus: they wanted to turn Jesus into Socrates.

Some of the chief points of the Enlightenment reconstruction of Christianity are the following: (1) There is a God and his existence can be established by reason. (2) This God organizes the universe according to universal laws of reason, including the laws of ethics. (3) The true essence of Christianity was Jesus' ethical message. (4) This ethical message could be distinguished from theology and from stories about miracles. (5) Enlightenment made it possible to properly understand Jesus' ethical message, while also helping us to go beyond Jesus in order to establish an ethical theory that has truly universal application.

The ideas were connected as part of a general view known as "deism." Deism holds that God, as the rational creator of the laws that govern the universe, cannot intervene directly in the universe. This is true because God cannot violate the laws of nature, which he created. This view thus keeps God out of history and denies the possibility of miracles. Such a view is derived from a general commitment to science, law, and reason. And ultimately it is opposed to much of the dogma of traditional Christian faith.

Deism results from modern skepticism about God such as we find in Descartes. Although it is a bit of a historical stretch to include Descartes in the Enlightenment, it is clear that the modern philosophical commitment to a rational humanistic method for doing philosophy begins with Descartes. Descartes approaches religion from the perspective of reason. Using reason, he proves that God exists. Although he is very careful not to argue directly against revealed religion, it is clear that he views its claims as circular, and only convincing to those who already accept the authority of the religious tradition. The faithful believe the revealed story because it comes from God, but it is the revealed story that gives us reason to believe in God. Descartes' goal is to avoid this circle by using reason to prove God directly. But the sort of God we get by this proof has very little in common with the God of revelation. The result of Descartes' proof is the "God of the philosophers": a perfect, omniscient, and omnipotent being, what deists would later refer to as the supreme being. But this God has no connection to the God who entered into history with Abraham, Moses, and Jesus.

After Descartes, thinkers such as Locke considered the relation between religion and political power. One impetus for this interest in the relation between religion and politics was religious violence in Europe after the Lutheran Reformation. Locke acknowledges the tendency of religions to become intolerant when they are connected with political power. For Locke, religion is a private matter of what he calls "inward and full persuasion of the mind." From this, Locke concludes that the civil authorities should have no interest in forcing people to believe a particular revealed religion. Moreover, Locke thinks that it is possible to derive moral law from reason. We have certain rights that come from God. But these rights are knowable by reason and are not known only by way of revelation.

With this brief introduction to Descartes and Locke, let us turn directly to the Enlightenment's greatest proponent of deism, Jean-Jacques Rousseau. In *Emile*, Rousseau lays out a vision—articulated in the "Profession of Faith of the Savoyard Vicar"—of Enlightenment deism that includes the five ideas listed above. Rousseau also criticizes miracles, provides an argument for religious tolerance, and discusses the similarities and differences between Socrates and Jesus. *Emile* was published in 1762. It represents a high point for Enlightenment thought and had a profound influence on Kant, who is rumored to have disrupted his normally disciplined life to finish reading the book.

In *Emile*, Rousseau's Savoyard vicar discusses his ideas about religion under the rubric of "natural religion," which is what natural reason (as opposed to revelation) tells us about the order and structure of the universe. According to this perspective, revealed religions actually undermine the rational idea of God as described by natural religion. Rousseau criticizes revealed religions as follows: "Their revelations have only the effect of degrading God by giving Him human passions. I see that particular dogmas, far from clarifying the notions of the great Being, confuse them; that far from ennobling them, they debase them; that of the inconceivable mysteries surrounding the great Being they add absurd contradictions; that they make man proud, intolerant, and cruel; that, instead of establishing peace of earth, they bring sword and fire to it."[1] Natural or rational religion is thus supposed to cure the evils of revealed religion.

Rousseau's basic idea is that revealed religions are stories about God that are generated by human beings according to their local, tribal interests. These stories are partial and require irrational belief in hearsay and authority. Moreover, as Rousseau's friend Hume put it, human beings transfer human qualities and infirmities to God. Thus they "represent him as jealous and revengeful, capricious and partial, and, in short, a wicked and foolish man in every respect but his superior power and authority."[2] As opposed to this, reasonable natural religion should make God out to be truly universal, rational, and just. If God is the rational ruler of the universe, all humans should be able to find God directly in nature and the moral law.

But revealed religions are partial, particular, and for the most part intolerant. Rousseau argues for tolerance by indicating how odd it is to claim that God appears in history at a certain place and time and that others who do not have access to this specific revelation are damned. This makes God both cruel and arbitrary. But since God is neither cruel nor arbitrary, this sort of intolerance must be the result of the human invention of revelation and religion; it has nothing to do with God.

The use of reason as the sole vehicle that provides us with access to God also leads to the rejection of miracles. Miracles violate the reasonable order of nature that God himself created. According to Rousseau, God wants us to develop our reason and our rational understanding of the divine order. God does not want us to corrupt our reason by believing absurdities. Part of Rousseau's focus in making such claims is that sort of authoritarian religion that demands unthinking belief. "The God I worship is not a god of shadows. He did not endow me with an understanding in order to forbid me its use. To tell me to subject my reason is to insult its Author. The minister of the truth does not tyrannize my reason; he enlightens it."[3]

These arguments against revealed religion led Rousseau to struggle to articulate the importance of the person of Jesus. The Savoyard vicar loves Jesus and finds the scriptures to be amazing and holy. Indeed, he claims that the story of Jesus surpasses even the story of Socrates. He says: "When Plato depicts his imaginary just man (in Book 2 of the *Republic*), covered with all the opprobrium of crime and worthy of all the rewards of virtue, he depicts Jesus Christ feature for feature."[4] For the vicar, the moral problem of Jesus is that his virtuous life is not rewarded in this world. Although the same is true of Socrates, Socrates led a long and productive life, while Jesus' life is cut short, despite his virtue. This is why Jesus' story is of higher worth. As Rousseau has the vicar say, "Yes, if the life and death of Socrates are those of a wise man, the life and death of Jesus are those of a god."[5] Nonetheless, the vicar indicates that the revealed religion is limited, in part because the Gospels introduce miracles and mysteries. The vicar's solution is to look to the moral heart of Jesus' story, which the vicar identifies as compassion. Here is the vicar's conclusion, which quotes the two commandments given by Jesus in Matthew 22:37–44:

> My son, keep your soul in a condition where it always desires that there be a God, and you shall never doubt it. What is more, whatever decision you may make, bear in mind that the true duties of religion are inde-

pendent of the institutions of men; that a just heart is the true temple of divinity; that in every country and in every sect the sum of the law is to love God above everything and one's neighbor as oneself; that no religion is exempt from the duties of morality; that nothing is truly essential other than these duties; that inner worship is the first of these duties; and that without faith no true virtue exists.[6]

These same sorts of ideas are expressed by a wide variety of thinkers in this period, including many early Americans. Thomas Jefferson noted that Jesus and Socrates were similar: they both wrote nothing. And he recognized that Jesus fell victim to the closed-minded zealots of his age. But Jefferson was interested in purifying Christianity in a way that made it consistent. He did this by rewriting the Gospels along more rational lines, in part by eliminating the miraculous elements. Another American, Thomas Paine, suggested more forcefully that Jesus was simply a virtuous and amiable man and not a God. Paine held that the miraculous stories of the virgin birth were mere hearsay without proof and that the epithet "son of God" was an honorary title meant to express Jesus' virtue and importance. Benjamin Franklin expressed doubt about the divinity of Jesus while maintaining that Jesus was a moral exemplar.

As noted, Hume expressed doubts about claims that were made about miracles, and he directed our attention to the tendency of human beings to believe in superstitious, anthropomorphic accounts of the gods. Voltaire went so far as to claim that some stories about Jesus were acceptable, such as those that make Jesus out to be militant and self-righteous. Voltaire holds that Jesus was an advocate of the morality of compassion, on a par with Socrates, Zoroaster, and Pythagoras. Like Rousseau, Voltaire claims that the basis of religion is simply the two commandments from Matthew: "Love God and your fellow creatures as yourself."[7]

KANT

Immanuel Kant is one of the names most closely associated with the Enlightenment. It is not too much to say that the German philosopher's *Critique of Pure Reason* revolutionized Western philosophy. Kant's contribution in ethics was his theory of duty (or deontology), which remains an essential idea in philosophical ethics. And Kant was also involved in the Enlightenment's revolutionary approach to Christianity. Kant was one of the most forceful proponents of the idea that Jesus was a great moral teacher and an important moral exemplar. But Kant remained agnostic about whether Jesus was the incarnate divinity. Indeed, Kant goes so far as to claim that it is better to consider Jesus as a human being, if we are looking to him as a moral exemplar.

The goal of Kant's ethical system is to defend an absolute and objective theory of duty. Such a theory must, according to Kant, be derived directly from reason; it cannot be built up from examples. Kant's basic idea is quite similar to the idea found in Plato's *Euthyphro*: we must decide what good is first, before we can say whether a particular example is an example of the good. Kant applies this idea directly to the question of the ethics of Jesus by claiming that reason's prior idea of what is good allows us to say that Jesus is good. "Even the Holy One of the Gospels must first be compared with our ideal of moral perfection before we can recognize Him as such."[8]

Kant's deontological system seeks to identify absolute moral duty (the root of "deontological" is *deon*, which means "duty"). Kant asks whether it is possible to say of a behavior that it should be done by everyone. In Kant's language, this is the Categorical Imperative: "Act only on that maxim whereby thou canst at the same time will that it should become a universal law." If it is possible to say that everyone should behave in a certain way, then the behavior is morally acceptable. Kant also formulates a second version of this moral principle, which focuses on respect for persons: "So act as to treat humanity in thine own person or in that of any other, in every case as an end in itself, never as means only." In other words, we are to respect persons as "ends in themselves" and not use or exploit them. This idea conforms to the Categorical Imperative, since it is possible to universalize it without contradiction: it is possible to say without contradiction that all persons should be respected.

Like other Enlightenment thinkers, Kant claims that the principles of ethics could be discovered by reason alone, without aid from revealed religion. Indeed, he asserts that moral philosophers should be free to develop the ethics of reason without reference to the Bible. Nonetheless, Kant praises the Christian approach to ethics because its idea of moral duty is so demanding and uncompromising. Kant interprets Jesus' twin command, "Love God above all and thy neighbor as thyself," as a command that pushes us beyond mere self-love and toward the absolute and categorical idea of moral law.[9] For Kant, we should do this, not because we like it, but because it is the right thing to do. This is essential to his idea of duty: duty is what we must do, even if we don't want to. According to Kant, the point of the Christian message is that the demands of duty are so great that we should view them and ourselves with humility.[10] In this way, Kant opposes the Christian moral message to a kind of moral and religious fanaticism that does not take the demands of morality seriously. For Kant, the task of duty requires sobriety and ongoing self-criticism.

Kant claims that we do learn by examining moral exemplars, and that the narrative structure of the life of Jesus provides us with an example of the triumph of morality. But the "archetype" of morality is "already present in our reason."[11] In other words, we do not need revealed religion to show us what is morally good. Indeed, Kant implies that stories and examples have a subjective element. Each of us evaluates the stories of revealed religion according to our own criteria. Thus, "each man ought really to furnish an example of this idea in his own person."[12] The point is that the example must be selected and interpreted so that it reminds us of morality. In other words, morality is prior to the example, since it is the idea of morality that helps us properly to choose and interpret the example.

Kant goes on to claim that the example of Jesus is more pertinent to us if we conceive of him as a human exemplar and not as the incarnate God. "The elevation of such a holy person above all the frailties of human nature would rather so far as we can see, hinder the adoption of the idea of such a person for our imitation."[13] If Jesus is divine, then he is not really a suitable model for *human* imitation—since no human being can realistically aspire to divinity. But Kant also realizes that the superhuman demands of morality point beyond the capacity of human agents, who are often motivated by self-love and not purely by morality. The story of Jesus can thus be used to remind us of the possibility of going beyond self-love toward total dedication to the moral law.

Kant goes on to say that the theological interpretation of Christ's sacrifice as atonement for sin is not necessary. Rather, in line with the spirit of the Enlightenment, Kant maintains that evil "can be overcome only through the idea of moral goodness in its entire purity."[14] Kant hopes that reason is powerful enough to resist evil without the intervention of God. Jesus provides us a model for how far we may have to go to maintain moral purity—that is, all the way to an ignominious death. This demonstrates the significance of the task. But human beings can be moral without divine intervention.

Kant goes on to state that the miraculous and mystical elements of revealed religion actually serve to undermine the importance of the Christian message. The Christian moral message is "completely authoritative" for a reasonable person because reason tells us that the basic ethical commands of Jesus are in fact reasonable.[15] In Kant's words, Jesus' moral teachings do not require "external certification" because they will be known to be true by reasonable persons.[16] The appeal to divine command and miracles to establish the credibility of the moral message makes it seem that the message is not reasonable but that it needs support from other sorts of certification.

Kant believes that Jesus' moral message is contained in the Sermon on the Mount and especially in the two commandments. After discussing with approval the Sermon on the Mount, Kant concludes: "Finally he combines all duties (1) in one universal rule, namely: Perform your duty for no motive other than unconditioned esteem for duty itself, i.e., love God (the Legislator of all duties) above all else; and (2) in a particular rule, that, namely, which concerns man's external relation to other men as universal duty: Love every one as yourself, i.e., further his welfare from good-will that is immediate and not derived from motives of self-advantage."[17] Kant's concern with the proper motive for acting morally shows up here again. The real point of his emphasis on doing duty for the sake of duty is to push us beyond that sort of immature obedience that easily becomes fanaticism. For Kant, the goal of morality is to understand why the moral law is good and why it is our duty. If we think that it comes from divine command only and that we must comply because of fear of hellfire, then we are not yet fully moral. To obey the moral law because you want a reward from God is to turn religion and morality into what Kant calls a "fetishism." Kant concludes that "true enlightenment" is the process by which "the service of God becomes first and foremost a free and hence a moral service."[18] We truly serve God when we are moral for the right reasons.

MILL

John Stuart Mill is, along with Kant, another of the most influential ethical thinkers of the past few centuries. Unlike Kant, who emphasized abstract duty and respect for persons, Mill focused on happiness and social welfare. Mill expanded upon Jeremy Bentham's Utilitarian theory of ethics and postulated that the moral law was to do whatever created "the greatest happiness for the greatest number."

Mill makes an explicit connection between Utilitarianism and Christian ethics in his book *Utilitarianism*. He says, "In the golden rule of Jesus of Nazareth we read the complete spirit of the ethics of utility. To do

as one would be done by, and to love one's neighbour as oneself, consti-
tute the ideal perfection of utilitarian morality."[19] However, Mill realizes
that Utilitarianism may seem anti-religious because it allows for a rational
foundation for ethics that is not grounded in Christianity (even though
it is sympathetic to the Christian ideal). Mill claims that God must desire
the happiness of his creatures, and Utilitarianism is the best way to create the most happiness for God's creatures. Mill goes further in claiming
that God created us with the capacity to discover this for ourselves. "The
Christian revelation was intended, and is fitted, to inform the hearts and
minds of mankind with a spirit which should enable them to find for
themselves what is right, and incline them to do it when found, rather
than to tell them, except in a very general way, what it is." He concludes
with a remark that hearkens back to the problem indicated by Socrates in
the *Euthyphro*: we need a system of ethics, "to interpret to us the will of
God."[20] The point is, again, that we need to clarify our theory of ethics
in order to know what our ethical God wants us to do.

Mill goes further in *On Liberty*. Here he states the case for going
beyond Christianity in terms of the incompleteness of Jesus' ideas about
ethics. Mill does not reject Jesus' teachings. Indeed he agrees with them,
saying, "They are irreconcilable with nothing which a comprehensive
morality requires." But he goes on to say that "it is quite consistent with
this, to believe that they contain, and were meant to contain, only a part
of the truth; that many essential elements of the highest morality are
among the things which are not provided for, nor intended to be provided for, in the recorded deliverances of the Founder of Christianity."
His conclusion from this is that "it a great error to persist in attempting
to find in the Christian doctrine that complete rule for our guidance,
which its author intended it to sanction and enforce, but only partially
to provide."[21] One of the things that is missing is a more robust analysis
of politics and the importance of human liberty. Christian texts, for example, appear to sanction slavery and the subjection of women. This is
not acceptable, which is why we must go beyond Christianity.

In other places Mill explains the limits of Christian ethics by claiming that the Gospels' ethical claims are like "poetry or eloquence" and
that they lack the "precision of legislation."[22] The Gospels contain some
inspirational spiritual ideas. But Mill also notes that Christianity depends
on the more developed moral ideas found in both the Old Testament
and in the Greco-Roman culture of the first century—without these
there would be no social and political content to Jesus' general idea of
loving one's neighbor.

A further problem for Mill—and indeed for everyone who values democracy—is that Christianity appears to emphasize passive obedience and submission to established authority without embracing democracy.[23] Mill goes on to criticize Christian intolerance, which he believes is based on the authoritarian tone that is found in Christianity. He claims that Christians must tolerate other belief systems in the name of justice. And indeed, he goes farther in claiming that non-Christians have profound ethical insight: "A large portion of the noblest and most valuable moral teaching has been the work, not only of men who did not know, but of men who knew and rejected, the Christian faith."[24]

CONCLUSION

Since the Enlightenment, some philosophers and religious thinkers have reacted negatively to the idea that reason is the key to morality and religion. Postmodernists deny that reason is one thing for everyone. And religious fundamentalists claim that revelation and tradition are more fundamental than reason and natural religion. The recent retreat to a view of the Bible as inerrant and literally true is a direct response to the worry that Enlightenment deism has little or nothing to do with traditional Christianity.

There are reasons to listen carefully to at least some of these challenges to the Enlightenment. The postmodern critique reminds us that our knowledge is always limited. And religious fundamentalism reminds us of the importance of tradition. However, those who completely reject the Enlightenment project often retreat into an embarrassingly untenable corner of irrationality. Some who reject the Enlightenment end up espousing a sort of relativism that leads to an inability to defend moral values such as the idea of human rights. Some also end up absurdly rejecting science and the scientific method itself.

One example can be found in William Spohn's book on Christian ethics, *Go and Do Likewise*, which is an odd combination of postmodern and fundamentalist ideas. Spohn claims that questions of historical truth are irrelevant to the study of Christian ethics. He writes: "Nineteenth-century scholars aimed for a scientific history that could objectively determine the truth about the past. That project has been met with skepticism in a postmodern age that rejects Enlightenment pretensions to universal truth. Historical method cannot demonstrate the truth of assertions about what Jesus of Nazareth did and said." One might think that such claims would lead us to reject Christianity outright. If we do not know what Jesus did and said, what's the point of continuing to think about him? But Spohn explains this as follows: "We have moved from a culture that prized historical fact and objectivity to one that evaluates systems of ideas primarily by their capacity for transforming individuals and society."[25]

Thus one might retreat to traditional stories and texts without worrying about whether they are true! But such an approach rejects the basic human interest in truth. Most of us want to know the truth about the world. It is true that it is difficult to know exactly what the historical Jesus said and did. But the larger question is whether the claim that the moral life involves loving God and loving the neighbor is true.

It is not hard to see that the task of knowing the truth is intimately connected to the ethical task of living well and doing right. When we answer ethical questions, we make truth claims. The idea that human beings have inherent rights is claimed as a universal truth, as is the claim that all human beings require food, shelter, and water to survive. The danger of focusing, as Spohn does, on transformational power while ignoring truth is that we can end up adopting misguided and pernicious ideas simply because of their transformative power. There are many ideas that have the capacity to transform our lives, but the only question that matters is whether the message contained in these ideas is true. It seems that Spohn and others who advocate a postmodern approach to religion are really trying to insulate their faiths from rational criticism. Although they would be loathe to admit it, this is the same problem found in religious fundamentalism. Radical Islamists claim, for example, that the Koran advocates terrorism and that God promises a reward in heaven for those who martyr themselves for Islam. This, too, is a transformational belief. But it must be criticized from the perspective of truth. It is false that terrorism is justifiable. And it is false that any God who is worthy of worship would advocate terrorism and reward terrorists. We know that these moral claims are false by consulting reason and our rational systems of ethics.

The Enlightenment project begins, then, with a commitment to truth and to the idea that reason is the way to reach it. Enlightenment thinkers admired Jesus and his ethical message, even when they were critical of other aspects of Christian belief and even as they pointed beyond a dogmatic fundamentalist approach to Christianity. As we've seen, the two great ethical systems of the Enlightenment—Kantian deontology and Mill's Utilitarianism—both trace their basic idea back to Jesus' ethical commandments, and they make use of the idea, first developed by Paul, that natural reason can provide us with access to moral truth.

NOTES

1. Rousseau, *Emile* (New York: Basic Books, 1979), 295.

2. David Hume, "The Origin of Religion," in *The Portable Enlightenment Reader*, ed. Isaac Kramnick (New York: Penguin, 1995), 114.

3. Rousseau, *Emile*, 300.

4. Rousseau, *Emile*, 307.

5. Rousseau, *Emile*, 308.

6. Rousseau, *Emile*, 311–312.

7. Voltaire, *Philosophical Dictionary* entry on "Religion," in *The Portable Enlightenment Reader*, 124.

8. Kant, *Foundations of the Metaphysics of Morals* (New York: Macmillan, 1990), 26.

9. Kant, *Critique of Practical Reason* (New York: Macmillan, 1956), 85–86.

10. Kant, *Critique of Practical Reason*, 89.

11. Kant, *Religion within the Limits of Reason Alone* (New York: Harper Torchbooks, 1960), 56.

12. Kant, *Religion within the Limits of Reason Alone*, 56.

13. Kant, *Religion within the Limits of Reason Alone*, 57.

14. Kant, *Religion within the Limits of Reason Alone*, 78.

15. Kant, *Religion within the Limits of Reason Alone*, 79.

16. Kant, *Religion within the Limits of Reason Alone*, 150.

17. Kant, *Religion within the Limits of Reason Alone*, 148.

18. Kant, *Religion within the Limits of Reason Alone*, 167.

19. John Stuart Mill, *Utilitarianism*, in *On Liberty and Other Essays* (Oxford: Oxford World Classics, 1998), 148.

20. Mill, *Utilitarianism*, 154.

21. John Stuart Mill, *On Liberty* in *On Liberty and Other Essays*, 57.

22. Mill, *On Liberty*, 55.

23. Mill, *On Liberty*, 56.

24. Mill, *On Liberty*, 58.

25. William C. Spohn, *Go and Do Likewise: Jesus and Ethics* (New York: Continuum, 2003), 18.

13

SIN, GRACE, AND HUMANISM
AFTER THE ENLIGHTENMENT

> For the law was given through Moses; grace and truth came through Jesus Christ.
>
> —John 1:17

In the previous chapter we saw how Enlightenment thinkers aimed to reconstruct Christianity according to a more rational and humanistic ethical ideal. Some would argue that Enlightenment deism is actually no longer Christian, since it downplays the importance of Jesus as the unique savior of humankind and the literal incarnation of God. Moreover, the Enlightenment weakened Christianity's universal claims: the ideal of toleration allowed for diverse revelations of truth not only within Christian culture but also beyond. Many Enlightenment thinkers saw Jesus as a moral teacher like Socrates. In the nineteenth and early twentieth centuries, there were more blatant attacks on Christianity as well as attempts to reinvigorate Christianity. Much of this debate had to do with the relationship between ethics and Christianity. And it focused on the question of whether human beings were capable of helping themselves to become good. At issue here is the question of sin and the possibility of overcoming sin. A traditional view of this question claims that human beings are by nature sinful and that sin is only overcome by the grace of God.

Philosophers of the Enlightenment had faith in human power, including the human ability to live well. Kant famously hoped that human beings could create a "kingdom of ends" in which mutual respect would be the rule of life. This kingdom of ends was connected to Kant's hope for perpetual peace. If human beings became moral by educating themselves about moral philosophy, if they established republican systems of government and instituted a federation of nations, then war would end and peace would prevail. Kant believes that human beings have the capacity to solve their own problems through ethical and political reform. But this idea runs counter to the traditional Christian idea that sin can only be overcome by the grace of God made manifest in Christ's sacrificial act of atonement. Thus one of the ways that Christians resisted the lure of Enlightenment deism was to reemphasize original sin while also distinguishing Jesus—the lamb of god—from Socrates, a mere moral teacher. Thus in the generation or two after Kant, diverse ways of thinking about faith and ethics developed. In the present chapter we will discuss Georg Wilhelm Friedrich Hegel (1770–1831), Søren Kierkegaard (1813–1855), and Ludwig Feuerbach (1804–1872).

HEGEL

For Hegel, Enlightenment reason alone was too abstract to lead us to the ethical life. Hegel claimed that reason is always already part of a history and tradition that includes religion. Enlightenment thinkers were interested in reconstructing the tradition according to universal moral principles. They still looked to Jesus as a moral exemplar, but they made sense of (and criticized) stories about Jesus from the vantage point of rational morality. Hegel realized that the Enlightenment reconstruction of the tradition threatened to push us completely beyond the tradition: Enlightenment deism was so abstract and humanistic that it risked becoming un-Christian. But ethical and religious life only made sense, according to Hegel, within a tradition in which the abstract truths of ethics were given flesh. Moreover, Hegel claimed that the Christian revelation was the most adequate expression of the human spirit. Christianity led to the idea that human beings are spiritual beings living both in the world and apart from the world. And Christianity was closely tied to the idea that human beings are free, have dignity, and are worthy of respect. Hegel thought, in fact, that in the Protestant world of Western Europe, these Christian ideas had entered into history, and that the secular world had in fact come to resemble the Christian ideal. This is the gist of Hegel's idea that history was at its end: the idea of the human spirit as set forth in Christianity had finally become actual.

Hegel agrees with much of the content of the Enlightenment reconstruction of Christianity. This is especially true when it comes to ethics and politics. Ethics and politics should, according to Hegel, be grounded in reasonable principles, especially the principle of the inherent dignity of free human beings. But the Enlightenment reconstruction of Christianity went too far when it denied the importance of Jesus and when it used ethics to criticize religion. The Enlightenment critique of Christianity came primarily from the perspective of scientific or empirical naturalism. But it was also linked to the optimistic idea that human nature could be divorced from its history and culture. Rousseau had held that human beings are basically good and that civilization—including the stories and myths of religion—corrupts us. But Hegel rejects this point of view. For Hegel, Christian civilization is the key to progress. Human beings are historical and cultural beings, and Jesus is an essential part of Western culture. Hegel maintains that education must make use of stories or images (what he calls representations): we begin to learn both morality and metaphysics from these stories. Thus Hegel does not want to do away with religious stories, as Rousseau seems to want to do in *Emile*.

Hegel goes further in maintaining that the Christian story is superior to other stories because it begins with the idea of original sin. Hegel says: "The Christian doctrine that man is by nature evil is superior to the other according to which he is good."[1] This is true because "when he exists in an immediate and uncivilized condition, he is therefore in a situation in which he ought not to be, and from which he must liberate himself. This is the meaning of the doctrine of original sin, without which Christianity would not be the religion of freedom." The virtue of Christianity is that it begins with the idea that we are free, which Hegel here defines as the fact that we are free to sin. Human dignity is found in the capacity to freely overcome evil by a self-conscious choice to be good. Of course, this choice is facilitated by Jesus, who provides us with the possibility of choosing the good despite the temptation to do evil.

But Jesus' ethical model is more than the model of how a good person should behave. Rather, the Christian story shows us the ultimate sacrifice, God's sacrificial love, and the deep anguish of death on the cross. Moreover, Hegel recognized that a naturalized Jesus is no longer religious: "When Christ is viewed in the same light as Socrates, then he is regarded as an ordinary human being, just as in Islam he is regarded as a messenger of God in the general sense that all great men are messengers of God. If one says no more of Christ than that he is a teacher of humanity, a martyr to the truth, one is not adopting the religious standpoint; one says no more of him than of Socrates."[2] For Hegel, religion is primarily about the spiritual aspect of human life and the truth that God is love and that the kingdom of God is present in the hearts of believers. This idea transcends ethics. "The issue is not a moral teaching . . . rather what is of interest is an infinite relationship to God, to the present God, the certainty of the kingdom of God—finding satisfaction not in morality, ethics, or conscience, but rather in that than which nothing is higher, the relationship to God himself."[3] This transcendent or numinous aspect of religious experience was forgotten by the Enlightenment critique. In the Enlightenment, religion was viewed primarily through the lens of ethics. But for Hegel, ethics and religion are distinct realms of human experience; religion cannot be reduced to rational ethics or to the mundane explanations of empirical naturalism.

Despite his critique of the Enlightenment, Hegel was also an advocate of Enlightenment principles in ethics and politics. He defended constitutional monarchy, he argued for the separation of church and state, he rejected slavery, and he maintained that all men should be free. But he wanted to reintegrate the naturalism of the Enlightenment critique of religion into a larger theological point of view. For this reason, we might call Hegel a Romantic. Romanticism can be understood as a reaction against the Enlightenment that emphasizes a return to tradition and a reemphasis on the numinous or mysterious. But this reaction is not an outright rejection of the Enlightenment. Hegel criticizes the "abstract" nature of Enlightenment ethics even while claiming that it was substantially correct. While affirming the general ethical principle of Kant's categorical imperative, Hegel claims that ethics must take into account the given historical life of a community: its history, traditions, and religion.

One of the most basic historical facts to be considered is the family and the institution of marriage. Ethical life is grounded on the spiritual relation between two individuals united by love. Marriage and family relations are so important that they have a religious quality and are a source of piety.[4] This is why, Hegel says, Christ prohibited divorce: marriage is the model for other ethical commitments that create bonds between individuals. These bonds should not be subject to the passions (as in adultery). Rather, the passions should be channeled by the ethical idea that aims to create social entities united by love.

Despite his emphasis on the connection between religion and ethical life, Hegel remains committed to Enlightenment ideas about the separation of church and state. Hegel says, "Religion as such should not hold the reins of government."[5] Religious piety is subjective and arbitrary and Hegel is aware of the dangers of intolerance that would follow if religious piety were joined with political power. According to Hegel, then, piety and religion have their proper place in the totality of human life. But religion should be distinguished from ethics and politics. It is sufficient that political life should recognize the Christian idea that all men are free without then imposing a religious view. Indeed, individuals should be free to come to religious conclusions for themselves, even though the correct conclusion is that Christianity is the highest religion.

KIERKEGAARD

This attempt to distinguish ethics and religion can also be found in Kierkegaard, who represents the next generation after Hegel. But while Hegel wanted to synthesize both Enlightenment ideals and more traditional religious notions, Kierkegaard deliberately rejected the Enlightenment in favor of a return to Jesus. Kierkegaard emphasized that there was an explicit contrast between the reasonable demands of ethics and the unreasonable demands of religious faith. According to Kierkegaard, ethical commitment is related to the process of becoming a substantial self: we realize ourselves by establishing and keeping ethical commitments. In his book *Either/Or*, Kierkegaard locates this process of commitment in the context of love and marriage. Indeed, he uses love and marriage as preliminary stages on the way toward the higher sorts of commitment that are required by religious faith. Love requires a leap of faith: there is always a risk involved in giving oneself to another. The risks, the doubt, and the uncertainty are infinitely higher when making the leap of religious faith. Thus ethical commitment is a model for the sorts of commitment that are required by religion.

Kierkegaard recognizes that it is possible to remain aloof and uncommitted. One of the risks of Enlightenment humanism is that its emphasis on the human individual can turn the self into a self-contained unit whose choices are egoistic and arbitrary. Reason may lead us to emphasize a sort of ethical egoism in which individuals are encouraged simply to pursue their own self-interest while letting the invisible hand of the economy take care of larger social issues. Kierkegaard realizes that this can lead to a life of disengagement in which an individual remains disconnected from others and incapable of a higher sort of ethical love. This was obviously not what Jesus had in mind. The Good Samaritan was not an ethical egoist, and Christ's sacrifice provides a model which obliterates all such egoisms. And yet, egoism remains compelling, in part because it seems so reasonable. If reason is our only guide, then we may conclude that we should maximize pleasure for ourselves by controlling our passions and remaining essentially detached from ethical commitment. In *Either/Or*, Kierkegaard argues against this sort of egoism by emphasizing the sort of substantial self that is achieved when we make ethical commitments. The marriage vow, for example, helps us to become stable: by committing oneself to a person and to a principle (the principle of fidelity itself), the self thickens and settles. Without these commitments, the self is thin, fickle, and evanescent.

However, this kind of ethical personhood is not the final end of human existence. Rather, there is a higher end for human beings that transcends ethical commitment. Ethical commitment can be a model for the thickening of the self; however, the most substantial sort of selfhood is achieved through communion with and commitment to God. This idea is fleshed out in Kierkegaard's thought about the difference between Socrates and Jesus. Socrates gets us to the level of ethical commitment. But Jesus takes us beyond ethics and opens the possibility of religious dedication. Socrates teaches *about* the truth, but Jesus *is* the truth. In John, this idea is expressed as "I am the way, and the truth, and the life; no one comes to the Father but by me" (John 14:6). The problem for Kierkegaard is that for a genuine and radical transformation of the self to occur, we need help from the source of being who lies beyond ourselves. The ethical tradition of the Enlightenment held that it was possible to achieve ethical substantiality by oneself: you simply have to make commitments and keep them. In Kant's terms, you have to do your duty. Even though this can be difficult, it is not impossible. The ethical tradition that extends from Socrates to Kant teaches us how and why to be ethical. But the teacher—Socrates or Kant—is not essential to this message. Rather, one can become ethical through one's own exertions.

Christianity is different, according to Kierkegaard. To go beyond ethics toward the higher consummation of religion, the teacher of truth must make this transformation possible. A finite mortal human self cannot overcome itself without divine intervention. Thus Jesus not only points toward the truth but also provides the condition of transformation. "The teacher before beginning to teach, must transform, not reform, the learner. But no human being is capable of doing this; if it is to take place, it must be done by the god himself."[6] For Kierkegaard, sin and error are closely linked. But we cannot overcome sin or error by ourselves: no amount of instruction can lead us beyond sin. Rather, what is necessary is God's grace and the gift of forgiveness, which comes through Jesus.

While the teachings of Socrates or other humanistic philosophers can help us to become an ethical person, Jesus allows us to achieve an even higher good: Jesus allows us to move beyond ethics toward a higher sort of existence. Thus, for Kierkegaard, the Enlightenment takes us only so far: religion carries us farther.

This is the crucial difference with which Kierkegaard directs us back to faith. But Kierkegaard makes it quite clear that there are alarming consequences when we pursue faith beyond ethics. In his discussion of faith in *Fear and Trembling*, Kierkegaard reminds us of Abraham as the "father of faith." Abraham's faith went so far as to include the deliberate sacrifice of his promised and beloved son (even though God provided an alternative at the last minute, Abraham was fully prepared to kill Isaac). In Kierkegaard's words, this was a "teleological suspension of the ethical": God's commands represent a *telos* or end that is beyond ethics. From this perspective, faith requires that we obey God even if God orders us to violate the basic principles of ethics.

In a sense, this idea is a response to the idea that Socrates develops in the *Euthyphro*. According to Socrates, the gods should be subject to ethical law, and the ethical law is known by reason. If the gods commanded something unethical, a reasonable being would stop and say that the gods were wrong to make such a command. In other words, for Socrates, ethics is prior to religion, and human reason can know ethical truth and use this knowledge to criticize the supposed commands of God. But Kierkegaard reverses the order of priority. From this perspective, faith is prior to ethics. Of course, this faith includes the belief that God would not really command something evil—it includes the idea that God is good. But it is not for us to judge God's wisdom or his goodness. Rather, we must trust that God's commands always aim at the good, even when it seems that they do not.

FEUERBACH

Opposed to this point of view is the outlook of Ludwig Feuerbach, a contemporary of Kierkegaard and another post-Hegelian. Kierkegaard and Feuerbach were both attempting to get to the bottom of the relation between Christianity and ethics. While Kierkegaard emphasized the transcendence of religion beyond ethics, Feuerbach returned to the Enlightenment idea that ethics was the heart of religion. Feuerbach reinterpreted Christianity in such a way as to reassert the Socratic and

Kantian ideas about the importance of ethics. In this sense, he is directly opposed to Kierkegaard.

Feuerbach defended an unabashedly anthropological idea of God. Ideas about God are merely the highest human ideas. We judge what is godly by focusing on our ideas about what is good. Feuerbach puts it this way, in a passage that echoes Plato's *Euthyphro*:

> The idea of God is dependent on the idea of justice, of benevolence; a God who is not benevolent, not just, not wise, is no God; but the converse does not hold. The fact is not that a quality is divine because God has it, but that God has it because it is in itself divine: because without it God would be a defective being. Justice, wisdom, in general every quality which constitutes the divinity of God is determined and known by itself independently, but the idea of God is determined by the qualities which have thus been previously judged to be worthy of the divine nature.[7]

From this perspective, God is a limited being: his limits are the concepts and values of ethics. Moreover, human beings are able to make judgments about what is worthy of the divine nature because we have access to ethics outside of God, by way of human reason. Thus, in an important sense, the idea of God is subject to human reason. One might say that this idea is a creation of human reason. However, Feuerbach's goal is not to turn God into a work of the human imagination. Rather, Feuerbach recognizes the importance and "objectivity" of human ideas about justice and wisdom: we do not make these up as fantasies; rather, they are products of the objectivity of reason. The point is that what we know about God must cohere with what we know about ethics. God is the idea that unites our ideas about ethics, and ultimately God is the highest symbol for our ideas about ourselves.

Unlike Kierkegaard, then, Feuerbach thinks that God and ethics are one and the same. However, unlike his Enlightenment predecessors, Feuerbach does not think that this equivalence results in an easy and obvious ethical system. Rather, Feuerbach recognizes that God remains in part mysterious because human nature—and ethics—points beyond itself toward something that is infinite and of infinite value.

Feuerbach points out that Christianity is unique in emphasizing the importance of human individuality and salvation. This is all combined in the idea of love. Love is the heart of Christianity, which is concerned with the ultimate happiness of human beings. As Feuerbach puts this, "If God loves man, man is the heart of God."[8] The idea that God loves us is the idea that God wants us to be happy. Now for Feuerbach, this is an anthropological ideal. The basic idea is that we love ourselves, and our idea of God is of a God that loves us in return. God's love is, in part, a symbol of our high regard for ourselves: we want a religion in which God loves us because we love ourselves and view ourselves as worthy of the love of God. This love of God for humanity culminates in the Christian story of God's sacrifice through Jesus. God loves us so much that he is willing to give his only son (and in essence himself) for us. As Feuerbach interprets this, love is higher than God himself. In the Christian story, God "renounced his Godhead" out of love for human beings. Thus love is a higher power and truth than deity. Love conquers God. It was love to which God "sacrificed his divine majesty."[9]

It is important to recall at this point that Jesus' two commandments are love God and love your neighbor. Love is the heart of Jesus' ethical ideal. Feuerbach recognizes this, and he interprets Jesus' claim that he came to "fulfill the law" (Matthew 5:17) as follows. The moral law (as found in the Old Testament) was a law of commandment and condemnation. When we confront the Old Testament moral law directly, we find ourselves to be weak and incompetent. The law tells us that we are sinners and morally worthless. This ancient moral ideal is thus anti-human, painful, and terrifying. But the Christian story of love and compassion tempers this terrible aspect of morality and creates a more fully human idea of ethics. This is the basic idea articulated in the quote from John that is the epigraph for this chapter: the law of Moses showed us that we all sin; the love of Jesus represents forgiveness and atonement for sin. Feuerbach says: "No man is sufficient for the law which moral perfection sets before us; but, for that reason, neither is the law sufficient for man, for the heart. The law condemns; the heart has compassion even on the sinner. . . . Love gives me consciousness that I am a man; the law only the consciousness that I am a sinner, that I am worthless. The law holds man in bondage; love makes him free."[10]

This idea shares much in common with Enlightenment humanism. From this perspective, the goal of religion and ethics is to elevate human beings, not to degrade us. Feuerbach admits that love is the primary ethical idea. But he claims that this idea is not unique to Christianity. He claims that the Stoics had this idea, as did others in the ancient world. Indeed, he claims, "Love is an independent idea; I do not first deduce it from the life of Christ; on the contrary, I revere that life only because I find it accordant with the law, with the idea of love."[11] This conclusion thus pushes Feuerbach beyond Christianity. Unlike Hegel, who emphasized the need for both religion and ethics, Feuerbach affirms ethics as primary and religion as a mere instance of the ethical idea. Unlike Kierkegaard, who maintained that human beings were essentially insufficient and needed the external help of Jesus, Feuerbach maintains that human beings created the idea of Jesus as a model of the sort of love that is primary and essential.

Thus, with Feuerbach, the Enlightenment critique of Christianity is in a sense complete. Feuerbach concludes, "He therefore who loves man for the sake of man, who rises to the love of the species, to universal love, adequate to the nature of the species, he is a Christian, is Christ himself. He does what Christ did, what made Christ Christ. Thus, where there arises the consciousness of the species as a species, the idea of humanity as a whole, Christ disappears, without, however, his true nature disappearing."[12] In other words, with Feuerbach, Jesus' model becomes fully human. We can each become ethical, and when one becomes ethical, one becomes Christ.

CONCLUSION

With Feuerbach, we see the logical conclusion of the Enlightenment's attempt to humanize ethics. Those who think that we can overcome evil through our own power no longer have need of Jesus as the redeemer. While some, like Kierkegaard, continue to claim that metaphysical grace is needed because of sin, humanists attempted to do away with the description of human nature that led to the idea that we needed grace. This idea develops further toward the end of the nineteenth century and is transformed into a more pointed critique of the Christian tradition that holds that the Christian tradition itself was the source of the idea of sin. As we shall see in the next chapter, this led to a full-blown critique of Christian ethics in an attempt to make human beings feel less inadequate and less guilty while also empowering human beings to discover and create value for themselves.

NOTES

1. Georg Wilhelm Friedrich Hegel, *Elements of the Philosophy of Right* (Cambridge: Cambridge University Press, 1991), sec. 18 Addition.

2. Georg Wilhelm Friedrich Hegel, *Lectures on the Philosophy of Religion* (Berkeley: University of California, 1988), 458.

3. Hegel, *Lectures on the Philosophy of Religion*, 464.

4. Hegel, *Elements of the Philosophy of Right*, sec. 163.

5. Hegel, *Elements of the Philosophy of Right*, sec. 270 Remark, 304.

6. Søren Kierkegaard, *Philosophical Fragments* (Princeton, NJ: Princeton University Press, 1985), 14–15.

7. Ludwig Feuerbach, *The Essence of Christianity* (New York: Barnes and Noble Books, 2004), 24.

8. Feuerbach, *The Essence of Christianity*, 60.

9. Feuerbach, *The Essence of Christianity*, 56.

10. Feuerbach, *The Essence of Christianity*, 50–51.

11. Feuerbach, *The Essence of Christianity*, 268.

12. Feuerbach, *The Essence of Christianity*, 270–71.

14

ANTI-CHRISTIAN ETHICS

And if your right hand causes you to sin, cut it off and throw
it away; it is better that you lose one of your members than
that your whole body go into hell.

—Matthew 5:30

Cultural changes during the nineteenth century facilitated attacks
on Christianity. Biblical scholarship raised questions about the
status of the "historical Jesus." A better understanding of non-Western
culture led people to wonder whether Jesus was the unique incarnation of God. Darwin's view of evolution and Lyell's view of geological
time challenged the Genesis account of creation. Old traditions like
slavery were being abolished. And socialists, communists, and anarchists
condemned Christian culture for its hypocrisy and social injustices.
Radicals came to equate atheism with progress. The Russian anarchist
Bakunin, for example, claimed that God and the state must both be
abolished because both were based on an ideology of domination. And
Marx—who was a devotee of Feuerbach—famously called religion "the
opiate of the people" because religion promised otherworldly rewards
that pacified the population and prevented them from rising up to fight
injustice in this world. Such developments in the nineteenth century
owed something to the Enlightenment insofar as they used reason to
criticize revelation and ethical ideas to criticize religion and politics.
But they went beyond the Enlightenment in turning directly against
Christianity.

Important proponents of this attack on Christianity include
Ralph Waldo Emerson (1803–1882), Friedrich Nietzsche (1844–
1900), William James (1842–1910), Sigmund Freud (1856–1939), and

Bertrand Russell (1872–1969). The gist of this general assault was that Christianity was anti-human and unethical. Nietzsche suggested that Christianity was the greatest source of unhappiness in the world. And Freud agreed that Christianity was at the heart of psychological and social disorders that haunt civilization. At issue for both of them is the ubiquity of guilt in Christian culture and the corresponding sort of self-mutilation that occurs in an attempt to overcome sin. In Jesus' recommendation to cut off one's hand (or pluck out one's eye) to avoid sin, we see the heart of the unease that troubles Western culture. No one is adequate to Jesus' demand for purity; thus we constantly mutilate ourselves in pursuit of an ideal that we can never attain. Passages such as this lead Nietzsche and others to reject Christian ethics as cruel and self-deceptive. Here is Nietzsche's interpretation of this passage:

> At times the founder of Christianity's methods seem like those of a dentist whose sole cure for pain is to pull out the teeth; as, for example, when he combats sensuality with the advice: "if thy eye offend thee, pluck it out."—But there is this difference, that the dentist at least attains his object, the cessation of pain in his patent; in so clumsy a way, to be sure, as to be ludicrous: while the Christian who follows that advice and believes he has killed his sensuality is deceiving himself: it lives on in an uncanny vampire form and torments him in repulsive disguises.[1]

Unlike Feuerbach and Enlightenment philosophers who thought that the Christian story showed us that we could obtain happiness and goodness, Nietzsche, Freud, and other critics of Christianity thought that this story taught us the exact opposite. Christianity creates the vampiric specter of guilt and self-loathing that sucks our very life energy from us. For this reason, Christianity needed to be overcome.

The danger of attempting to overcome Christianity is that it can lead us into evil and vice, as we set our inner vampire free—to use Nietzsche's metaphor. This is not to say that one must be Christian to be good. Rather, the point is that some of those who deliberately turn against Christian ethics can end up going too far in the opposite direction and affirming evil, or at least espousing relativism. As we shall see, Bertrand Russell offers perhaps the best attempt at avoiding the problem of "throwing the baby out with the bath water." Russell thinks that the basic values of Christian ethics can be sustained but also that they should be grounded in a new way.

EMERSON AND NIETZSCHE

American transcendentalism developed as the American response to European Romanticism. Emerson, the major figure in this movement, was a Unitarian minister who resigned his post because he questioned the truth of the rituals and sacraments of the church. In his turn away from religion, Emerson advocated the idea of "the God within." This idea has much in common with Feuerbach's ideas about Christianity. But Emerson goes farther in advocating a sort of pantheism that sees God's presence everywhere. The difficulty of this view is that the God who is found in nature is unstable and changing. This makes it tough to discover ethical truths that are not susceptible to being overcome.

In a controversial address to the Harvard Divinity School in 1838, Emerson claimed that Jesus was a man who "saw that God incarnates himself in man."[2] Emerson also argued that the religion of Christianity was founded on a "noxious exaggeration about the person of Jesus."[3] Emerson claims that ideas about the uniqueness of the incarnation of God in Jesus were related to the cult and ritual of Christianity. Through the rituals, sacred texts, and cultic practices, Emerson thought, the church attempts to subdue individual genius and subordinate individuals to the church.

Although Emerson did think that Jesus was an important moral teacher, what Jesus taught, according to Emerson, was self-reliance, authenticity, and autonomy. Emerson writes, "Jesus was better than others because he refused to listen to others and listened at home."[4] Emerson believes that it is possible to love God and discover ethics directly in nature and without the mediation of Jesus. This anti-Christian approach to Jesus and ethics risks becoming deliberately antinomian and unethical. Emerson says in "Self-Reliance": "Nothing at last is sacred but the integrity of your own mind."[5] While this sounds like noble self-assertion, Emerson goes on to assert: "If I am the Devil's child, I will live then with the Devil." In turning against the straight-jacket of the Christian religion, Emerson ends up with a kind of relativism in which "Good and Bad are but names."

This view was typical of nineteenth-century critics of religion. Indeed, it was articulated most famously by Dostoevsky, who claimed: "If God is dead, then everything is permissible." Dostoevsky believed, however, that since we want to preserve ethics, this shows us that God must not be dead. But critics such as Emerson and Nietzsche—who was directly influenced by Emerson—argued that God was, to some extent, dead. The old traditions of Christianity were being called into question by expanding knowledge of both the natural world and human culture. If it were true that God was dead, then perhaps it was time to give up on absolute notions about good and evil.

Nietzsche is the most famous proponent of the idea that God is dead. For Nietzsche, this claim is a source of joy or gaiety: indeed the claim is made by Nietzsche in a book called *The Gay Science*. Nietzsche thinks that the death of God will allow us to move beyond the guilt and self-loathing that he believes is typical of Christian ethics. However, Nietzsche provides us with very little detail about whether there is ethics beyond Christianity. Rather, Nietzsche's focus is polemical. Nietzsche claims that Western culture's interest in science, history, and psychology has led to the realization that the old God is dead. Nietzsche's endeavor is primarily to help spread this "good news." The difficulty of moving beyond Christian ethics is that for 2,000 years, moral concepts in Western culture have been defined in Christian terms. Thus Nietzsche hopes for the creation of a new set of values that is "beyond good and evil," by which he means a set of values that is no longer stuck in the Christian framework. But like Emerson, Nietzsche's effort to escape from Christian morality leads him to advocate relativism and to flirt with evil, vice, and cruelty.

While Nietzsche grudgingly admired Jesus' charismatic power, he criticized the ascetic ideal of Christian morality. According to Nietzsche, all of human culture is based on the psychology of the will-to-power. Human beings want power and they develop twisted and insidious ways of obtaining it. For Nietzsche, the most subtle and the most successful pursuit of power is found in Christianity. Nietzsche calls Christianity a "slave-morality." This is, in part, a historical claim. Christianity evolved from the pursuit of power by slaves: the Jews and Christians who suffered under the yoke of Roman bondage were the founders of this new moral idea. According to Nietzsche, these slaves turned inward to create a moral and cultural revolution, since their masters were strong enough to prevent a political revolt. The key to this revolution was a moral system that praised the slavish virtues while condemning the virtues of the masters.

This idea provides Nietzsche with a method for interpreting the values expressed, for example, in the Sermon on the Mount. Jesus claims that in the kingdom of God, the slaves—the meek, the poor, the powerless—will be rewarded, and that the evil masters who now rule—the rich and the powerful—will be punished. Turning the other cheek, tolerating others, and loving your enemies are all ideas that befit slaves.

Masters have the power to retaliate, but slaves have no other choice but to comply, tolerate, and submit. According to Nietzsche, the clever ploy of Christianity is to praise the powerless while creating a system that devalues the strength and virtue of masters. One way that Nietzsche puts this in his polemic *The Antichrist* is as follows: "Christianity is a rebellion of everything that crawls on the ground against that which has height: the evangel of the 'lowly' makes low."[6]

Nietzsche locates the origin of Christian morality in the psychology of vengeance and resentment. According to Nietzsche, the slaves (the ancient Jews and early Christians) felt a hidden and submerged hatred toward their masters. This hatred could not be expressed because of impotence. Since the slaves could not revolt against their masters in a material sense, they were forced to stage a spiritual revolt. However, this revolt also expressed self-loathing that festered along with resentment toward the masters: the slave hated the masters for oppressing them, while also hating themselves for their powerlessness. This self-loathing produced guilt, which Nietzsche thinks is part of the essence of Christianity.

Nietzsche does not believe that Jesus offered a path toward peace, forgiveness, and love. Rather, Nietzsche sees hypocrisy and duplicity in the claims of the prince of peace: "This Jesus of Nazareth, the incarnate gospel of love, this 'Redeemer' who brought blessedness and victory to the poor, the sick, and the sinners. . . . Did not Israel attain the ultimate goal of its sublime vengefulness precisely through the bypath of this 'Redeemer'?"[7] Nietzsche derives this interpretation from his psychology of the will. Nietzsche cannot believe that anyone would give up power without expecting something in return. The psychology of what Nietzsche calls will-to-power emphasizes egoism and self-interest. Nietzsche argues that one of the ways to obtain power is to convince others to be altruistic while secretly preserving one's own egoism. Nietzsche implies that Jesus is the best example of one who has actualized the will-to-power: by convincing humanity to worship him, Jesus has satisfied the human longing to be a master and God.

However, for Nietzsche, the result of the Christian revolution is the further enslavement of humankind. Eventually the vengeance of the slave revolt was used to keep the priestly caste in power through the mechanism of a sort of guilt that could only be expiated by the priests who mediate with God. Guilt is employed by Christian ethics in two ways, according to Nietzsche. The first sort of guilt is metaphysical. The sacrifice of Jesus creates a situation of profound and inexpungible guilt. God's self-sacrifice is a gift that can never be repaid by human beings.

Thus we are always beholden to God for his grace. The second sort of guilt is created by the moral law itself. According to the rigors of Jesus' moral idea, even the *thought* of doing evil is evil. We see this, for example, in Jesus' claims about anger and lust in the Sermon on the Mount. We are culpable if we feel angry or think lustful thoughts, even if we do not actualize these thoughts or emotions. This creates an ethical standard that no mortal can live up to. Thus we always fall short of the moral ideal. And thus we always feel guilty. Jesus counsels self-mutilation as the path to purity, and this impossible ideal makes us beholden to Jesus (and his priests), since only they provide the key to releasing us from guilt.

Nietzsche argues this point by looking at the history of asceticism. Christians have martyred themselves and mortified their flesh in pursuit of a sort of moral purity that is unattainable for ordinary mortals. The model of this behavior is Jesus himself, whose crucifixion provides the primary example of the Christian life. But this model is repeated throughout the history of asceticism. It should be noted that while Nietzsche's primary polemical focus is Christianity, he admits that the same critique can be applied to Buddhism and other forms of asceticism.

Morality provides a way of disciplining the masses (what Nietzsche calls "the herd") by demanding conformity to mediocrity: no one is allowed to become a master, and we are all required to comply with the rules of herd-morality. Thus morality is used to ensure that certain classes remain in power—primarily the priestly class. In this sense, Nietzsche's critique is similar to Marx's. Marx claimed that "the ruling ideas have always been the ideas of the ruling class." What he means by this is that the ruling class disseminates certain ideas that help it to remain in power. The ruling ideas of Christianity make the masses feel guilty, and this empowers the priestly class because the priests have sole power to cure guilt. Moreover, by claiming that the poor and the weak and the miserable will be rewarded when they inherit the kingdom of God, any further revolutionary fervor is defused: the otherworldly focus of Christianity makes it easier for the oppressed to accept their oppression.

JAMES AND FREUD

In America, the pragmatist William James—a near contemporary of Nietzsche and another admirer of Emerson—pioneered the psychology of religion. This effort would be taken up by Freud a few decades later. According to James, the mystical or ecstatic experience (what he also calls rapture, enthusiasm, and wonder) helps to explain the ethics of Jesus. Love of enemies and nonresistance to evil are linked by James to the unifying state of mind that occurs in mystical experience. James says, for example, "Jubilation is an expansive affection, and all expansive affections are self-forgetful and kindly so long as they endure."[8] One significant conclusion of James' ideas is that the mystical ground of ethics is not unique to Christianity: James argues that it can be found in Buddhism and Stoicism and other religions. Like Nietzsche, James indicates that this mystical foundation of ethics can lead to an obsession with inner purity and asceticism.

The problem of Christian ethics is that is appears to be an ethics for saints but not for the real world.

> We must frankly confess, then, using our empirical common sense and ordinary practical prejudices, that in the world that actually is, the virtues of sympathy, charity, and non-resistance may be, and often have been, manifested in excess. . . . The whole history of constitutional government is a commentary on the excellence of resisting evil, and when one cheek is smitten, of smiting back and not turning the other cheek also. You will agree to this in general, for in spite of the Gospel, in spite of Quakerism, in spite of Tolstoi, you believe in fighting fire with fire, in shooting down usurpers, locking up thieves, and freezing out vagabonds and swindlers.[9]

James is ambivalent about this defense of commonsense morality: the saintly morality of the Gospels is inspiring even if most of us will not choose to follow it. Thus James is not as adamantly opposed to Christianity as Nietzsche. James quotes Nietzsche's critique of ascetic saints in some detail in his *Varieties of Religious Experience*. But James points out that Nietzsche's critique itself represents an "antipathy" that "is itself sickly enough."[10] According to James, we can admire the ascetic ideal of the saint. But "each of us must discover for himself the kind of religion and the amount of saintship which best comports with what he believes to be his powers and feels to be his truest mission and vocation."[11] While James does not stray as far into relativism as Nietzsche, this quote reminds us that he was a pluralist about religious experience as well as about morality.

Freud's consideration of religious ethics is similar to James' and Nietzsche's. Like James, Freud is interested in the "oceanic experience" that is typical of religious experience. Like Nietzsche, Freud thinks that religion produces guilt in relation to asceticism. However, Freud's account of the historical evolution of religion and religious ethics is tied to his concern with the traumas of psychological development. Freud thinks that religion originates within the family drama. Freud claims that religion begins with the rebellion of the son against the father. This results in the murder and cannibalism of the father (either in fact or in symbol), which then creates guilt. This primitive process is repeated throughout the history of culture. It eventually becomes the myth of Christianity: sinful man kills God, their father, and then memorializes this murder by consuming God' body through the eucharistic ritual. This simultaneously assuages our guilt while keeping us beholden to God and the church. As a result, religion functions as a sort of "obsessional neurosis" that focuses on the ritual repetition of compulsive behavior, the creation of fetish objects that are invested with psychological power, and a negative process in which the thing that we desire continually makes us feel inadequate.

Freud looks at the phenomenon of religion from the perspective of a psychologist interested in disease. He thinks that religious ethics lies at the heart of many psychological disorders. Indeed, Freud thinks that religion is an illusion that we believe because of a psychological need. It is what Freud calls a wish fulfillment. We want nature to be comprehensible, we want there to be a reason that things happen the way they do, we want a moral purpose for the universe, we want a benevolent deity, and we want immortality. Religion satisfies these desires. But wanting religion to be true does not make it true. And there is a psychological price to pay for belief in religion in terms of inadequacy and guilt. Freud thinks that many of the neuroses of modern culture are caused by the stringent nature of religious ethics. This is especially true because religion imposes sexual restrictions that inhibit the natural flow of sexual energy. When this flow is impeded through repression, there are psychological disturbances.

Freud rejects both the Golden Rule and the internalized sexual repression that is typical of Christianity. With regard to the Golden Rule, Freud says that "not merely is the stranger in general unworthy of my love; I must honestly confess that he has more claim to my hostility and even my hatred."[12] The Christian commands—to love your neighbor, to help the stranger, to forgive, and to return love for evil—are all absurd. However, Freud's point is not only that this is bad advice; rather, these commands set up an impossible standard that runs counter to our natural instincts. Our natural instincts are toward sex and aggression, but the Christian ideal demands that we refrain from sex and aggression. We will always fail to live up to the ideal, and we will always feel guilty.

Christian ethics internalizes the need for purity. It is not enough that one should abstain from actually committing adultery (as in the Old Testament). Rather, Jesus demands that sexual purity encompass one's unactualized intentions. In Matthew, Jesus says that one may commit adultery "in one's heart." Now, Freud thinks that the sex drive is natural and inevitable. Thus this commandment makes us all into adulterers. And Jesus recommends that the remedy for this failure is self-mutilation: one should cut off the offending organ. Self-mutilation happens, according to Freud, in many of the neuroses and psychological disturbances that were his primary interest.

Some Christians accept affliction and suffering as a path to piety. Guilt and psychic pain can lead us to desire forgiveness and to accept God's grace. Thus sin and guilt can be seen by some Christians as an essential part of the path toward redemption and fulfillment. Freud worries, however, that this process reinforces the problem of what he sees as an obsessional neurosis. Guilt causes us to turn to the rituals and fetish items of religious practice. But since none of us are perfect in our worship and prayer, we fall short. As we turn to these rituals with more and more zeal, we feel more and more guilty.

The solution for Freud is to replace religion with science, including his own psychological theory. We don't need more religion; rather, we need a better understanding of the self. However, Freud recognizes that religion has led to the production of civilization itself, including its magnificent artworks and scientific achievements. Thus Freud's conclusion is ambivalent. Freud says, "The price we pay for advancement in civilization is a loss of happiness through the heightening of the sense of guilt."[13] Guilt is useful. It forces people to conform to moral rules. And it allows for the sublimation of the drives that causes people to produce great cultural achievements. Guilt inspires us to work harder, to produce more, and to strive for what Nietzsche called "self-overcoming." But Freud also notes that guilt comes with a cost: the general feeling of inadequacy and dis-ease that we feel when confronting the great moral commandments of the Christian tradition.

RUSSELL

Like Freud, Bertrand Russell admired science and the progress that scientists had made in examining the natural world and in understanding psychology and ethics. Christian ethics is problematic because

Christianity itself is vague and contradictory when it comes to ethics. Russell's most famous polemic against Christianity was entitled "Why I Am Not a Christian." The gist of Russell's critique of religious ethics was the same as Plato's and Feuerbach's: right and wrong have a meaning that is independent of God's fiat. Russell also notes that Christianity in particular has long been associated with intolerance, cruelty, and war. While praising some of Jesus' virtues—such as his idea of giving to the poor—Russell maintains that these virtues are not unique to Jesus. In fact, Russell maintains that Buddha and Socrates are more worthy of our respect as moral exemplars than Jesus is. One of the reasons for this is that, like Nietzsche, Russell maintains that Jesus' idea of hell and eternal damnation was vindictive and cruel. "I must say that I think all this doctrine, that hell-fire is a punishment for sin, is a doctrine of cruelty. It is a doctrine that put cruelty into the world, and gave the world generations of cruel torture; and the Christ of the Gospels, if you could take Him as his chroniclers represent Him, would certainly have to be considered partly responsible for that."[14] According to Russell, Socrates and Buddha did not have the sort of vindictive fury that Russell finds in Jesus' apocalyptic language. Thus they are better models of the ethical life.

Russell's critique of Christianity is not as vitriolic as Nietzsche's. In his essay "A Free Man's Worship," Russell is sympathetic to the idea that renunciation and asceticism, as found in Christianity, are part of genuine progress in ethics. But one problem is that Christian renunciation is grounded in the idea of future redemption. Russell's goal is to go beyond religious renunciation toward a sort of tragic heroism that recognizes that the universe is indifferent to our struggles. The difficult task is to remain committed to values such as sympathy, kindness, and generosity in the face of an indifferent universe.

Russell's goal is to continue to strive to assert human value despite death and oblivion. Unlike Nietzsche, however, Russell is not interested in cruelty or power. Indeed, Russell's humanistic values are quite similar to the values of the Gospels, even though the basis for these values is human solidarity in the struggle against the cruel indifference of the vast, purposeless universe.

> Very brief is the time in which we can help them [our comrades], in which their happiness or misery is decided. Be it ours to shed sunshine on their path, to lighten their sorrows by the balm of sympathy, to give them the pure joy of a never-tiring affection, to strengthen failing courage, to instill faith in hours of despair. Let us not weigh in grudging scales their merits and demerits, but let us think only of their need—of the

sorrows, the difficulties, perhaps the blindnesses, that make the misery of their lives; let us remember that they are our fellow-sufferers in the same darkness, actors in the same tragedy as ourselves.[15]

This passage echoes the Gospels in some ways. However, for Russell, the moral task is to discover and actualize these values while also admitting the truth of scientific reason. Religion should be rejected because it provides a false story of what the universe is, where it came from, and where it is headed. A true moral hero is one who is able to retain humane values despite the indifference of the universe that science describes.

CONCLUSION

By the middle of the twentieth century, critiques of Christian ethics were fueled by the horrors of two world wars and a growing awareness of religious diversity around the globe. At the same time, some Christian thinkers began to consider that the troubles of the twentieth century could only be healed by a renewed commitment to Christianity. Thus the twentieth century produced a variety of choices for thinking about religion and ethics. Some took the path of outright atheism. Existentialists such as Sartre and Camus struggled to find a way to live in a world without God and in which ethics was completely divorced from religious tradition. Others retreated to traditional fundamentalism in a way anticipated by Kierkegaard, in which faith trumps reason and in which religious imperatives are superior to ethical ideals. The great "culture wars" of the past several decades owe much to the philosophical struggle during the past several centuries to properly relate religion and ethics.

The question is whether it is worth going back to the Bible in order to generate a truly Christian ethical ideal, or whether we should look to the past as a model that we have to overcome while attempting to ground ethics in modern sciences such as psychology, anthropology, history, and philosophy.

NOTES

1. Friedrich Nietzsche, *Human All Too Human* (Cambridge: Cambridge University Press, 1986), 330.

2. Ralph Waldo Emerson, "Harvard Divinity School Address," in *The Essential Writings of Ralph Waldo Emerson* (New York: Modern Library, 2000), 67.

3. Emerson, "Divinity School Address," 68.

4. Ralph Waldo Emerson, "The Sovereignty of Ethics," in *The Complete Writings of Ralph Waldo Emerson* (New York: William H. Wise, 1929), 1006.

5. Ralph Waldo Emerson, "Self-Reliance," in *The Essential Writings of Ralph Waldo Emerson*, 135.

6. Friedrich Nietzsche, *The Anti-Christ*, in *Viking Portable Nietzsche*, ed. Walter Kaufmann (New York: Viking Penguin, 1982), sec. 43, 620.

7. Nietzsche, *On the Genealogy of Morals* (New York: Vintage, 1989), I:8, 35.

8. William James, *The Varieties of Religious Experience* (New York: Modern Library, 1994), 307.

9. James, *The Varieties of Religious Experience*, 389.

10. James, *The Varieties of Religious Experience*, 407.

11. James, *The Varieties of Religious Experience*, 411.

12. Sigmund Freud, *Civilization and Its Discontents* (New York: Norton, 1989), 67.

13. Freud, *Civilization and Its Discontents*, 76.

14. Bertrand Russell, "Why I Am Not a Christian," in *Why I Am Not a Christian* (New York: Touchstone, 1967), 18.

15. Russell, "A Free Man's Worship," in *Why I Am Not a Christian*, 115.

15

ETHICS BEYOND JESUS

Think not that I have come to abolish the law and the prophets; I have come not to abolish them but to fulfill them.

—Matthew 7:15–16

Jesus claims that his ethical vision fulfills the old law. Jesus intensifies,
enriches, and deepens the ethical sensibility of the ancient tradition.
My effort here has been to further deepen and intensify your ethical reflection by engaging in a critical encounter with Jesus. Unlike Nietzsche
or Freud, I do not maintain that Jesus is irrelevant or pernicious. Indeed,
the spirit of ethics can be found in Jesus' idea of loving one's neighbor
as oneself. But we need to go beyond Jesus in the same way that Jesus
went beyond Moses. Jesus provides a wonderful and inspiring model of
a life of service and an ethic of love. But he simply fails to provide us
with answers to the tough questions of ethics.

Since the death of Jesus, human beings have made substantial
progress. Our ethical ideas have become more compassionate. Our political systems have come to accept the idea of human rights. We have
abolished slavery and established equality for men and women. Some
of this progress can be attributed to a better understanding of Jesus'
basic teachings. We are continually learning to love one another better. Although we often fail to live up to the idea of love, we have made
progress. But our recent progress, especially in the realm of human rights,
extends Jesus' ideas in ways that were unimaginable in his time. We have
also made advances in terms of science and technology. Our lives are
longer, healthier, and more comfortable. Most of this progress should be
attributed to reason and not to religion. Christianity has often been a
counterweight, holding back progress. One need only recall the inquisi-

tion of Galileo to get the idea. Reason has given us dentistry, vaccines, scientific agriculture, the internal combustion engine, and the Internet. And it was the liberal philosophy of Enlightenment deism that gave us the U.S. Constitution and other progressive political reforms.

The world is still imperfect: there is terrorism, war, pollution, and environmental degradation. There is no utopia. Science cannot conquer death. And liberty does not necessarily produce happiness. But very few of us would want to give up the results of science, technology, and modern political and economic systems. We should be skeptical, then, of those "false prophets" (Matthew 7:15) who claim that we should return wholeheartedly to the values of the Bible. What could be gained by a return to Jesus that comes at the expense of the developed human wisdom of Western culture? Such fundamentalism would have to accept a return to the ignorance and brutality of the ancient world. But would we really want this? To cite one pertinent example, we no longer crucify dissidents and political agitators. But arguments against "cruel and unusual punishments" such as crucifixion are not found in the Bible. Nor do we find there arguments against monarchy, slavery, or the subordination of women.

Nonetheless, Western culture remains indebted to Jesus' ethical ideas. Christian virtues such as forgiveness, mercy, tolerance, and love are closely linked to modern liberal ideals. The modern liberal idea that individual human beings are of infinite and equal worth can be derived from the Christian idea that God loves all of us equally. As Martin Luther put it in his essay "Concerning Christian Liberty," all who believe in Jesus are "kings and priests" with inherent and eminent dignity. But it took several centuries for Luther's idea to be incorporated in institutions, and it has taken even longer to extend this idea to include the dignity of all persons, regardless of race or religious faith. The idea that "all men are created equal and that they are endowed by their creator with certain inalienable rights" is a very late development in Christian thought. This universal claim about human dignity was a product of the Enlightenment's interpretation and extension of Christian ideas. It has been a long struggle, but this idea has gradually been extended to include all human beings of all races, genders, and religions.

One end point of this development is Martin Luther King Jr.'s hope that one day human beings "would not be judged by the color of their skin but by the content of their character." We've still got room for progress, but we are on our way toward this ideal. This ideal is clearly linked to the idea of loving your neighbor. As King put this in his discussion of Christian love (*agape*): "*Agape* means recognition of the fact that all life is interrelated. All humanity is involved in a single process, and all men are brothers."[1] While King locates this ideal in Christian sources, it was the development of this ideal in secular society and modern liberal philosophy that allowed us to actualize it.

LIBERALISM AND CHRISTIANITY

The basic idea of liberal democracy is that structures of authority should be limited in order to protect individual liberty and ensure equality of consideration. This idea has been clarified by modern political philosophers and institutionalized in European and American states during the last several centuries. This idea represents a substantial development beyond both the imperial order of ancient Rome and the sacral feudalism of the Christian Middle Ages. One of the most important modern developments is the idea of religious freedom. This idea grew out of a process that privatized religious belief in the name of tolerance: political power was prohibited from interfering in the private religious belief of citizens, and states no longer sought to establish a public religion. Of course, this development was viewed negatively by those who wanted conformity of belief in hope of creating the purity of a "new Jerusalem." A traditional name for religious diversity is, after all, *heresy*. The sacral ages show us a long history of intolerance toward heretics, including their exclusion and extermination. But the liberal tradition in philosophy and politics has helped us overcome this sort of intolerance.

We might think that freedom is a uniquely Christian idea. We read about freedom in the Gospels. For example, Jesus says: "If you continue in my word, you are truly my disciples, and you will know the truth, and the truth will make you free" (John 8:32). But the difference between this sort of freedom and liberal freedom is important. In the Christian tradition, you are free when you love God and follow his law. But in the liberal tradition, you are free when the state allows you to decide for yourself about religion and ethics. The philosophical founders of modern liberalism—Locke, Rousseau, Kant, and others—were Christians, although we have already seen (in chapter 12) that the Enlightenment version of Christianity was humanistic and more concerned with ethics than with theology. Moreover, liberal developments in the West were also influenced by interest in classical Greek and Roman thought. When the American founders wanted models for the U.S. system of government, they did not look to the Christian or Hebrew traditions. Rather, they looked to Greece and Rome. The history of the Hebrews was one of kingship and a firmly united church–state complex. The history of the Christians—once they obtained political power—was also based on kingship and hierarchy. The ideas of individual liberty, restraint of state power, and separation of church and state do not follow directly from Christian sources.

When Jesus claims that he is the truth and that his truth will set us free, the sort of freedom indicated here is freedom from sin or the freedom that comes with moral perfection. It is not the freedom to make mistakes, think one's own thoughts, or behave according to one's own best judgment. The freedom of Christianity is what the philosopher Isaiah Berlin called "positive liberty." The idea is that without God, one is not really free; rather, true liberty is obtained when one properly communes with God. As Paul puts this, "The Lord is the Spirit and where the Spirit of the Lord is, there is freedom" (2 Corinthians 3:17). Or, "For freedom Christ has set us free; stand fast therefore and do not submit again to the yoke of slavery" (Galatians 5:1). This seems to run counter to Paul's defense of slavery. But the point is that there is a different sort of freedom beyond the limits of earthly slavery. Paul goes on to clarify that true freedom occurs when one obeys the moral law of love. "For you were called to freedom brethren; only do not use your freedom as an opportunity for the flesh, but through love be servants of one another" (Galatians 5:13).

The difficulty is that positive liberty is often connected to authoritarian and totalitarian systems of government, as state power is used to force people to be free, or to force them to accept the truth. Liberalism is based on what Isaiah Berlin called "negative liberty," which limits state power in defense of basic human rights. This liberty is negative because it is about limits and boundaries—it is about what the state cannot do. This idea is not clearly present in the ancient Christian tradition. One of the reasons that the Christian tradition has historically had a hard time accepting the idea of negative liberty is that this is a specifically secular idea. It is an idea designed for a public life that is neutral with regard to religion, and indeed, which treats religious belief as a merely private choice. This ideal runs counter to both the ancient Hebrew and medieval Christian traditions in which church and state were united. Christianity is an all-inclusive religion: Christ makes demands of one's entire life. But liberal politics asks us to ignore our religious views and come together to develop consensus about the common good despite our religious differences.

The basic idea of secular liberalism is that diverse members of society can use reason to reach agreement on political values that will allow them to govern their communal life. This idea was defended most famously by John Rawls, the late Harvard philosopher, who followed the Catholic philosopher Jacques Maritain in developing the idea of "overlapping consensus." The idea of overlapping consensus is that people of different religious backgrounds can come together, despite their fundamental differences, in support of a common set of political values. They do this by appealing to what Rawls called public reason. Public reason is the common language of those of us who communicate despite differences of religion. One of the basic values derived through public reason is liberty itself: we agree that each of us should have the freedom to pursue our own faith, so long as we respect the freedom of others to do so as well.

The First Amendment to the U.S. Constitution can be justified in this way: freedom of speech and the disestablishment of religion should be a value for each of us because we can each imagine that we might be a minority who would want our rights defended against the possible tyranny of the majority. It is easy to imagine that Jesus and the early Christians would be sympathetic to such an idea, since they were on the receiving end of religious intolerance. But there is no direct statement supporting religious toleration and the disestablishment of religion to be found in the Bible.

The values of liberalism developed during the Enlightenment as a reaction to protracted wars that were fought during the struggle to reform European Christianity. The idea of toleration developed as people began to see the futility of killing each other over religious differences and agreed to disagree about these issues. This pragmatic justification of freedom of religion can be supplemented by a deeper emphasis on the private nature of religious belief. As John Locke insisted over three hundred years ago, religious belief requires a sort of inward commitment that is not amenable to public coercion. The idea here is that each person's religion is his or her own concern. So long as individuals do not violate the basic outlines of the social contract, we should agree to allow them the freedom to worship their own God in their own way. Locke's primary focus is, in fact, toleration among reformed Christians. The limit of Locke's approach is found in the fact that he denied toleration to Catholics and to atheists. For Locke, Catholics have an allegiance to Rome that made him suspicious of their loyalty to the secular Protestant state. And according to Locke, atheists who deny the divine foundation of ethics could not be trusted.

Hopefully, we have made further progress since Locke in understanding toleration. Christianity is not monolithic; there is substantial diversity within Christianity. Locke and others, such as Thomas Jefferson, developed the concept of toleration in light of the fact of diversity *within* Christianity. When we open the question of diversity beyond Christianity toward a global culture that includes Jews, Muslims, Buddhists, Hindus, animists, atheists, and others, we find even more need for toleration and the project of developing overlapping consensus.

Even if we accept the idea that Christian values should be fundamental, these values push us in the direction of toleration. The idea of tolerance can be grounded in the Christian virtues of humility and love. Jesus said, "Judge not, that you be not judged" (Matthew 7:1; Luke 6:37). Paul also advises us not to judge others (Romans 14). Moreover, Jesus also claimed that we should be modest in our claims about piety, and we should beware of the "false prophets" who claim to have unique and special access to religious truth. The modern liberal tradition institutionalizes values such as tolerance in a way not imagined in Jesus's era. But it is possible that he might have approved of the idea that individuals should be free to fulfill the first commandment—to love God—however they see fit.

PROBLEMS FOR THE ENLIGHTENMENT VISION

For some, Enlightenment liberalism has negative connotations. In the twentieth century, postmodern thinkers turned against the Enlightenment project. Some critics claimed that the project of the Enlightenment was flawed by the patriarchal and occasionally racist views of important Enlightenment thinkers—flaws that were inherited from the patriarchal and racist views of the entirety of Christian culture. Others claimed that the very idea of the Enlightenment was a bourgeois hoax, that it was ethnocentric, or that it was another phase of Western imperialism. More importantly, others argued that the very idea that human reason could attain universal truth was hopelessly flawed. And others worried that the extension of liberty and tolerance results in an "anything goes" sort of relativism.

One result of the Enlightenment project is what Max Weber called the "disenchantment" of the world. The universe revealed by humanistic philosophy and natural science is a vast and indifferent one in which, after Copernicus, human beings are not at the center. Even the world of human culture turned out to be more complex than Western Christians had previously imagined. During the Enlightenment, Europeans developed their knowledge of the varieties of human experience around the world. This showed them that the Christian revelation was not unique and that there were other impressive developments of human culture that had nothing to do with the events in Roman Palestine in the year zero. Indeed, other systems of dates exist, fixed by the creation stories of other religious systems. The fact of diversity led some to the conclusion that none of these systems had the final interpretation of God or of his commandments about ethics. Christianity thus became merely one story among others. Historians of Christianity came to doubt the authenticity of the biblical stories as it became clear that the canon of biblical texts had been honed and shaped by human authorities for specific purposes. This problem has been exacerbated by biblical archaeology, which has discovered alternative stories about Jesus.

As natural science developed, it became obvious that the miracles and healings that occur in the New Testament were either exaggerations by credulous and self-interested observers or that they could be given scientific explanations. When reason was applied to the Bible, most of the miracles had to be denied. To cite one example, Joshua's miraculous power to stop the sun in its tracks would have resulted in the destruction of the earth, as it would have meant that God would have had to suddenly and violently stop the rotation of the planet. Nature is an integrated system, and if the laws of nature are violated in one place, this violation will have a cascade of effects throughout the world. Moreover, modern cosmology contradicted the Genesis creation story. Lyell and Darwin showed that the age of the earth was far older than the authors of Genesis could have imagined, and that species were not created as distinct "natural kinds."

The Enlightenment project thus leaves us with skepticism about the truth of the biblical tradition. Similar skeptical conclusions may also be directed toward Socrates and other figures in the history of Western culture. The difference is that Jesus has a more central role in the life of the Christian than Socrates does to the life of a philosopher. Christians orient their entire lives around the person of Jesus and the revelation of truth that is supposed to be embodied in him. Jesus says, "I am the way and the truth and the life. No one comes to the Father but by me" (John 14:6). If we become skeptical of this claim, the worry is that perhaps there is no truth or no way to obtain the truth. Thus the worry is that there is no truth of ethics, and that the relativists may be right, that anything goes.

Our challenge is to find a way to defend values like tolerance, liberty, and love without succumbing to relativism. One way to do this is to recall that when we claim that liberty is good, this does not mean that anything goes. We should be free to develop our own consciences, but this freedom cannot impinge on the freedom of others. And tolerance can be defended by distinguishing it from relativism. Tolerance is a nonrelative value that everyone should cultivate. One reason for this is that we want to allow others the freedom to develop their own lives and make their own mistakes. But another reason is that we should be concerned with our own virtue first and not worry about what others are doing. We see a defense of tolerance and a sort of negative liberty in some of Jesus' teaching. For example, Jesus says: "Why do you see the speck that is in your brother's eye, but do not notice the log that is in your own eye? Or how can you say to your brother, 'Let me take the speck out of your eye,' when there is the log in your own eye?" (Matthew 7:3–4). And Jesus' ideas about forgiveness and mercy provide further support for tolerance and respect for the liberty of others. But Jesus' defense of these values is not a sort of relativism: he thinks that these values are essential to a good human life.

One of the most important values for Jesus is love. In 1 John 4, we read that "God is love" and that we should love our brothers because God loves us. But it is important to note that God expressed his love for us by creating us with free will. Love requires that we help each other to discover the good life for ourselves and to support one another as we work to become virtuous. This sort of love may in fact have to patiently allow others to make their own mistakes. Indeed, since none of us is perfect, and since the ethical questions we face are often quite complex, love requires us to allow others to answer ethical questions in their own way. Love can be understood as a kind of respect for autonomy. But love itself is not a relative value: it is essential for human flourishing. We grow together in virtue and goodness by loving one another and by learning from each other as we engage in the communal project of finding the truth for ourselves.

Even if modern science and philosophy somehow disenchant the world by eliminating magic and miracles, it is still possible for individuals to find value and meaning in life. Reason and experience show us that a rewarding human life is one that is organized around "Christian" values such as peace, forgiveness, mercy, and love. But we do not need Jesus to tell us this. Jesus and the Christian tradition remind us of these values. But if they are truly valuable, their value can be seen directly without reference to any specific authority. The modern liberal state allows us the freedom to explore the meaning of life in unprecedented ways. Since we are free from the obligations of public religion, we are free to discover meaning for ourselves. It is true that no one is forcing us to be moral, and we are free to make our own mistakes. This sort of freedom is to be celebrated, since it is the sort of freedom that is required to become fully human. And it helps to free us from the angst and guilt that are produced by Christian authority, as described by Nietzsche and Freud. But it is now up to us to learn to use our freedom well.

CONCLUSION

For some who are raised Christian, skepticism about Jesus and his message can produce despair. This is more than the disenchantment that occurs when we discover that there is no Santa Claus or when we look behind the wizard's curtain. Rather, those who question the faith of their childhood can experience deep and profound anguish. Our entire worldview can be called into question, including moral values and much else that at one time helped us make sense of life.

But one need not throw the proverbial baby out with the bath water. We should allow reason to lead us toward the truth. And we should remember that the truth that is discovered by reason shares much with the claims of faith. Jesus' model of mercy, peace, and love remains inspiring because experience shows us that a life based on such values is a good one. And these values are found in a wide variety of traditions that are not Christian or even particularly religious, as for example, in Betrand Russell's pacifism or in the ideas found in the Dalai Lama's *Ethics for a New Millennium*. The Golden Rule is in fact the basic principle of almost every moral system that is worth consideration. We've seen that Jesus' idea about loving our neighbor provides a model for the two most important modern moral philosophers: it is found in Kant's deontological approach as well as in Mill's Utilitarianism. Thus despite the many questions that Jesus does not answer, his model of virtue and his broad altruistic concern can help us begin to work toward answers. Although Jesus says nothing directly about many of the issues we've discussed in this book, he reminds us of the sort of care and compassion that is required as we approach these issues for ourselves.

It may seem that philosophical questioning leaves us with no answers to the tough questions. I have noticed that students often reach such a conclusion after taking their first philosophy class. But the real conclusion is not that there are no answers to life's big questions. Rather, the point is that there are several very good answers to these questions. Most good answers to ethical questions will remind us that we should care about others and work to cultivate virtues that allow us to live in peace with others. In the chapters of this book that were focused on applied ethical issues, more questions were raised than were answered. But this is simply the way life is: there are often more questions than answers. We've seen that the Bible provides only limited guidance for thinking about these topics. Jesus says little or nothing about abortion, euthanasia, the death penalty, homosexuality, or political rule. He espouses pacifism and direct handouts for the needy. But he also acquiesces to tyranny and apparently permits slavery. In the face of these conclusions, one might be tempted to give up entirely on ethics (or at least on Christian ethics). But silences, inconsistencies, and unanswered questions should not be viewed as dead-ends. Rather, they are opportunities for us to find better answers. To find such answers, we need to cultivate philosophical virtues such as courage, moderation, wisdom, and a sense of justice.

Ethical reflection did not end with Jesus. In fact, life has become more complicated and more interesting. We are confronted today with amazing new technologies and profound questions about life, death, and our place in the universe. To answer these questions, we must cease to idolize Jesus and go beyond him by using reason to develop better ideas about how to deal with contemporary questions. For this to happen, we need an open society that values reasoned dialogue and open debate. One of the difficulties of freedom is that we may end up with different answers to the big questions. This makes the task of judging that much more difficult. It also reminds us of how important it is to be tolerant of others, to forgive their mistakes, and to offer them our loving concern as they struggle to find answers.

Although the Golden Rule is a useful moral principle, the difficult task is figuring out how to love our neighbors as ourselves. This task becomes more complicated when we realize how diverse our neighbors are. The challenge of the future is to think more carefully and more deeply about how to deal with diversity without succumbing to relativism. Jesus' model should inspire us to take up this challenge. Jesus did not simply retreat to the law of Moses. Rather, he creatively reinterpreted this law in light of the circumstances of his time and place, while reminding us of the importance of love. We would do well to follow this model as we confront the ethical challenges of the twenty-first century.

NOTE

1. Martin Luther King Jr., "Pilgrimage to Nonviolence," in *A Testament of Hope: The Essential Writings of Martin Luther King Jr.*, ed. James Melvin Washington (San Francisco: Harper and Row, 1986), 20.

INDEX

SCRIPTURE INDEX